LOW INCOME SELF-EMPLOYMENT

CASH AND CARE

Editors: Sally Baldwin and Jonathan Bradshaw

Cash benefits and care services together make a fundamental contribution to human welfare. After income derived from work, they are arguably the most important determinants of living standards. Indeed, many households are almost entirely dependent on benefits and services which are socially provided. Moreover, welfare benefits and services consume the lion's share of public expenditure. The operation, impact and interaction of benefits and services is thus an important focus on research in social policy.

Policy related work in this field tends to be disseminated to small specialist audiences in the form of mimeographed research reports or working papers and perhaps later published, more briefly, in journal articles. In consequence public debate about vital social issues is sadly ill-informed. The series is designed to make the details of important empirically-based research more widely available.

THE AUTHORS

Tony Eardley, formerly a Research Fellow in the Social Policy Research Unit at the University of York, is now a Senior Research Fellow in the Social Policy Research Centre at the University of New South Wales, Australia.

Anne Corden is a Research Fellow in the Social Policy Research Unit at the University of York.

Low Income Self-Employment

Work, benefits and living standards

TONY EARDLEY
ANNE CORDEN
Social Policy Research Unit
University of York

Avebury
Aldershot • Brookfield USA • Hong Kong • Singapore • Sydney

Published by
Avebury
Ashgate Publishing Limited
Gower House
Croft Road
Aldershot
Hants GU11 3HR
England

Ashgate Publishing Company
Old Post Road
Brookfield
Vermont 05036
USA

British Library Cataloguing in Publication Data

Eardley, Tony
Low Income Self-employment: Work, Benefits and Living Standards
I. Title II. Corden, Anne
362.50941
ISBN 1 85972 241 5

Library of Congress Catalog Card Number: 95-83044

Typeset by
Social Policy Research Unit
University of York

Printed and bound in Great Britain by
Ipswich Book Co. Ltd., Ipswich, Suffolk

Contents

Figures and tables

Acknowledgements

A good many people have contributed to the completion of this book and we would like to express our gratitude to them.

The book draws on research commissioned by the Department of Social Security. Continuing help and support have come from our liaison officer, Tony Martin, from Family Credit policy makers and from staff in the Family Credit Unit at North Fylde, who were patient with our frequent requests for help with selection of cases and helpful in answering our queries about benefit administration. We would also like to acknowledge the help of the local authority housing benefit officers who contributed to our workshop. Any opinions expressed are, however, those of the authors and not necessarily those of the Department of Social Security.

Joan Brown provided advice and help in the early stages of our work, and Steve McKay and Alan Marsh at the Policy Studies Institute gave us useful access to early data from their survey of low-income families.

Rebecca Boden from the University of Manchester was an important member of the research team, contributing her expertise in accountancy and small business finance. Within SPRU a number of colleagues made essential contributions. Sandra Hutton organised the family credit administrative dataset and carried out analyses which contributed to Chapter Four. Gill Dix conducted around one-third of the in-depth interviews for the living standards study and made many useful suggestions at the planning stage. Computing and technical support came from Maureen Astin, Julie Williams and Steve Johnson. Typing and manuscript preparation were by Sally Pulleyn and Jenny Bowes, to whom we always owe many thanks. Lorna Foster proof read the text.

We are also grateful to the ESRC Data Archive for permission to use data from the Family Expenditure Survey and General Household Survey.

Finally, particular thanks go to all those people who agreed to take part in our research, without whom none of it would have been possible. They gave freely of their time in spite of the pressures of their busy working lives and notwithstanding, in some cases, serious financial problems. We enjoyed meeting them. This book is about them and for them.

1 Introduction

The decade of the 1980s in Britain and elsewhere in Europe was marked by profound changes in the nature of work and the labour market. The pace and intensity of change has differed across countries, but trends common to all the developed economies have included greater participation in paid work by women, a shift from manufacturing to service industries, and growth in part-time, temporary and other forms of 'atypical' work (Blackwell, 1994). Some of these are long-term trends, but in the UK one of the most striking features of rapid change during the 1980s was the growth in work described as self-employment. Between 1979 and 1990 the number of people recorded as self-employed rose by 95 per cent, to more than 3.4 million (Department of Employment, 1993). It fell back in the recent recession, but since 1992 it has risen again to around 3.3 million, or about one in eight of all those active in the labour market. The signs are that as the economy recovers, the upward trend in self-employment is resuming.

The activities embraced by self-employment range from those of the liberal professions or lucrative and technologically-advanced small enterprises to the most marginal and insecure forms of work. Growth has taken place at both ends of this continuum, leading to a wider dispersion of incomes within the self-employed sector itself and contributing significantly to patterns of growing inequality which have characterised the last 15 years in the UK (Goodman and Webb, 1994; Jenkins, 1994). Rapid increases in the service sector have also masked long-term stagnation or decline in traditional areas of self-employment, such as agriculture and fishing.

This book is concerned with the lives and work of the people behind these statistics. More specifically it is concerned with the lower income self-employed. For many commentators these terms can appear contradictory: there is still a widespread and persistent idea of self-employed people as an affluent and self-sufficient *petite bourgeoisie*. Moreover, the difficulties in measuring self-employed earnings in ways that provide figures comparable with the wages of employees have given rise to largely untested assumptions of widespread, and sometimes purposeful, under-reporting of income. It is our contention that there is a substantial and growing section of the population, amongst whom families with children are over-represented, who spend part or all of their working lives in forms of independent or semi-independent work which often bring very low financial rewards. In this group we find people who have responded to calls to embrace the 'culture of enterprise' but have found it difficult to compete in an overcrowded service sector. It includes others whose sources of employed work have dwindled in the industrial restructuring of the 1980s, or who have found that the only available work has been redesignated as self-employment in the name of 'flexibility'. There are also traditional forms of self-employment, such as farming and fishing, where incomes are highly dependent on external economic or environmental forces, or on policy decisions taken at a European level. Finally, the low-income self-employed increasingly include women, who have found in the flexibility offered by working for themselves a way of combining work and caring responsibilities.

Why is this important? There have always been people working for themselves and some of them have always had low earnings. Indeed this was recognised as long ago as 1942 in the Beveridge Report:

> Many independent workers - small shopkeepers, crofters, fishermen, hawkers, outworkers - are poorer than many of those employed under contract of service and are much dependent on good health for their earnings. (Beveridge, 1942, para.118)

This book argues that a shift in the pattern of work on the scale that has taken place since the beginning of the 1980s has potentially profound consequences which are only now beginning to be assessed. The growth of self-employment has taken place in parallel with, and partly linked to, an expansion in other forms of 'non-standard' employment, including part-time, temporary and sub-contracted work. One defining characteristic of this non-standard or atypical work is that it tends to provide less security and legal protection than conventional full-time employment and brings more limited access to employment-related social security benefits (Hakim, 1987a). However, many of these 'atypical' work patterns are actually normal and traditional for women and the growth of non-standard work is partly a consequence of more women entering the labour market. What is atypical, and apparently more controversial, is men being faced with similar 'flexibility' of employment. This is one way in which self-employment perhaps differs from other atypical work forms. Although the biggest proportionate increases in the 1980s were among women, the self-employed sector is still predominantly a male arena, but one in which, as the book shows, women often play an essential but largely invisible role.

There is no one simple explanation for the exceptionally strong resurgence of self-employment in Britain but the main contributory factors appear to have been industrial restructuring and changes in contractual employment relationships. The link with unemployment is contentious, but political efforts to establish a 'culture of enterprise' also have to be seen as part of the equation. In practical terms the ideology of enterprise has been underpinned by schemes like the Enterprise Allowance (subsequently renamed Business Start-up), which have encouraged people to move from unemployment into small business ventures, and by other initiatives to reduce fiscal or bureaucratic burdens on small business. Yet we know little at present about the nature of the work of the new self-employed, the organisation of home life and household activity which derives from it, or about the long-term financial consequences for the individuals and families involved.

Brown (1992) has suggested that self-employed people have been particularly disadvantaged in their exclusion from key social security provision such as unemployment benefit and the state earnings-related pension (SERPS), and from access to industrial injuries compensation. The question of retirement incomes is especially important. The exclusion of self-employed people from SERPS is premised on their ability to make private provision for themselves, and tax concessions have been made available to encourage private protection. However, there is growing evidence that amongst the lower earning self-employed at least, such a policy may be ineffective, as both national insurance contributions and private pension premiums are payments which attract low priority in times of financial difficulty. In a recent study of income distribution among the self-employed, Meager et al. (1994) found that retired people who had experienced spells of self-employment tended to have both lower savings and poorer pension entitlements than ex-employees. In general, Brown (1992) has argued that a 'policy vacuum' has existed in relation to the self-employed, based on perceptions which are no longer valid. Partly these perceptions stem from a lack of understanding of the work and living circumstances of many self-employed people. Until its resurgence in the 1980s, self-employment as a form of labour market activity had been largely stagnant if not in long-term decline. Sociologists of work and the labour process were pre-occupied mainly with the firm and the Fordist production process, and self-employment provoked little research interest. This began to change in the mid-1980s and there is now a growing body of work from legal, sociological, gender and labour market perspectives, as well as, more recently, a new focus on the financial circumstances of the self-employed. Yet there is still relatively little research which specifically links the working and family lives of self-employed people in a way that illuminates the connections between them. There has also been little attention given to the role of social security in the lives of self-employed people - not least because of the notions of self-reliance and independence which attach to this work status and the assumptions made about earnings derived from it.

Our book attempts to address this gap in knowledge, through research on self-employed people claiming family credit - the means-tested in-work benefit for lower income parents.

The research

The book is based on a programme of research commissioned by the Department of Social Security and carried out between 1991 and 1993 by the Social Policy Research Unit (SPRU) at the University of York. The study developed from earlier work on family credit (Corden and Craig, 1991), in which it was noted that applications for family credit by self-employed people appeared to cause special problems both for claimants and for the administration. At a policy level, there were several concerns. The number of self-employed families receiving family credit (and its predecessor family income supplement) had been growing steadily since the mid-1980s and self-employed families consistently received higher average payments than families with employed earners. This raised questions as to whether the assessment of earnings by the Family Credit Unit was representing accurately the 'true' incomes and living standards of these families because of inconsistencies in the assessment process and potential under-reporting of income by self-employed people.

The rising number of claims from self-employed people was also a focus of administrative interest. Staff difficulties in reaching consistent interpretations of the financial information supplied by self-employed claimants were matched by the problems claimants faced in trying to provide the information in the form required. In spite of the growing number of claims, it was thought that take-up amongst the self-employed could still be lower than for employees. Meanwhile there was a build up of representations from accountants, MPs and organisations acting on behalf of self-employed people, highlighting anomalies in the treatment of some groups. These concerns were coming to the attention of the Department at a time when the Government was placing increasing emphasis on maintaining work incentives in the benefit system and on smoothing the transition to work. Policy makers therefore required detailed information about the living and working situations of lower income self-employed people and their families.

The research was designed to illuminate the nature of low-income self-employment, the living standards generated and sustained with the help of family credit, the role of in-work benefits in providing incentives to work, and the process of applying for and establishing eligibility for benefit. It also focused specifically on the assessment of self-employed earnings, evaluating DSS regulations and procedures from an accountancy perspective. To achieve these goals the study included five main components:

- a review of research on self-employment and social security
- secondary analysis of administrative data on family credit recipients
- a conceptual study of the assessment of self-employed earnings for family credit
- a qualitative study of self-employed recipients of family credit and their occupations
- a qualitative study of the household living standards of self-employed recipients of family credit.

Methods

A preliminary review of the literature was required since so little was known about low-income self-employment in general and the use of social security benefits by the self-employed in particular. The aim was to locate the research within the existing body of knowledge about self-employment and to identify avenues of enquiry needing to be addressed in the empirical studies.

It was also clear that considerable information on both employed and self-employed family credit recipients was held on the administrative database at the Family Credit Unit in North Fylde. This had previously received little analysis beyond the basic tabulations, drawn from a five per cent sample of claims in payment on a particular day each month, produced for the Department of Social Security's annual statistical report. Secondary analysis of these data was designed to explore the differences and similarities between families with different employment statuses, and to pursue the question of why self-employed recipients consistently received higher levels of benefit. Monthly extracts were re-analysed, comparing information on employed and self-employed recipients between 1989 and 1991. More detail is given of the processes involved in Appendix A.

The analysis of administrative data provided a quantitative framework for the three other empirical elements of the research. For several reasons, the emphasis in these studies was on qualitative techniques. First, the conceptual study of the procedures for assessment of self-employed earnings required an in-depth analysis of a number of cases involving people in different kinds of work. It involved collaborative work with an academic accountant, examining administrative regulations and procedures from a business accountancy perspective, interviewing self-employed people and inspecting their workplaces and accounts. The discussions with recipients were carried out as part of the same interview which explored their experiences of applying for family credit. The findings from this study have been reported elsewhere (Boden and Corden, 1994).

Secondly, as was mentioned earlier, research on self-employment as a whole was relatively underdeveloped and the use of social security benefits by self-employed people in particular was a new area requiring initial exploration. The nature of the research questions required an understanding of self-employed people's experiences, their motivations for work and attitudes towards the social security system, and their understanding of the family credit assessment process and the rules of eligibility. All these aspects of the research - exploratory, diagnostic and evaluative - are prime territory for in-depth, qualitative techniques (Miles and Huberman, 1994).

The use of qualitative interviews to examine living standards is perhaps more unusual and requires some explanation. Conventionally, living standards are measured quantitatively by means of large-scale, representative surveys, since the purpose is generally to establish a statistical picture of the prevalence of different levels of living, either in the population as a whole or in particular sub-groups. There are a few exceptions to this norm, such as the study by Ritchie (1990) on living standards in unemployment, but this too was linked to a quantitative survey. For the present study it was decided that the complexity of the issues relating to self-employment required a different approach. In order to explain why in-depth, qualitative methods were felt to be most appropriate, it may be useful to review briefly the debate on the measurement of poverty and living standards.

One of the key arguments has been whether living standards can be measured 'objectively'. Early pioneers of poverty research like Rowntree (1901, 1937) attempted to assess the extent of poverty by measuring income and resources against an absolute minimum standard. Although there has been some debate about how Rowntree viewed the purpose of the subsistence minimum (see, for example, Veit Wilson, 1986), 'absolute' measures of living standards set by experts tended to hold sway until the late 1960s when this approach began to be challenged by the concept of 'relative deprivation'. Townsend (1979), one of the most influential proponents of this approach, argued that the living standards of individual people or families have to be seen in the context of the wider life of the community. A body of social expectations exists which is defined by particular societies to which people belong. These expectations change over time and create a set of norms by which people's ability to participate in society may be measured. Townsend's early attempts to turn the concept of relative deprivation into a measurable phenomenon met with some criticisms. Piachaud (1981), for example, argued that Townsend's choice of indicators suggested an unrealistic consensus around people's lifestyles and cultural expectations. Consequently some of the observed disparities in living standards could be seen as reflecting *choices* as much as financially-imposed *constraints*. A subsequent strand of work has attempted to meet this criticism by incorporating measures of public consensus around the importance or necessity of goods and participatory activities (Mack and Lansley, 1985; Brownlee and MacDonald, 1991).

Another aspect of the debate concerns the scope and breadth of the indicators which should be used to measure living standards. There has been a general acceptance of the relativist position that measures of deprivation should be broadened to include social and environmental factors such as participation in social activities and access to services. There has been less agreement on the use of more 'subjective' criteria such as personal well-being, stress, or individual self-evaluation of living standards. It has been argued that subjective feelings of unhappiness or frustration may carry little weight in policy terms compared to demonstrable deprivation of decent housing or adequate food (Sen, 1987). Other critics have doubted the value of attempting to measure the 'subjective domain' (Ringen, 1988), which it is suggested may not properly be the responsibility of the state. Against this position, others such as Townsend (1987) and Donnison (1988) have argued that the interconnection of the public and private spheres legitimates the inclusion of aspects of life beyond just those which are directly amenable to state intervention.

More recently attention has returned to the need for objective measures of living standards which incorporate aspects of both the relativist and the consensual approaches. Sen, for example, has argued that such measures are essential if the question of adequacy of state benefits is to be addressed (Sen, 1987). This is a point taken up by Bradshaw and Morgan (1987) in arguing the case for budget standards research, whereby experts compile household budgets for model family types using survey data on items considered essential or desirable by the general public. The budgets can be set at a minimum level or at any higher level required for particular policy purposes. In the UK the most developed application of this approach has been in the work of the Family Budget Unit (see, for example, Bradshaw and Ernst, 1990; Yu, 1992; Oldfield and Yu, 1993). Budget standards have been used in a number of other countries to aid decisions on benefit levels and are central to recent proposals for a new set of poverty lines for the USA (Citro and Michael, 1995).

A different direction was taken in recent work by Townsend which suggested that there were levels of income for different types of households where falling resources resulted in a sharp and measurable increase in deprivation and a withdrawal from social participation (Townsend and Gordon, 1989). This attempt to establish an objective poverty line has, however, been disputed on methodological grounds by the Department of Social Security.

Both the consensual and the budget standards approaches have attempted in different ways to deal with problems such as the influence of taste and preference on living standards and the establishment of objective measurement criteria. Difficulties still remain, however, with both the use of expenditure patterns as a proxy for consumption and of possession of consumption items as indicators of living standards. These problems cross all household types, but for reasons outlined below they may be particularly salient among families engaged in self-employment.

One problem lies in taking account of the periods of time during which people experience different levels of household income. The OPCS survey of living standards in unemployment found that levels of expenditure and consumption tended to be higher during unemployment among households where the head had been in full-time employment for most of the previous year than among those who had experienced interrupted work (Heady and Smyth, 1989). Patterns of consumption of a range of items were thus associated with pre-unemployment patterns of income, and subsequent rises in consumption following a return to work were also linked with factors such as pre-unemployment credit-worthiness.

Similar patterns of expenditure and consumption can be observed among people working in self-employment. For example, consumption may be inconsistent with current incomes where families have recently moved into self-employment from the relative security of higher paid employment, or where business fortunes have improved or declined. It is also not uncommon for self-employed people to experience earnings which fluctuate substantially over time. The value of housing property (and the size of mortgages) may also bear little relation to current earnings, since they may be the result of inheritance or of investments made in more comfortable times. Moreover, there can often be a time-lag between the period during which particular levels of expenditure or consumption are observed and the out-turn of actual business profit for this period. Such fluctuations and time-lags may in practice be absorbed by the rundown of capital and savings, by the use of credit, or by a build-up of other debts. Whether self-employed people have access to means of credit or other borrowing may depend on the nature of their enterprise, on previous income or on housing tenure, but the use of overdraft facilities are a common feature of financial management in small enterprises. Borrowing may be used to provide finance for household expenditure or to reduce drawings in order to help the business to ride out periods of market fluctuation. Such borrowing may not be regarded as problematic until there is clear evidence of a decline in business turnover or a change of policy by lenders, and the level of expenditure and consumption it allows may bear little resemblance to the pattern of profits actually made through the business over a period of observation.

A similar problem exists with the use of household goods or domestic capital as indicators of living standards. It is simple enough to ask whether households possess certain consumer durables, and a degree of consensus has arisen in recent years over the inclusion of a core of common items (see, for example, Table 6.7 in *Social Trends* (OPCS, 1994)). It is less obvious that meaningful conclusions can be drawn from such indicators. Possession of domestic capital may be suggestive of certain standards of living. However, even if adequate adjustments can be made to account for family size, need and individual choices or priorities, value, age, condition and circumstances of acquisition of some consumption items could be seen as more pertinent criteria than simple possession, particularly where the items concerned are present in the vast majority of households and are widely regarded as virtual necessities. In many cases the ability to repair or replace important items in the event of breakdown or deterioration may be the crucial test, a point which a number of studies have tried to incorporate (see, for example, Bradshaw and Holmes, 1989).

For the self-employed, it may be that ownership of certain consumption items is intrinsically linked into the nature of working for oneself. Access to some form of vehicle, for example, is vital in certain kinds of work, and this is recognised as an allowable expense in both taxation and in the assessment of income for means-tested benefits. Telephones too are often essential for people providing services to the public. Home ownership is closely associated with being self-employed, one reason for which may be the possibility of using housing as security for loans. There are also certain types of traditional self-employment, such as farming and fishing, where assets in the form of land, housing or equipment is handed down between families and where it is commonplace for parents and grandparents to continue their involvement in the development of new businesses. More generally, the achievement of a suitable home from which to work, a certain level of living standards and a secure stock of household goods may for some people be a prerequisite for entering the insecure arena of self-employment, rather than necessarily a product of the enterprise itself.

This brings us to a final feature of self-employment, which is the potential for overlap between 'business' and 'household' monies, both in income and expenditure. The ambiguity of different flows of money may be especially evident in the kind of modest, sole-trader or home-based enterprises common in the lower income self-employed sector. There is little known about how people separate these in practice, how much leakage there is between them, or how the allocation of money to different forms of expenditure may affect living standards. Earlier work on family credit has shown that among employees there are distinct gender dimensions in the claiming and use of benefit (Corden and Craig, 1991). We need to understand whether there are any special features of self-employment which affect the allocation of household resources between partners and how this might affect the use of family credit among these families.

The way that living standards are conceptualised in this book is not, therefore, solely based on measures of income, expenditure and possession of consumer goods, although some information of this kind is included. It relies additionally on respondents' own accounts of how their present material standards came about. How was this process linked with work decisions or experiences in the past? How much were present standards maintained by current incomes, or were they a residue from more affluent times? What difficulties, if any, did families have in managing on their present low incomes and how were their living standards changing? What choices were they making about future financial security in old age or ill health? By pursuing these questions the study attempts to identify the expectations, choices and constraints facing different families, the strategies of managing on low earnings, and the degrees of insecurity or satisfaction felt about respondents' present circumstances.

Appendix B explains the methodology of the in-depth studies in more detail, including the selection of samples for the qualitative interviews. In all, interviews were carried out with 73 self-employed people and wherever possible, in the case of couples, their domestic partners. With a few exceptions interviews were tape-recorded and transcripts were analysed manually, using a system of card indexation under key themes.

The structure of the book

The book is organised as follows. Chapter Two sets out the wider context for the study, looking at the legal and sociological approaches to defining and categorising different forms of self-employment, and reviewing the evidence on the rapid upsurge of self-employment in Britain during the 1980s. We discuss the arguments about the causes of this resurgence and examine the characteristics of the 'new' self-employed. One point which emerges clearly is that there has been growth in both forms of professional and higher paid self-employment and in marginal enterprises which are likely to be insecure and poorly rewarded. Chapter Three takes up this issue in a discussion of the financial circumstances of the self-employed and the problems involved in conceptualising and measuring the resources available to them. The next chapter focuses on the lower income groups, drawing on the analysis of family credit administrative data and providing a quantitative comparison between the circumstances of employed and self-employed recipients. Chapter Five is about the working lives of families in self-employment. We look at what people do and how work is organised, their routes into self-employment and their motivations, the role of other family members and the special role self-employed work can play in the lives of lone parents, disabled people and those with special caring responsibilities. This is followed, in Chapter Six, by an analysis of the role of social security benefits in the lives of self-employed people, focusing particularly on family credit. Chapter Seven examines the construction and maintenance of living standards in the lower income self-employed families, tracing the links between previous work and family circumstances and current income. It also looks at patterns of managing and budgeting, and at how these are linked with the allocation of resources within households. The book concludes, in Chapter Eight, with a discussion of risk and insecurity in an enterprise culture, an evaluation of the role of in-work benefits for self-employed people and an assessment of the implications for social security policy.

2 The resurgence of self-employment in the 1980s

The working lives of low-income families supported by self-employment in the early 1990s have to be understood against the background of the remarkable upsurge in work of this kind which took place during the 1980s. This chapter provides a contextual background for the qualitative study of low-income families by examining the statistical evidence on the growth of self-employment both in Britain and elsewhere. We also discuss the characteristics of people entering self-employment since the beginning of the 1980s in the light of recent sociological research. As we suggested in Chapter One, self-employment was somewhat neglected as a research issue until the mid-1980s. Hakim (1988, p.421) described it as 'one of the Cinderellas of labour market research, only recently invited to the ball'. Since then, however, a substantial body of work has emerged, particularly from the labour market and business studies disciplines. Meanwhile, debates on social policy and 'atypical' work patterns within the European Union, and more widely within the OECD, have stimulated new comparative analyses of self-employment, both as a form of labour market participation and as an issue within the area of social protection.

First, however, it is necessary to face the problem of defining self-employment. The difference between being employed and self-employed may appear self-evident, but definitions can vary according to the purposes for which a distinction is being drawn. This question is of more than academic interest because it represents the central dichotomy of employment status which determines treatment in labour law, income tax, national insurance and social security. It also affects both the measurement of change in the labour force, the evaluation of data on earnings and income distribution and estimations of take-up of social security benefits.

What is self-employment?

Conceptual problems

The limited attention previously given to self-employment as an area for study has been ascribed to the dominance of sociological interest in the industrial processes of mass production and the firm (Curran, 1990). This focus was in turn influenced by marxist sociological theories on class and the relations of production (Bogenhold and Staber, 1991). Within this theoretical framework self-employment was regarded as an anachronistic work form which was destined for an inevitable historical decline, while the self-employed themselves tended to be seen as a unitary '*petit bourgeois*' grouping. This traditional sociological approach to self-employment has depended on the idea that working 'on one's own account' is linked intrinsically with ownership, autonomy and control over production, clearly distinguishing craftspeople, independent professionals and small business proprietors from waged workers. Evidence on the changing nature of self-employment in the last decade suggests that such a clear distinction is no longer tenable. In fact one could argue that it never was: concern has existed since at least the end of the last century about the conditions of 'lump' workers, outworkers and other forms of sweated labour whose employment status was ambiguous (Harris, 1972).

What appears to have happened more recently is a marked increase in the number of people whose legal and contractual status is that of self-employment, but whose actual work situation may be far from that of the *petit bourgeois* small business owner (Dale, 1986). This new 'quasi self-employment' includes people engaged in homeworking, franchising and other forms of outworking, freelancing and casual agency work for which self-employment status has become widespread, as well as labour-only subcontracting in construction and agriculture (Creigh et al., 1986; Casey and Creigh, 1988; Hakim, 1988; Felstead, 1991; Rainbird, 1991). For many, the working environment may be markedly different from that of the 'autonomous' small trader and the level of individual control over work may be less than with many traditional employees (Cragg and Dawson, 1981; Hakim, 1985; Steinmetz and Wright, 1989). On the other hand, research suggests that some notionally self-employed workers see freedom from control by an employer as a more conclusive test of their status than that derived from their formal tax or national insurance position (Hakim, 1987a). Certainly the conventional definition based on tax and national insurance status does not always correspond either with the real world of work or with people's perceptions of their own status.

Legal definitions

Legislation defines self-employment in a number of ways. For taxation purposes, for example, the Inland Revenue classes those 'in business on their own account' as self-employed and the rest as 'dependent employees'. For national insurance purposes, the Social Security Contributions and Benefits Act 1992, like its predecessor the 1975 Social Security Act, defines self-employed people negatively as being employed 'otherwise than in employed earner's employment' (s.2(1)(b)). 'Employment which is not employed earner's employment' is further defined 'in somewhat circular terms' (Luckaus, 1991, p.10) by reference to another legal construct, the 'contract of service'. The contract is also a determining factor under the 1978 Employment Protection (Consolidation) Act (EPCA), which defines a dependent employee as having a 'contract of service' and a self-employed person as having 'contracts *for* services' or 'contracts of their own kind'. Neither the Social Security Act nor the EPCA offer a precise definition of these contracts and it has been left to the courts to decide on a case-by-case basis (Casey and Creigh, 1988).

Although the courts have regularly had to adjudicate on the employed/self-employed distinction in order to determine employment rights, rates of social security contributions and entitlements, and protection under health and safety regulations, no clear or settled definition has emerged (McCarthy, 1993). Leighton (1986) argued that the courts had failed to provide adequate guidance and that self-employed workers consequently remained marginalised from the mainstream of legal protection. The marginality of the self-employed in labour law is reinforced by associations of self-employment with the 'informal' or 'irregular' economy. It is also maintained by the courts' continued view of commercial contract law as the appropriate arena for determining relations between apparently self-employed workers and other employers or contracting bodies. Although a form of legal checklist has emerged for determining employment status, covering factors such as how workers are paid, how tax is paid, how supervision is maintained and whether more than one employer is involved, Leighton (1983) argued that the courts have nevertheless continued to privilege the contractual 'label'. Many of the checklist factors are themselves legally uncertain and the failure of the courts to resolve problems of the exclusion of many marginal workers from protection has led some commentators to argue that the distinction should be abandoned altogether (Hepple, 1986).

One particular problem lies in the status of company directors. Owners of incorporated businesses should be classified as employees, but often think of themselves as self-employed. Each year the Inland Revenue reclassifies a substantial number of directors who attempt to enrol in the Schedule D taxation scheme or to pay Class 2 or 4 National Insurance Contributions. This suggests a continuing area of uncertainty or ambiguity in the status of small business owners. The same difficulty arises in the definitions of self-employment used in national surveys.

Defining self-employment in surveys

Although both the courts and individual workers may see control over work as an important element in the employment/self-employment dichotomy, such a test is not specifically applied in surveys. The main source of national employment data, the Labour Force Survey (LFS), bases its classification of respondents primarily on self-definition and then by reference to tax or national insurance status if the respondent is in doubt. This has two main effects: first it includes within the ranks of self-employment large numbers of labour-only subcontractors whose employment status could be seen as ambiguous; secondly, it attempts to exclude directors of incorporated businesses, whose tax and insurance status is officially that of employees, but who are arguably much closer to the traditional image of the *petit bourgeois* small business owner.

In the LFS, those who say they are self-employed but subsequently describe themselves as company directors are reclassified as employees. This approach is consistent with both taxation and social security practice, but it is not unproblematic. For the purposes of assessing eligibility for means-tested benefits it is an issue of some importance, because claimants who differ little in practice from many other self-employed people, except in having registered their business as a limited liability company, have to be assessed as employees of their company. The problem with the LFS classification is that an unknown number of company directors may describe their occupation in other terms more closely related to the activity of their particular business and will thus not be reclassified. Some idea of the difference this issue can make to statistics of the self-employed can be found from a checking exercise carried out on the 1981 Census. This resulted in a reclassification of some 300,000 company directors who had assessed themselves as self-employed, reducing the census figures for self-employment by 13 per cent (OPCS, 1984). It is not known how many company directors correctly assess their legal status in either the census or in the LFS, but as Hakim (1988) has pointed out, those who do are more likely to be found in larger enterprises. This is one of the reasons why surveys show that most self-employed people have no, or very few, employees.

Household surveys, such as the Family Expenditure Survey (FES), recognise that it is insufficient just to ask people whether they are employed or self-employed and instructions to interviewers are designed to allow employment status to emerge, according to subsequent answers. There are also some predetermined rules for categorising specific occupations or ways of working. There are early instructions to FES interviewers to treat company directors as employees and other questions later in the schedule are designed to re-route people who have identified themselves incorrectly as self-employed. However, even if all company directors are identified correctly and dealt with as employees, the question remains whether this really is the appropriate categorisation, particularly for analysis of income data. Thus it has been argued that directors' control of their companies allows them access to financial resources which places them in a situation analogous to that of a self-employed person, and that their treatment as employees for social security purposes may place them in a relatively privileged financial position (Boden and Corden, 1994; Hallam, 1994).

There are a number of other areas of uncertainty or ambiguity in defining people as self-employed in household surveys. In the FES, for example, as little as one hour per week of self-employed work qualifies as conferring self-employed status. But there is currently an administrative bench-mark of 16 hours work per week for social security purposes, which separates the conditions for claiming out-of-work benefits (income support) from those entitling people to in-work benefits (family credit, disability working allowance). Uncertainty about work status can often be found among people in transitional situations between unemployment or inactivity and self-employment. People trying to start a small business and to move out of unemployment sometimes find it hard to know on which side of an apparent line they stand, especially if the process has been gradual.

People working below the level of earnings at which they become liable for national insurance contributions and income tax may receive few official 'prompts' as to their employment status. Many of these are women, whose work status can be particularly ambiguous. In the FES, people earning small amounts from occasional work as babysitters or catalogue mail order agents are classified as unoccupied: the 1980 Women and Work Survey found 13 per cent of 'non-working' women between the ages of 16 and 59 were engaged in such work, earning an average of £4.10 per week for about five hours work. In the General Household Survey (GHS), by contrast, mail order agents are included in the self-employed category. Discrepancies between datasets, or reclassifications, can have important implications. When, in 1982, self-employed people with no other employment and small earnings of £3.50 per week or less were reclassified for FES as unoccupied, the self-employment rate fell sharply from over 11 per cent in 1981 to eight per cent in 1982 (Hakim, 1989a).

While labour-only subcontracting and other forms of 'quasi' self-employment are known to have grown, precise figures have been hard to obtain. It is possible, however, to make a broad estimate drawing on LFS data for the period when self-employment growth was at its peak. Since 1989 the LFS has included a question asking whether people defining themselves as self-employed were the owner or manager of the business in which they worked. This has been taken as an approximate indicator of a distinction between 'true' self-employment and labour-only subcontractors. In 1989, some 690,000 people said they did not own or manage their business, or 20 per cent of all the self-employed (and more than a quarter of self-employed women) (Daly, 1991a). This question was not asked in earlier years, so the expansion of this group over time cannot accurately be gauged. One hypothesis is that people may have been switching from employment to self-employment while continuing to carry out the same work, often under pressure from employers aiming to take advantage of their more limited liabilities towards the self-employed. There is in fact little evidence to suggest that this has been happening on a large scale, at least in the early 1980s. LFS data show that only nine per cent of those moving from employment to self-employment in the course of 1984, when self-employment was increasing particularly rapidly, remained in both the same occupation and attached to the same firm (Creigh et al., 1986).

There are some other data available on specific industries or occupational groups. The legal position of labour-only subcontractors in the construction industry, for example, has long been an area of concern (Ministry of Labour, 1966; Austrin, 1980) and an increasing casualisation of labour was noted in the mid-1980s (Bresnen et al., 1985). Construction was one of the areas of particular growth in self-employment during the 1980s. Even at the beginning of this period it was clear that a high proportion of building workers were nominally self-employed while providing only their labour to other contractors. A survey of male labour mobility in the construction industry (Marsh et al., 1981) found that 20 per cent of the hireable workforce were self-employed for the purposes of tax and national insurance, but two-fifths of these worked only for other contractors. Forty per cent of building workers provided their own labour only, and of these over four-fifths worked directly for other contractors. Similar trends have also been noted in a number of manufacturing industries, including steel (Fevre, 1987). In agriculture and fishing the overall numbers of people in work have declined, but the proportion who are self-employed had risen to well over half by the summer of 1994 (Department of Employment, 1994). It is likely that many are subcontractors. One result of these ambiguities in employment status is that social security and Inland Revenue statistics consistently record fewer self-employed people than the Labour Force Survey. Casey and Creigh (1988) have suggested a number of explanations for this: first, the LFS may pick up some of those working in the informal economy who do not pay tax and insurance; secondly, the publicity accorded in the 1980s to the idea of the 'enterprise culture' may have encouraged those on the margins between employment and self-employment status to emphasise the latter; thirdly, some married women in self-employment may still be opting out of national insurance contributions, as is permitted if they chose to do so before 1977. Finally, many self-employed people have earnings below tax and national insurance thresholds and might not be recorded (this question is discussed further in Chapter Three). Although people earning below the national insurance thresholds are meant to apply for formal exemption from contributions, there is evidence that many self-employed people are unaware of this or do not apply for other reasons (Brown, 1992). Given that part-time self-employment is not uncommon, particularly for women, this may well account for much of the discrepancy. Hakim (1989b) has also argued that failure to recognise this group of low earners is one cause of widespread over-estimation of the size of the informal economy.

The examples given of problems in defining work status illustrate the difficulty of discussing the representativeness of survey data as applied to self-employed people. It is the analysts' definitions of self-employment, especially at lower earnings levels, which determine who is included or excluded, and the rules can differ from one survey to another. This is likely to be especially important in considering the composition of the lower income deciles and in setting income survey data into wider contexts such as labour market behaviour or take-up of benefits.

The rise in aggregate self-employment

Even allowing for ambiguities in the classification of employment status, it is clear that the UK experienced an exceptional boom in self-employment during the 1980s. Labour Force Surveys for Great Britain[1] show that between 1979 and 1990 the total number of people recorded as self-employed (in their main or second jobs) rose by 95 per cent, to 3.47 million in the first quarter of 1990, or 13.4 per cent of all those in work (Department of Employment, 1993). This increase followed a long period in which self-employment was virtually static in numbers and declining as a proportion of the employed workforce. The Institute for Employment Research (1987) has estimated that over the 30 year period from 1949 the number of people self-employed fluctuated only between 1.8 and 2.0 million. This picture does, however, conceal shorter periods of growth such as in the late 1960s when self-employment increased from 1.7

million, or 6.4 per cent of the workforce, to just over two million, or 8.4 per cent, between 1965 and 1971. During the 1970s the self-employment rate also fluctuated, but finally declined again to 1.8 million, or 7.3 per cent of the workforce, in 1979.

Another way of measuring the increase in self-employment is to look at Value Added Tax (VAT) registrations by small businesses. The threshold of business turnover above which small businesses have to pay VAT (£35,000 in 1991/2) excludes many businesses from liability. Thus the level of registrations is always lower than the figures recorded for self-employment from other surveys. Nevertheless, VAT registrations during the 1980s followed the same upward trend as found in the LFS (Daly, 1990).

Table 2.1 shows the total number of people recorded as self-employed in their main job in the Labour Force Surveys between 1979 and 1994, and the percentage they made up of all those in paid work.

This table illustrates two main points. First, it is clear that while the increase evident since 1979 was halted in the recession of 1990-1992 (reaching a low point of 3.05 million in the winter of 1992), the upward trend has now resumed. The fact that the self-employment rate has not increased significantly is due to the parallel increase in the number of employees since the recession ended. Secondly, the table shows that rate of growth in the 1980s varied considerably. Year-to-year changes tend to be prone to sizeable fluctuations, partly caused by sampling errors, but it is evident that the most rapid rises occurred in the early 1980s. There was an increase of 442,000, or more than 20 per cent, between mid-1981 and mid-1984, of which around 315,000 occurred in 1983/4 alone (Daly, 1991a). In the later years of the 1980s the numbers of self-employed people continued to grow, but at a much slower average rate of around two per cent per year.

Table 2.1
Trends in aggregate self-employment, Great Britain, 1979-1994

		Self-employed (thousands)	*Self-employment rate (%)*
Spring	1979	1,778	7.3
	1981	2,201	9.3
	1983	2,301	10.2
	1984	2,618	11.4
	1985	2,714	11.6
	1986	2,727	11.6
	1987	2,997	12.6
	1988	3,143	12.8
	1989	3,426	13.4
	1990	3,472	13.5
	1991	3,318	13.2
	1992	3,131	12.8
	1993	3,103	12.7
	1994	3,208	13.1
Summer	1994	3,216	13.0

Note: Figures are not seasonally adjusted

Sources: *Labour Force Survey Historical Supplement*, April (Department of Employment, 1993)

Labour Force Survey Quarterly Bulletin, No. 10, December (Department of Employment, 1994a)

The pace of change in self-employment during the last three decades is illustrated in Table 2.2, which shows the number of people self-employed in their main job between 1961 and 1991, together with the percentage changes between decades. While there was a gradual net increase in self-employment between 1961 and 1981, the upsurge began at the beginning of the 1980s.

Table 2.2
Self-employment 1961 to 1991: numbers and percentage increase over decades

	1961	*1971*		*1981*		*1991*	
			% +		% +		% +
Men	1,338	1,556	16	1,745	12	2,512	44
Women	327	398	22	455	14	806	77
Total	1,665	1,954	17	2,201	13	3,318	51

Note: Before 1981 self-employment figures were calculated on a different basis. See *Employment Gazette*, Department of Employment, February 1983, pp.55-56 for an explanation of the pre-1981 figures.

Sources: Labour Force Surveys, Department of Employment
Census 1981 (OPCS, 1984)

The involvement of women in self-employment is discussed in more detail later, but it is worth noting here that the large percentage increase among women, while significant, was partly a reflection of their greater overall labour market participation. The self-employment rate for women increased from just under five per cent in 1981 to just over seven per cent in 1991, but the sector remains predominantly a male arena. The latest LFS estimates put the total number of self-employed people in the second quarter of 1994 at 3,216,000 (not seasonally adjusted), of whom 25.4 per cent were women. In addition, some 342,000 people held second jobs in self-employment, of whom two-fifths were women (Department of Employment, 1994). Finally there were an estimated 144,000 'unpaid family workers', mainly involved in small self-employed businesses, of whom two-thirds were women.

The increase in self-employment in Britain is all the more remarkable when the experience of other comparable countries is taken into account. Although some other countries also experienced increases during the 1980s, the UK's rapid and sustained growth was unique. There are some difficulties with international comparisons of self-employment because of different definitions and variations in the inclusion or exclusion of people such as homeworkers and company directors. There are wide variations between countries, for example, in the proportion of people working in incorporated and unincorporated businesses (OECD, 1986). Even the Community Labour Force Survey, which aims to collect a core of information on a common basis, is not immune from problems of definition (Glover, 1995). Some comparison is, nevertheless instructive, and Table 2.3 gives the rates of self-employment in 1988 in the member countries of the European Union, along with the percentage changes in the level of self-employment since 1979. Denmark and Luxembourg experienced a drop in self-employment over the decade, while for others the rate of growth varied considerably. Britain still had a rate of self-employment in 1988 which was below the EU average in spite of the rapid growth after 1979.

Table 2.3
Self-employment rates in 1988 and percentage changes 1979-88 in the European Union

	1988 rate %	*Percentage change 1979-88* %
Belgium	13	+13
Denmark	6	-24
France	11	+ 2
Germany (West)	8	+ 5
Greece	27	+ 1
Ireland	13	+13
Italy	22	+28
Luxembourg	8	- 7
Netherlands	8	+ 2
Portugal	17	+10
Spain	18	+22
UK	11	+68
Unweighted average	*14*	*+11*

Source: Daly (1991a), based on national labour force surveys

Perhaps a better comparison comes if we exclude agricultural self-employment, since this sector has demonstrated a steady secular decline in most European countries. Table 2.4 gives the self-employment rates outside agriculture in the OECD countries which are members of the European Economic Area. Again it is evident that the magnitude of change in the UK was unique, though substantial increases were recorded in some countries, such as Portugal and Sweden and Ireland, while nearly half the countries experienced a drop in the self-employment rate.

Table 2.4
Percentage rates of non-agricultural self-employment in countries of the European Economic Area, 1979 and 1990

	1979	*1990*
Austria	8.9	6.4
Belgium	11.2	12.9
Denmark	9.2	7.2
Finland	6.1	8.8
France	10.6	10.3
Germany	8.2	7.7
Greece	32.0	27.2*
Ireland	10.4	13.3
Italy	18.9	22.3
Netherlands	8.8	7.8
Norway	6.6	6.1
Portugal	12.1	18.5
Spain	15.7	17.2
Sweden	4.5	7.0
UK	6.6	11.6

* 1989
Source: OECD (1992) Table 4.1

Another way of judging the importance of self-employment in different countries is to look at the proportion of average income derived from it, compared to the share derived from wages and other income sources. Table 2.5 provides data on the composition of average incomes for selected countries, using the Luxembourg Income Studies. The data have to be regarded with some caution both in the light of comparability problems discovered in the early LIS datasets and the difficulties involved in assessing incomes from self-employment which are discussed in the next chapter. The table does, nevertheless, give a further illustration of the relatively low base from which the 1980s growth in the UK was starting. In 1981/2 the UK derived an average of only 4.5 per cent of income from self-employment. Of all the LIS countries, only Sweden derived less from self-employment, with 3.7 per cent of total incomes. By the mid-1980s, however, the share of incomes derived from self-employment had fallen for all of the countries.

Table 2.5
Percentage of average incomes derived from wages, self-employment and other sources in selected Luxembourg Income Study countries, 1981/2 and mid-1980s

	Wages and salaries		*Self-employed earnings*		*Other sources*[a]	
	1981/2	mid-1980s	1981/2	mid-1980s	1981/2	mid-1980s
UK[b]	72	65.2	4.5	6.9	23.5	27.8
Germany[c]	63.1	70.1	16.7	8.3	20.2	20.5
Sweden[d]	64.5	65.1	3.7	2.7	31.8	2.2
Australia[e]	69.9	72.1	13.5	8.7	16.6	19.2
USA[d]	75.8	75.1	6.7	6.4	17.5	18.4
Canada[d]	75.7	75.4	5.4	5.8	18.9	18.8

[a] Includes property income, social security benefits, private and occupational pensions and other transfers
[b] 1986
[c] 1984/5
[d] 1987
[e] 1985/6

Sources: Saunders et al. (1989) Table 9; Smeeding et al. (1990) Table 2.1; Whiteford and Kennedy (1994) Table 5.1

Explanations for the upsurge in self-employment in Britain

The particularly strong growth in self-employment in the UK requires some explanation, especially since it so clearly diverges from the trends elsewhere in Europe. Various attempts have been made to construct a robust macro-economic relationship between self-employment and the business cycle in different economies over time which would allow some accurate prediction of future trends, but these have had only limited success.

Broadly speaking, the argument is that the expansion of self-employment and small enterprise generally is a counter-cyclical response to recession, closely related to unemployment levels, and that a period of economic growth may be expected to be accompanied by a slowdown or decline in self-employment. This has happened before in the UK with the slump of the 1930s followed by the post-war economic revival. Using time-series data mainly from the USA, Steinmetz and Wright (1989) found evidence to support this theory, but also found that the relationship between self-employment and unemployment appeared to have declined over time. They speculated that the widening earnings distribution in many OECD countries meant that self-employment was not just a consequence of an absolute lack of wage employment opportunities, but was also a structural response to declining opportunities for good, well-paid jobs. More recently Bogenhold and Staber (1991) carried out a similar analysis for eight OECD countries with data from 1957 to 1987 and found a strong positive correlation between unemployment and self-employment for all countries except Belgium and Sweden, where the correlations were positive but weaker. Meager (1992a, 1992b, et al., 1994), however, has criticised these approaches to the question and argues that no single factor can explain the varying trends across countries, particularly because the heterogeneity of the self-employed makes it unlikely that their activities can be captured within one theoretical model.

The national aggregate statistics on which such analyses are based are not sufficiently detailed or accurate to account for movements in and out of self-employment at a micro level. Such changes are inevitably more closely related to particular features of national labour market, government policies and other localised developments. Nevertheless, such studies do suggest that at a macro level self-employment tends to increase at times of high unemployment, supporting the idea of a countercyclical response (Curran, 1990). Hakim (1988), however, has suggested that the counter-cyclical effects demonstrated in the OECD countries have been insufficient to account for the growth of self-employment in Britain.

Daly (1991b) too is sceptical about the explanatory power of economic modelling in this area. He pointed out that there is recent evidence that self-employment may also respond positively to a *decrease* in unemployment (as has happened in the UK since 1992). Both these apparently conflicting theories may have some elements of truth, because recession brings both opportunities and dangers for self-employment and small businesses. Similarly, an upturn in the economy may encourage some people to risk starting a business, whereas others may take the safer option of a better chance of waged employment. Thus both economic cycles can foster certain kinds of self-employment if other conditions are favourable. Either way, it appears to be the balance of particular national conditions interacting with the economic cycle which influences the flows into and out of self-employment in any given period.

The most important factors appear to be the level and direction of structural change in the economy, and shifts in employers' contractual arrangements. The restructuring of industry away from manufacturing and towards services, which has taken place in most of the OECD countries, tends to favour the growth of self-employment, since the service sector offers the greatest opportunities for individuals to try working on their own. The general shift towards services in the UK has been widely noted (e.g. Pollert, 1988), and more specifically the Institute for Employment Research (1987) has also highlighted the growing demand for services in competitive markets which favour small enterprises. Some of these services are in areas which were previously provided by the public sector, but have been contracted out as a result of public spending constraints. In terms of changing contractual arrangements, it has already been argued that employers have specifically encouraged the substitution of employee jobs with 'flexible' work arrangements through subcontracting, franchising and other forms of self-employment (Atkinson, 1985; Fevre, 1987, 1991; Hakim, 1985, 1988; Wood and Smith, 1989), though Pollert (1991) and others have disputed whether such practices represent a significantly new development.

While these arguments are persuasive, they do not fully account for the exceptional increase in self-employment in Britain, since similar shifts towards services have taken place in many other EU member countries within a broadly similar macro-economic environment. Two other influences have been suggested as contributing to the UK trends. The first relates to changes in the country's demographic structure. The argument is that since different population groups are more or less likely to enter or stay in self-employment, changes such as women's growing labour market participation, the ageing of the population and growth in the minority ethnic population of working age might have tended to swell the ranks of the self-employed. However, as Meager et al. (1994) point out, such tendencies as there are act in opposite directions and cancel each other out. In any case the changes have not taken place at a scale or pace which would account for the trend in the UK.

The second factor, which is perhaps more contentious, is the promotion by government of an 'enterprise culture'. Curran (1990) and Curran and Burrows (1991), among others, have queried the validity of this concept, arguing that its suggestion of bold entrepreneurialism misrepresents the nature of much small-scale self-employment, which he characterises as cautious and conservative. Meager et al. (1994) are also dismissive of this notion, citing surveys such as that of Blanchflower and Oswald (1990), which find little evidence of an attitudinal sea-change on the part of the British public. The concept of the enterprise culture was, nevertheless, an integral part of the ideological currency of the 1980s in the UK. As such it was persuasive in the construction of a favourable political discourse on job creation during a period of high unemployment and business failure. In practical terms it led to the creation of financial incentives to take up self-employment, such as the Enterprise Allowance Scheme (now renamed Business Start-up), and other grants and concessions for small businesses. Rhetoric as much of the discourse around enterprise may have been, it also had practical consequences in the easing of an already relatively loose framework of regulation around business start-up and access to financial capital, which was cited by Meager et al. (1992c) as one of the environmental differences between Britain and Germany.

The influence of such factors on self-employment at the micro level can be better understood by looking at the 'flow' data, which records the numbers and characteristics of people moving into or out of self-employment in any one year. The next section examines these data and looks at other research evidence which sheds light on the changing nature of self-employment.

Flows into and out of self-employment

The total number of people recorded as self-employed in any one year represents the net difference between those joining and those leaving self-employment. The flow of people into and out of self-employment is measured in the Labour Force Survey by asking respondents what they were doing at the same time the previous year. Problems with accuracy of recall, proxy information and multiple changes of activity during the year suggest substantial margins of error. Consequently there are discrepancies between the figures for the change in the 'stock' of self-employed people derived from year-on-year comparisons and those measured by the difference between gross inflows and outflows. Daly (1991a) and Campbell and Daly (1992) attempted to deal with these problems by scaling the gross flow data to correspond with the net stock change levels. In another analysis, comparing flow changes across countries, Meager et al. (1994) preferred to work with the unadjusted data on the grounds that there was no clear methodological basis for the scaling process. There are, thus, some differences in the estimates derived from the two methods, but the data still provide important insights into the dynamics of self-employment and the changing composition of the self-employed workforce.

Labour Force Surveys over the decade paint a broadly similar picture, with fluctuations in the net change from year to year caused more by variations in entries than in exits. This is not surprising because people may have more choice about deciding whether or when to enter self-employment, based on their perceptions of economic opportunities and personal changes in their lives, than in leaving it, which is more likely to be involuntary. Both entry and exit rates over the period were higher for women than for men and for the 16-24 age group. Meager et al.'s (1994) comparative analysis shows that the UK flows have been particularly dynamic, with relatively high levels of both entry and exit. This suggests that more people in the UK than in other countries will have experienced a period of self-employment at some time in their working lives.

Of particular interest is the previous employment history of people coming into self-employment and those leaving it. The 1989 LFS showed that just over half of those entering self-employment during the previous year had switched from an employed job, 19 per cent had previously been unemployed and 23 per cent were economically inactive. For women, double this percentage had been economically inactive and correspondingly fewer had come from unemployment or another job. Much the same picture was observed from the 1987 LFS (Hakim, 1989a).

This means that in 1988/89 some 113,000 people entered self-employment from unemployment, of whom 16,000 were women. The figures do not tell us how long these entrants had been unemployed, but given that over 95,000 people took part in the Enterprise Allowance Scheme (EAS) in the course of 1988 (Unemployment Unit, 1991a), they highlight the importance of this scheme as a route to self-employment.

A somewhat different picture of the importance of self-employment as a route out of unemployment comes from a national survey carried out for the Department of Employment in 1987 (Bevan et al., 1989). They interviewed 472 people who were currently self-employed, had recently left self-employment or were planning to start a new business. Forty per cent of all those who had started self-employment in the previous two years had been unemployed before they started, and 54 per cent of the 'potential' self-employed were currently not working.

A number of smaller scale or qualitative studies have concentrated on redundancy as a spur to self-employment (for example, Johnson and Rodger, 1983; Lee, 1985; Leece, 1990). These studies tend to support an impression of the redundancy 'window' as used mostly by men in the 30-40 age bracket, with somewhat higher levels of redundancy payment than the average, more skills and often some previous direct or indirect experience in self-employment. The businesses created were mostly in the service sector, tended to remain one-person enterprises and often brought less in financial rewards to the founders, at least in the early years, than they had previously received in wages. The studies also shed light on the motivations and attitudes of those starting businesses: these are discussed in more detail below, but it is interesting to note that although they often expressed aspirations towards independence, many of these new entrepreneurs felt they had little choice and that self-employment was the only alternative to unemployment.

Evidence on the wider impact of redundancy on self-employment is inconclusive. The LFS suggests that such situations are actually quite rare. Since the mid-1980s a question about redundancy has been asked of all those in self-employment, or in employment in a new job, for less than three months. In 1989, only a tiny proportion of the self-employed in this position had been made redundant and even less had received any redundancy payment (Daly, 1991a). However, a national survey of self-employed people working from home found that 10 per cent gave redundancy from their last job as a reason for entering self-employment (Hakim, 1987a).

The relatively small proportion of people starting businesses from unemployment suggests that the role of self-employment in the 1980s as a route out of unemployment may have been somewhat exaggerated in the discourse around the enterprise culture. Nevertheless, given the difference in the overall numbers of people employed and unemployed, the proportion entering from unemployment was significantly larger than that of people switching from an employed job. Comparison with other European countries also shows that the probabilities of transferring from unemployment to self-employment were not only significantly greater in the UK than elsewhere, but also increased over the decade (Meager et al., 1994).

A similar picture emerges of exits from self-employment, but one that emphasizes the high turnover among women. Some 314,000 people stopped being self-employed in 1988/9, of whom 41 per cent were women. Over the period between 1981 and 1989 the average exit rate was 14 per cent for women and nine per cent for men, but the group with by far the highest exit rate was women aged 16-24, for whom the average was 30 per cent. Data from 1987/88 show that the destination of those leaving self-employment was distributed in a very similar way to the origins of those entering it, with around half moving back into employed jobs and the rest becoming unemployed or leaving the labour force in approximately equal numbers (Hakim, 1989a). This pattern of origins and destinations did not change significantly during the decade and the growth in self-employment resulted from new recruits consistently outnumbering those giving up .

It is not easy to identify the causes of people leaving self-employment, though it seems reasonable to suppose that a high proportion of exits into unemployment must result from business failures. There are costs involved in the failure of small businesses which fall not only on individuals, but also on creditors and the courts. The National Audit Office (1993) carried out research which highlighted difficulties faced by some former self-employed people who have to claim income support following the failure of their business. The fact that large numbers of people may only stay self-employed for a short time and then return to unemployment has also raised wider questions about the exclusion of self-employed people from unemployment benefit.

Women and self-employment

One of the significant features of the growth of self-employment in the 1980s was its comparatively rapid expansion among women. Between the first quarters of 1979 and 1990, net female self-employment rose by 151 per cent, as against 82 per cent for men (Department of Employment, 1993). Having said that, self-employment remains a predominantly male arena. In the second quarter of 1994 there were still only just over 808,000 self-employed women, compared with just over 2.4 million men. Less than 30 per cent of the overall increase between 1979 and 1990 was among women, and at the peak they still made up less than a quarter of all the self-employed. In 1989 seven per cent of women of working age were self-employed, as against 17 per cent of men (Department of Employment, 1990a). The particularly rapid growth of self-employment among women also levelled out in the mid-1980s, after which the net rate of increase was similar to that of men. This is partly, as we have seen, because their rate of exit from self-employment was particularly high in the latter half of the decade, even though their high rate of entry was sustained. One hypothesis is that newly self-employed women had difficulty surviving in self-employment, either because of having less access than men to financial and human capital or because they tended to enter sectors with poorer business prospects (Meager, 1993). Certainly, since 1987, the net increase in self-employment among women can be ascribed largely to changes in overall workforce participation, whereas among men self-employment has continued to grow as a proportion of all employment.

However, it may be misleading to rely too heavily on official statistics of women's self-employment. Women are often informally involved in small enterprises with husbands and partners, though their contributions may not always be acknowledged. Also, as Arber and Gilbert (1992) have pointed out, certain forms of self-employment, including child-minding, outworking and home production, lie on a continuum of economic activity between waged work and unpaid domestic labour, which can blur women's relationship with the formal labour market. The invisibility of this work is one reason why the involvement of women in self-employment may tend to be underestimated (Allen and Truman, 1992). Self-employment for women should also be seen as significantly different from that of men, because women are much more likely to be working part-time. Between 1981 and 1984, when self-employment grew most rapidly for women, four-fifths of the increase was among women working 16 hours or less per week (Casey and Creigh, 1988).

The attitudes and motivations of self-employed people

Another way of addressing the question of why self-employment has become so much more important in the UK is to consider what motivates people to become self-employed and whether there is anything special about the attitudes and views of those who do. This is a question of particular interest in view of Government policies of encouraging enterprise. It is also important as an aid to understanding how self-employed people may view their entitlement to, or disallowance from, social security benefits.

Curran (1990) has suggested that notions of entrepreneurialism have been rooted in sociological views of the entrepreneur as economic non-conformist - Schumpeter's (1934) 'prime economic mover' - or as the 'outsider', driven by exclusion or marginality to innovate. He argued that this approach misunderstands the nature of small business, much of which is conservative and traditional rather than revolutionary. Thus pragmatism is more common than innovation and the ethos might more accurately be described as a 'culture of survival' rather than a politically significant 'enterprise culture'. Similarly, Hakim (1988) and Blanchflower and Oswald (1990) noted a distinct similarity of views and attitudes on a wide range of issues between the self-employed and employees. Hakim did, however, detect some distinctive attitudes among owner-managers: these included a desire for autonomy and independence, a commitment to individualism rather than collectivity and an antipathy to large organisations, particularly the state and trade unions, but also big business.

In a study of self-employment among redundant steel workers, Lee (1985) also found differences in political attitudes between those he identified as 'aspirant' self-employed and those who were 'involuntary'. Although redundant workers who had become self-employed were more likely than others previously to have been Conservative voters, 'aspirants' were more likely to maintain these views and the 'involuntarily' self-employed were more likely to shift in favour of the centre parties or Labour. Overall, support for Labour remained strong among the group and Lee concluded that Conservative voting cannot be assumed among those who become self-employed where this represents occupational rather than social mobility.

A number of other studies have also identified the desire for independence as a motivation closely associated with the self-employed generally (Goldthorpe, 1980; Bevan et al., 1989; Goffee and Scase, 1985) and among women, in particular (Carter and Cannon, 1988a, 1988b), but these aspirations are not always clear cut or unambiguous. Hakim (1988) suggested that claims of independence and autonomy may sometimes mimic dominant stereotypes of enterprise and may be used 'to give moral value to, and rationalise a work situation which could otherwise be intolerable' (p.434). Lee (1985) also argued that aspirations towards independence may partly be a form of compensation for or a response to the constraints produced by redundancy. Thus, while a majority of his sample cited independence as a motivating force, a third also said they had no choice but to attempt self-employment.

This suggests that attitudes and motives may be closely linked to the route by which people enter self-employment and the actual level of autonomy available in the kind of work in which they are engaged. Bogenhold and Staber (1991) thus proposed an heuristic model of opposing 'logics' or recruitment channels. At one end of this spectrum lies 'autonomy', associated with those already occupying positions offering high earnings and job security, whose choice of self-employment is motivated by self-direction - the 'opportunistic entrepreneur'. At the other end is 'economic necessity', taking in people with limited chances to succeed as wage employees, or driven by unemployment or redundancy. Here businesses tend to be founded in industries with low financial barriers to entry (Allen and Hunn, 1985), such as small crafts and repair services, but also with intense competition, low profit margins and high failure rates.

Another version of this continuum has been proposed by MacDonald and Coffield (1991) in a study of business start-up by young people. They were sceptical of some of the claims of what they categorised as the 'enterprise movement', particularly as they applied to young people in an economically depressed area without a strong entrepreneurial tradition. In attempting to test whether their respondents could be seen as either 'aspirant' or 'involuntary' self-employed in Lee's terms, they found that motivations fell along a line between unemployment, with its negative connotations, and self-employment with the positive connotations of independence and control. 'Becoming your own boss' was a reason cited by many for starting their own businesses. However, for most it was a combination of the 'push' effect of unemployment and the 'pull' effect of the idea of independence which led them to self-employment. Few seemed to have started in order to put a particular business idea into practice. Other motivations included the 'stop-gap' development of hobbies, for example before going to college, the ability to fit in with domestic and childrearing work for young women, and racial discrimination experienced by some young Asians which excluded them from the local employee labour market.

Not all self-employment, of course, is directly affected by 'push' and 'pull' factors. Some types of work can virtually only be performed as self-employment and individuals choosing these careers may be making very specific choices based on their special interests, without being significantly influenced either by job insecurity or by notions of independence.

Where different individuals fit on the continua of motivation and channels of recruitment to self-employment is also likely to be influenced by their family, class and educational backgrounds. Self-employment is often assumed to be a means of upward social mobility as well as an opportunity for the expression of individual creativity. General Household Survey data in fact show that people self-employed in the mid-1980s were, overall, more likely than employees to come from non-manual backgrounds (Curran and Burrows, 1989). Only among self-employed men with no employees were their fathers more likely to have been manual workers than their employed counterparts, suggesting that it may be easier for many people to enter self-employment from a more privileged social background. There were also gender differences: self-employed women, particularly those without employees, were more likely than self-employed men to come from non-manual or professional backgrounds. This difference has been ascribed to the difficulties and barriers often faced by women starting businesses on their own, which may be offset by the advantages accruing from a more privileged background (Carter and Cannon, 1988a). Among women, the rate of self-employment is also highest among those qualified to degree or equivalent level (Daly, 1991a). For men, the highest rates are for those with A-level equivalents or those with no qualifications at all, although the overall proportion of self-employed people with no qualifications dropped during the 1980s from nearly two-fifths to under a quarter.

Another important factor identified by many studies as increasing the propensity towards self-employment is having parents or relatives already engaged in some form of small business (Goldthorpe, 1980; Hakim, 1988). A study of young self-employed workers (Payne, 1984) found that they were over twice as likely as an equivalent employee group to have fathers who were 'own account' workers. Carter and Cannon (1988a) found a similar inheritance effect among women in their study of female entrepreneurs, though their sample was skewed towards those with higher qualifications. More than three-quarters had some previous family connections with self-employment and two-fifths had husbands or partners who were also self-employed. Macdonald and Coffield (1991), on the other hand, found the inheritance effect largely absent from their study of young entrepreneurs on Tyneside, less than ten per cent of whom had a self-employed parent. In their view young people's economic behaviour was structured more by the contingencies of local labour markets than by their parents' occupations.

Unfortunately, none of the otherwise useful and detailed studies of transitions to self-employment among redundant workers, female entrepreneurs and young people addressed the role of social security and welfare benefits in decision making. Lee (1985) makes a passing reference to the concept of an 'income maintenance strategy', involving the use of benefits, but no survey data were collected on this topic.

The differing characteristics of people working in or entering self-employment during the 1980s are now explored in more detail.

Characteristics of the self-employed

The self-employed as employers

Nearly 70 per cent of all self-employed people have no employees and these 'sole traders' constituted four-fifths of the total growth during the 1980s. However, as was noted above, this figure is artificially boosted to some extent by the exclusion of owners of incorporated businesses. Thus as some businesses grow and take on employees, they may become incorporated and their owners cease to be counted by the official surveys as self-employed. Nevertheless, analysis of the 1983 and 1984 General Household Surveys by Curran and Burrows (1989) shows that self-employment with and without employees should be seen as two distinct types of business activity. Although some self-employed people may take on employees later, most remain one-person businesses or partnerships for as long as they continue in operation. Some of the disproportionate growth in sole trading during the 1980s is also likely, as we have seen, to be associated with the growth of labour-only subcontracting, franchising and other 'quasi self-employment'. The high proportion of sole traders among the self-employed is a feature common to many other countries, though the proportions vary considerably: in West Germany, for example, only 46 per cent worked on their own in the mid-1980s, as against 80 per cent in the USA (Bogenhold and Staber, 1991).

There is little difference in the proportion of self-employed men and women with employees, although many fewer women than men employ more than a handful of other people. Overall, it has been estimated that only about ten per cent of self-employed people have more than five employees (Hakim, 1989a). Bevan et al. (1989) also found that four-fifths of businesses identified were home-based and only a fifth had separate business premises. Women mostly worked at home, while men were more likely to use the home as a base but to work away from it.

Working hours

Another important distinction within the self-employed is in whether they work full- or part-time, though the picture of change is complicated. Overall, self-employed people tend to work longer hours on average than employees, leading to an identification sometimes made between self-employment and self-exploitation (Rubery, 1988). Self-employed men who employ others work the longest hours of all. Part-time self-employment has increased significantly, although the vast majority still work full-time. However, as we have seen, part-time work is particularly important for women and, as in employment generally, the rise in part-time work has accompanied the increasing labour participation by women.

Interestingly, however, since self-employment started to expand, it is the proportion of self-employed men working part-time which has actually increased and that of women has remained the same. LFS data show that between 1983 (the earliest year a comparable full-time/part-time split was recorded) and 1992 the proportion of self-employed men working part-time rose from five per cent to more than eight per cent, while that of women stayed at around 48 per cent. The numbers of women working part-time nevertheless rose because of the overall increase in self-employment among women. The biggest proportionate growth was among people working 12 hours per week or less, though these were still only seven per cent of the total in 1989. Nevertheless, 21 per cent of self-employed women worked these hours as opposed to only three per cent of men.

GHS data for 1983/4 showed a significant difference for women depending on whether they had employees or not (Curran and Burrows, 1989). More than

60 per cent of women without employees worked less than 30 hours per week, and on average this group worked fewer hours than women employees. However, excluding those who worked less than 30 hours, self-employed women as a whole worked longer hours than employees generally and about the same as self-employed men without employees.

A further aspect of working hours is the way they are distributed by industry. Curran and Burrows' analysis showed that the working of longer hours in self-employment by both men and women was most common in agriculture and the services and least common in construction. Over 30 per cent of women self-employed in the construction industry worked less than 12 hours per week, and construction has been one of the areas of biggest proportionate growth among women, albeit from a very small base. All these figures are of course averages and do not account for seasonal variation, which can itself be an important factor for some self-employed people.

One reason for the disproportionate concentration of short working hours among self-employed women may be their need to combine work and childcare responsibilities (Goffee and Scase, 1985) or to be available for the informal care of other relatives (Twigg and Atkin, 1991).

Age

Overall, the age profile of the self-employed is older than that of the working population generally. Self-employment is less common than being an employee among those under 25 and more common among those over retirement age, although there are some differences between men and women in this respect. The peak ages for male self-employment in 1989 were between the years 45-49 and for women between 30 and 45, while around 10 per cent overall were under 25 and five per cent 65 or older (Daly, 1991a).

Looking only at those self-employed at one point in time, however, gives a somewhat misleading picture. The age profile of *entrants* to self-employment during the 1980s was rather different to that of the total self-employed population. Thus taking the average for 1981-1989, 30 per cent of male entrants and 42 per cent of female entrants were under 25. Overall, twice as many new entrants were under 25 as the proportion among all self-employed people. For those over retirement age the difference was even greater: three times as many entrants were aged 65 or over. Curran and Burrows (1989) suggested that the higher proportion of self-employed people over retirement age may reflect their relative lack of access to pensions - both occupational and private - and is a consequence of postponing retirement. The high number of new entrants over retirement age, however, suggests a flow from employed work into self-employment (Daly, 1991a).

Meager et al. (1994) have also noted that the age profile of the self-employed in the UK is younger than of France and Germany, and that it also became progressively younger during the 1980s, as would be expected from the profile of the new entrants. However, we have seen that the high level of entry by younger people was almost matched by their exit levels, which is why the age distribution has not shifted even further towards the younger groups.

Family structures

Since this book is concerned with the working lives of self-employed families, the household characteristics of the self-employed are of particular interest. One feature frequently highlighted is the greater concentration of self-employment among people who are married. Thus in 1989, 79 per cent of both men and women in self-employment were married (or cohabiting), as opposed to 68 per cent of employees (Department of Employment, 1990a). However, much of this difference can be explained by the older age profile of the self-employed, which brings with it increasing likelihood of marriage. If the age distribution of the two groups were the same, the difference between self-employment among married and non-married people as a proportion of all employment would diminish from six to two per cent (Daly, 1991a).

More important than marriage itself are two main factors associated with it - the presence of children and the economic activity of partners. In 1989, 95 per cent of the husbands or partners of self-employed married or cohabiting women were also working, and this rose to 97 per cent of those with a dependent child under 16 (Department of Employment, 1990b). These data do not tell us the extent of husbands' employment, or who was the main earner, though there was little difference in the rate of husbands' employment where women were in part-time self-employment. It does, however, offer a perspective on the spread of part-time self-employed work among women and it indicates that this is often a secondary source of family earnings.

Another way of looking at this relationship is to compare self-employment rates by spouse activity (Table 2.6). This shows that for both sexes, having a self-employed spouse increases significantly their likelihood of being self-employed themselves - a point which is explored later in the book where we discuss the effect of self-employment on women's labour market participation.

Table 2.6
Self-employment rates by activity of spouse, 1989, (married or cohabiting people in employment only)

Economic status of spouse	*Self-employment as a percentage of all employment*	
	Male %	Female %
Employee	14.7	5.1
Self-employed	48.5	24.1
Unemployed	14.9	4.9
Inactive	19.5	5.8
All	*17.6*	*8.6*

Source: Daly, 1991a

Some previous small-scale studies have found a relatively high proportion of separated and divorced women among those self-employed and have suggested that self-employment offers special opportunities for independence for women (Goffee and Scase, 1985). Quantitative data do not, however, support the association between divorce and self-employment. As we have seen, the propensity for marriage is greater among self-employed women than employees (as the age distribution would suggest) and although self-employed women are more likely to be divorced or separated than their male counterparts, the proportion is similar to that among employed women (Curran and Burrows, 1989). Survey data on the working patterns of lone parents also suggests that self-employment is rare amongst this group: 40 per cent of Bradshaw and Millar's (1991) sample of lone parents were in full- or part-time work, but only one per cent were self-employed. This finding is consistent with our own analysis of family credit administrative data, which showed that while 37 per cent of recipients of family credit in April 1991 were lone mothers, only six per cent of them were self-employed. Lone fathers receiving family credit showed a much higher propensity to be self-employed (26 per cent), but there were relatively few of them.

The importance of self-employment for some minority ethnic communities in the UK is well known, though there are wide variations in the rate of self-employment among different populations. Much of the research in this area has concentrated on small-scale studies of business development in local areas, but LFS and GHS data also provide a national picture.

Using data from the 1981-84 GHS, Curran and Burrows (1989) found that a relatively high proportion of people with origins in the Indian sub-continent (India, Pakistan, Bangladesh, Sri Lanka and East Africa) were self-employed - 14 per cent compared to eight per cent of white British people. The group with the highest rate of self-employment, however, was that of people from the Mediterranean Commonwealth (Cyprus, Malta and Gibraltar), of whom 29 per cent were self-employed. At the other extreme, the rate was only three per cent for Afro-Caribbeans. The very high rate of self-employment among people from the Mediterranean Commonwealth is of particular interest. It is not clear, for example, whether this is a propensity they have brought with them from their countries of origin - their Mediterranean neighbour countries in the EC all have high rates of self-employment too (Table 2.3) - or whether it is a response to their position in Britain as small minorities facing difficulties in the labour market.

Since the early 1980s the number of people from minority ethnic groups who were self-employed increased rapidly, and the difference between their self-employment rates and those of the white British population has widened. Nevertheless, the overall profile of the different communities remains similar, except that self-employment among people whose origins are in the Indian sub-continent has overtaken that of the Mediterranean Commonwealth groups. Around one-fifth of the increase can be explained by the expansion of the ethnic minority population as a whole over this period, particularly for those of Pakistani and Bangladeshi origin. The different age structure of the ethnic minority groups from that of the white British population is also likely to have an impact on the numbers self-employed, because of the way self-employment varies with age. However, the only group significantly affected are those of Indian origin and the pattern of self-employment as a whole is not changed (Daly, 1991a). People of Indian origin make up the largest of the non-white groups in the LFS and at around 800,000 people they comprise 1.4 per cent of the whole population (Haskey, 1990). In 1987-1989, some 27 per cent of Indian men were self-employed. Table 2.7 shows the proportions of people who were self-employed in the various different ethnic groups, as defined in the LFS, taking the averages for the years 1979-83 and 1987-89.

Table 2.7
Proportion of the population self-employed, by ethnic origin

	1979-83	*1987-89*
White	9	12
All minorities:	10	16
West Indian/Guyanese	3	7
Indian	14	21
Pakistani/Bangladeshi	17	22
All other origins	11	16

Note: Under the classification used in the LFS, people with origins in the Mediterranean Commonwealth are included as White

Sources: Daly, 1991a; Department of Employment, 1991a

Both GHS and LFS data also show that self-employed people from the Indian sub-continent and those from the Mediterranean Commonwealth are more likely than their white British counterparts to have employees, though the differences declined somewhat during the 1980s. A fuller picture of the entrepreneurial experience for minority groups can be found in smaller scale, qualitative studies such as that by Wilson and Stanworth (1988), who studied 25 small businesses owned by Asian and Afro-Caribbean entrepreneurs. Features common to most of these businesses included a reliance on financial assistance, support unpaid work from families and other members of their communities. These family ties were particularly important for the Asian self-employed people: although two-fifths had no previous experience in the industry they had entered, nearly all had family members in other self-employed businesses. There was also little use of either public sector financial support for setting up the businesses or of borrowing from banks. There was also evidence, again particularly among in the Asian businesses, of privileged access to supplies, credit terms and premises through family or community connections.

Although it is clear that self-employment is a particularly important feature of economic activity in minority ethnic communities, the position of such activity in the economy as a whole should not be exaggerated. Ethnic minorities make up under five per cent of the population of working age and the proportion of the self-employed they represent is only slightly higher than this. Nevertheless, some groups may be of greater significance within family credit. Administrative statistics do not record the ethnic origin of claimants, but our analysis of family credit administrative statistics found that self-employed family credit recipients are concentrated in relatively high proportions in some areas such as the North West, which also have high ethnic minority populations. A trawl of self-employed recipients in the North West, carried out in order to construct a qualitative interview sample for our study, produced a high percentage of claimants with Asian surnames. This raises interesting questions, since other research evidence suggests that take-up of social security benefits is likely to be relatively low among such communities (Tarpey, 1984; NACAB, 1991a; Law, 1994).

Industrial and occupational distribution

One familiar feature of self-employment is that it is concentrated in certain industries and occupations - a concentration which is sharply gender-differentiated. We have suggested that the growth of self-employment in the 1980s resulted in some changes in the characteristics of the people involved and that at least part of the increase was among the more marginal forms of 'quasi self-employment'. It is of interest, therefore, to look at the kind of work the newer self-employed people went into and how far they differed from people already self-employed at the beginning of the 1980s.

Table 2.8 shows that between 1979 and 1990 there were substantial increases in all sectors except agriculture and fishing, but the two areas exhibiting the most powerful growth were the main service sectors of banking, finance and insurance, and 'other services'. The latter includes a wide range of personal and small-scale service enterprises, as well as a number of occupations in the public spheres of health and education. Some of the increases were due to the changing sectoral composition of employment in Britain, but the main cause appears to have been changes in the propensity within sectors for people to become self-employed (Meager, 1993).

Between 1990 and 1993 - a period covering the recession-linked drop in self-employment - all sectors except manufacturing saw a net fall, of which the largest proportionately was in construction.

Table 2.8
Self-employment trends, by industrial sector, Great Britain, June 1979-1993

Industrial sector	*Number of self-employed by sector (seasonally adjusted) (Thousands)*				
	1979 (June)	1990 (June)	% change 1979-1990	1993 (June)	% change 1990-1993
Agriculture and fishing	283	282	- 0.4	250	- 11.3
Manufacturing	168	335	99.4	344	2.7
Construction	391	819	109.5	654	- 20.0
Distribution, hotels, catering and repairs	645	826	28.1	727	- 12.0
Transport and communication	92	183	98.9	178	- 2.7
Banking, finance and insurance etc.	151	434	187.4	412	- 5.1
Other services	225	577	156.4	530	- 8.4

Source: Department of Employment (1994b)

The distribution of self-employment among sectors, however, is sharply differentiated by sex. In June 1993 just over 28 per cent of self-employed men worked in construction, as opposed to only two per cent of women, although the number of self-employed women in construction increased by over 150 per cent during the 1980s. Women were concentrated in 'other services' (35 per cent) and distribution and catering (32 per cent), where men were also well represented (21 per cent). However, in terms of the share self-employment takes of all employment in particular sectors, agriculture remain the largest at around 56 per cent, followed by construction (45 per cent). Another important cleavage in the industrial distribution is between those with and without employees. For those with employees - both men and women - 'distribution, hotels and repairs' is the most important sector.

Regional variations

Numerically, self-employment is concentrated most heavily in the South East of England, followed by the South West and the North West. The North, East Anglia and Wales have the lowest concentrations. Looked at in terms of the share of total employment and the relative growth during the 1980s, a slightly different picture emerges. Figure 2.1 shows the regional distribution of self-employment as a proportion of all employment in summer 1994, along with the percentage change in the number of self-employed people between 1983 and 1990 (the peak of the increase). The area with the highest rate in 1994 was the South West, with Wales, the South East and East Anglia all a little above the national average. There is a something of a North/South divide in self-employment, with above average growth in the Southern regions and Wales, and smaller increases in the Northern regions and Scotland. Yorkshire and Humberside was an exception in terms of numerical growth, but still has a relatively low self-employment rate.

One final issue to be explored in this chapter is how far people's choices to become self-employed are linked with health, disability or caring responsibilities.

Disability, health and caring responsibilities

It was suggested earlier that one of the attractions for women of part-time self-employment was the possibility of combining paid work with caring responsibilities. Work of this kind can also offer opportunities for people who are disabled or who have health problems which make it difficult for them to pursue work for an employer. Estimates of the number of economically active people with disabilities vary depending on the measures used, but the Employment and Handicap Survey carried out for the Government in 1989 put the total at between one and 1.2 million people (Prescott-Clarke, 1990). Disabled people face a range of difficulties in the employment market which make them almost four times more likely than the population in general to be unemployed (Department of Employment, 1990b). It might be expected that disability would also inhibit opportunities for self-employment, but what limited evidence there is suggests that this type of work is actually very important for disabled people. The Employment and Handicap Survey found that disabled people in work were actually slightly more likely to be self-employed than the general working population. This finding is supported by LFS data, which also found marginally higher rates of self-employment among respondents with health or disability problems which limited their opportunities for paid work (Daly, 1991a).

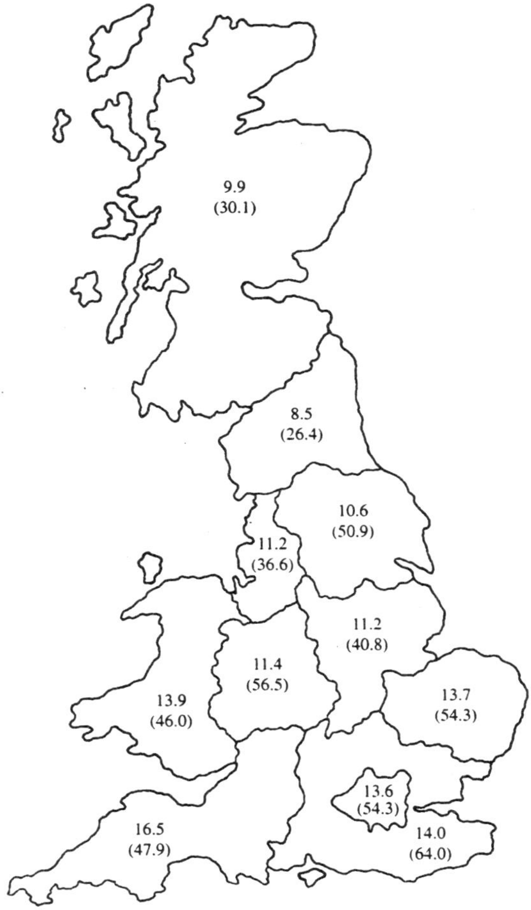

Figure 2.1 The regional distribution of self-employment in Great Britain

Note: In each region the figures given represent the percentage share of self-employment in total employment in Summer 1994, followed by (in brackets) the percentage increase in the numbers of self-employed between June 1983 and June 1990.

Rates of self-employment in themselves reveal little about the kind of work disabled people do or the hours they work, and the small numbers in general national surveys do not permit detailed analysis. It is likely that self-employment is of value to disabled people precisely because it allows them the flexibility to work from home and to structure their working hours around the nature of the particular occupational difficulties they face. Prescott-Clarke (1990) found that of the small percentage who were already in self-employment at the onset of their health or disability problem, three-fifths had managed to continue in the same work. Most of the rest had been obliged to give up work for health reasons. Just over two-thirds of those who were employees at onset had stayed in their jobs, eight per cent had switched to self-employment and the remaining quarter had become unemployed. Those who switched to self-employment accounted for more than half of the total self-employed, so about half of all those self-employed at the time of interview claimed that choice of work was influenced by their health problem.

Respondents in this survey were also assessed by Disability Registration Officers, who found little difference in the levels of occupational handicap between the two groups of employed and self-employed people. Similar results were also found using the OPCS disability scales. However, the levels of self-reported occupational difficulties were twice as high for the self-employed group as for the employees. The self-employed group also included many people whose condition was intermittent or variable, making it more difficult to work for an outside employer. Although the average hours worked by self-employed disabled people were greater than those of their employed counterparts, in line with the picture for the working population as a whole, a much higher proportion of the self-employed reported that they could not always work full hours. Self-employment thus afforded them the flexibility to take time off when they needed it.

A Government consultative document on employment and training for people with disabilities, issued in 1990, emphasized the importance of the flexibility offered by self-employment and the opportunities to develop a sense of independence (Department of Employment, 1990b). The document outlined the various schemes available through the Employment Service to help disabled people to enter or remain in self-employment. These included the Special Aids, Adaptations, Fares to Work, and Reader Services Schemes; the Business on Own Account Scheme, which provided set-up grants for people with severe disabilities; and the Blind Homeworkers Scheme, which provided grants and income guarantee subsidies through local authorities. Most of these schemes, however, have low coverage and declining levels of take-up, suggesting that they are no longer well suited to the needs of disabled people in the current labour market, and some are in the process of being wound up.

The Enterprise Allowance Scheme was always open to people with disabilities, and the consultative document estimated that between three and eight per cent of participants in the years up to 1990 were disabled people. In 1989/90, there were some 5,500 new participants with disabilities. There were some doubts as to whether the Business Start-up Scheme, which took over from the EAS in 1991, would continue to provide this level of help to disabled people because of its greater orientation towards business viability (Unemployment Unit (1991b). The evidence is not conclusive, but a follow-up study of participants carried out 18 months after they started their businesses did suggest that fewer disabled people were entering the scheme. The survey found that although seven per cent of participants said they had a long-term health problem or disability which affected the type of work they could do, less than one per cent overall were actually registered as disabled people (Tremlett, 1993).

An important development was the introduction of the disability working allowance in April 1992. This new benefit, modelled on family credit, aims to help disabled people enter or stay in lower paid work, and from the beginning the Department of Social Security has expected there to be substantial take-up by people taking on self-employed work. Disability working allowance is discussed at greater length in Chapter Five, but it should be noted here that while take-up of the benefit has so far proved disappointing, early findings from an evaluation of the benefit showed that some 25 per cent of recipients surveyed were self-employed (Rowlingson and Berthoud, 1994).

Overall, it is clear that self-employment is of considerable potential value to disabled people, but its importance should also be recognised for people with extra caring responsibilities towards others. There is a considerable body of work which has documented the range of costs falling on people providing informal care to disabled or infirm adults and children (see for example Baldwin, 1985; Equal Opportunities Commission, 1980; Joshi, 1987; Parker, 1990). The consequences of caring include the opportunity costs of paid employment given up in order to meet caring responsibilities. There is also evidence of the stress caused to carers who continue to work outside the home (Opportunities for Women, 1990).

Research on informal care has given little specific attention to self-employment as a way of reconciling the need for economic activity with caring responsibilities, but it appears from several small-scale qualitative studies that this is an option a number of respondents have pursued (Glendinning, 1989; Parker, 1989; Twigg and Atkin, 1991). Twigg and Atkin in particular found that although around a third of the carers they interviewed were in employment, most worked part-time or in work which allowed them control over their work circumstances - usually self-employment. Several had moved out of secure, employed positions into forms of relatively insecure self-employment, with considerably reduced earnings and career prospects. The flexibility which self-employment can offer to lone parents caring for children, and to disabled people, may thus be increasingly attractive also to people trying to juggle work with caring for elderly or disabled persons. However, the move to self-employment can be at some potential economic cost.

Conclusions

This chapter has reviewed the evidence on the growth of self-employment since the beginning of the 1980s and the changing characteristics of the participants. One of the main features identified has been increasing differentiation within self-employment, by gender, hours of work, stability and type of activity. Although, in the past, there has been a tendency for people starting self-employment to have some family connections with small business, the growing numbers of younger people, women and unemployed people becoming self-employed may be beginning to erode this pattern. This raises some questions about whether new entrants will be as successful in business as those previously involved - a doubt supported by the high rates of exit from self-employment over the decade. The high inflow and outflow levels also indicate that an increasing proportion of the workforce is experiencing short spells of self-employment at some time during their working lives. We have seen that the two main service sectors have had the fastest growth rates, but we might expect banking and finance to be considerably better rewarded financially than many of the marginal personal service enterprises. In general, the developments in self-employment are likely to have consequences both for people's earning potential in self-employed work and for their income security in retirement - issues explored in the next chapter.

Note

1. The LFS figures are for Great Britain only and exclude Northern Ireland.

3 The financial circumstances of self-employed people

It is likely, as was concluded in the previous chapter, that the growth of self-employment has had an impact on the distribution of incomes in Britain. In particular, the greater numbers of young people and women becoming self-employed, the prevalence of shorter spells of self-employment, and the marked expansion of the small-scale service sector along with that of banking and finance might all be expected to have increased the dispersion of self-employed incomes.

Understanding the financial circumstances of self-employed people, however, requires grappling with a number of problems which have tended until recently to be avoided by researchers and analysts. Self-employed people appear in national income surveys only in small numbers and are known to have a lower response rate than other groups. Earnings data are often incomplete and incomes are thought to be under-reported. Thus, since self-employment has been regarded as less important than other forms of work, those involved have often been excluded from survey analyses because of their problematic characteristics. For similar reasons the self-employed have also consistently been excluded from official estimates of benefit take-up, including family credit (Department of Health and Social Security, 1989; Department of Social Security, 1995), as well as from studies by independent researchers (see, for example, Hancock, 1988; Dorsett and Heady, 1991; Fry and Stark, 1992).

A change in this approach and a new focus on the problem of self-employed earnings are due in large part to recent evidence on the impact of the new self-employment on income distribution amongst the population as a whole. This evidence, which emerged from analyses of the Department of Social Security's Households Below Average Income series, suggests that households headed by a self-employed person are making up a growing proportion of the lowest income deciles, with many reporting zero or negative earnings (Department of Social Security, 1992, 1993a). While striking - and not inconsistent with the picture we have drawn of the changing face of self-employment - these findings actually highlight some of the difficulties with measuring the incomes of the self-employed which have led researchers to shy away from them in the past.

This chapter critically assesses the evidence on the incomes and resources of self-employed people and discusses the problems involved in reaching a clear understanding of their circumstances. We begin by reviewing the practical and conceptual difficulties which surround the interpretation of data on the self-employed in income surveys.

Problems in measuring earnings from self-employment

While all survey data on earnings have some limitations, estimates of the incomes of employees or people outside the labour force are generally regarded as sufficiently reliable for detailed analysis, both at an aggregate level and by age, gender, family type, industry, region and so on. Earnings from self-employment, however, present a number of difficulties, including:

- the definition of self-employment
- under-reporting of income
- differential response rates
- time-lags between survey dates and earnings periods
- the concept of earnings and the measurement of profits
- the treatment of income tax.

The boundary problems in defining self-employment were discussed in the previous chapter. Clearly any anomalies in the establishment of respondents' employment status will flow over into the analysis of their earnings - company directors being a prime example. Yet at the income analysis stage of research such anomalies are rarely regarded as problematic. Much more widely discussed is the problem of under-reporting.

Under-reporting of income

The assumption that self-employed people understate their incomes, both in tax returns and household surveys, is so widespread that it has been institutionally incorporated into national estimates of gross domestic product. Thus in Britain the national accounts are adjusted upwards by around 15 per cent of reported self-employed income to account for tax evasion, suggesting a discrepancy of around 1.5 per cent of GDP (Pissarides and Weber, 1989). Similar adjustments are made in a number of other countries (Hakim, 1989b).

One of the responses to this assumption amongst researchers is to disregard the income data on the self-employed derived from household surveys. Curran and Burrows (1989), for example, in an update of an earlier analysis of General Household Survey information on self-employment, decided to ignore the income data in favour of other indicators of living standards such as household possessions. Another response is to exclude the self-employed, or specific groups of self-employed people, from analyses. Rees and Shah (1986), for example, excluded all those in the agricultural sector from their empirical examination of determinants of self-employment on the basis that reported earnings of self-employed farmers 'are well-known to be notoriously inaccurate' (p.101).

While some under-reporting is put down to problems of recall or the lack of requisite information, much of it is commonly regarded as purposeful. It is associated with activity in the informal economy, within which it is often assumed that self-employed people are the main actors. The size of the informal economy is, not surprisingly, hard to assess and estimates have varied between one and 40 per cent of a country's GDP (Smith, 1981). More recent estimates put Britain's 'irregular' economy as between one and 35 per cent of GDP, with an average estimate of just under seven per cent (Dallago, 1991; Commission of the European Communities, 1990a). These estimates are mostly based on indirect evidence, referred to by Thomas (1988, p.169) as the 'statistical fingerprints of the black economy'. They attempt to measure discrepancies between reported income and expenditure, either at a macro-economic level, by reference to national accounts, or at an individual/household level using microdata. Such discrepancies are assumed to represent unreported economic activity. MacAffee (1980), for example, using the first method, estimated the informal economy in the 1970s as reaching a peak of around four per cent of GDP in 1974.

Several estimates of informal economic activity have been attempted using micro-data (for example, Dilnot and Morris, 1981; Atkinson et al., 1986; Smith, 1986; Smith and Wied-Nebberling, 1986; Pissarides and Weber, 1989; Baker, 1993). Although there are technical differences, the general approach is similar in that estimates are based on discrepancies between households' reported income and their expenditure. Using data from the Family Expenditure Survey, Dilnot and Morris, for example, put the extent of the informal economy in 1977 at an upper bound estimate of three per cent of GDP, involving some 15 per cent of FES respondents. As part of the process of constructing a tax/benefit model, Atkinson et al. made upward adjustments of 19.5 per cent of declared self-employed income in FES, based on estimates of unreported work derived from the Inland Revenue Survey of Personal Incomes.

The studies carried out by Pissarides and Weber, and by Baker, are of particular interest since they concentrate on the self-employed. This concentration is such, however, that they appear to ascribe all unreported taxable economic activity to self-employed people. Their estimates are based on expenditure on food, which they take to be the most accurately recorded item in the FES. Pissarides and Weber conclude that on average 'true' self-employed income was 1.55 times that of reported income, implying that the size of the informal economy was 5.5 per cent of GDP in 1982. Using a time-series analysis of data from the late 1970s through to 1990, Baker estimates under-reporting by the self-employed as between one-sixth and a third of 'true' income, though he found little evidence of a steady trend in the level of under-reporting over the decade.

A similar exercise was carried out in Australia by Bradbury et al. (1988) using the 1981/82 Income and Housing Surveys, in which they attempted to estimate the under-recording of self-employed income on the basis of housing expenditure. Their assumptions were that spending on commodities was more likely than declared earnings to reflect 'true' or permanent incomes, and that self-employed people were likely to have consumption tastes for housing that were identical to those of the non self-employed. They also disaggregated their results by industry. Their analysis suggested substantial under-recording of incomes across most industries, though with considerable variations. The only group of self-employed people who appeared to spend significantly *less* than predicted on their housing were small business owners in the construction industry, which is interesting given that this is an area where informal economic activity is generally regarded as widespread. The authors speculated that this discrepancy might reflect receipt of income in kind, such as access to construction materials for personal consumption.

Several criticisms have been made of both the general approach to the estimation of under-reported income and of specific studies. Commenting on studies such as that by MacAffee (1980), both Brown (1988) and Hakim (1989b) have pointed out that between 1978 and 1980, and later in the mid-1980s, income estimates from the national accounts exceeded those of expenditure, apparently indicating that the hidden economy had entered a negative phase. The residual error in the accounts appears to be the net effect of many factors, including undercounting of legitimate earnings below tax and insurance thresholds, and cannot be ascribed to one particular source.

Thomas (1988) has argued that the use of such indirect indicators cannot usefully say anything about the people involved or their patterns of behaviour. Hakim (1989b) has also pointed to the absence of any detailed empirical data to link this econometric work to people's everyday lives. This, she argues, encourages an unhealthy reliance on unreliable anecdotal evidence or surveys based on proxy information from people who 'know about' other people working 'cash in hand'. Hakim also points to the warnings in the FES handbook about comparisons between income and expenditure data: the handbook highlights limitations to analysis of this sort, particularly with regard to the absence of information about the accumulation or rundown of savings and the time discrepancies between income and expenditure data (especially relevant in a period of inflation). A further problem stems from trying to relate the behaviour of the head of household who supplied income data to patterns of household expenditure which may incorporate financial contributions from other earners.

The studies by Pissarides and Weber (1989) and by Baker (1993) rest on two somewhat robust assumptions: first that it is only the self-employed who under-report their income and secondly that the reporting of expenditure on food by all groups is accurate. It is conceivable that both assumptions are true, but there is no independent evidence to confirm them. The concentration on food expenditure appears to be based largely on food being the only item which clearly demonstrated the researchers' preconceptions of the scale of under-reporting by the self-employed (Pissarides and Weber, footnote 3). Pissarides and Weber draw on Smith's (1986) review to point to a concentration of informal economic activity among small family businesses, but their analysis does not permit a disaggregation which might indicate where under-reporting of income might be concentrated, apart from a simple blue collar/white collar distinction.

The study by Bradbury et al.(1988) based on housing consumption, is more sensitive to this question and also recognises some of the inevitable methodological limitations. First, housing expenditures, particularly those of owner-occupiers, are likely to be fixed in relation to the level of income prevailing when a house was purchased. The fact that a self-employed person is spending more than predicted on housing may simply reflect a recent drop in income. They tried to take account of this by creating a permanent income model based on national accounts figures for operating surpluses of unincorporated businesses in different industries. However, even when disaggregated by industry their results only give an average level of unmeasured income. As they point out, the actual level will vary considerably between individuals - a variation which is critical for understanding the distribution of incomes.

The main limitation of these studies lies in the relationship between current earnings and levels of consumption in self-employed families, which often depend on how far previous earnings and expenditure still cushion them from more recent falls in income. This question is explored in more detail in Chapter Seven, where we examine the construction and maintenance of living standards among the families interviewed in the qualitative studies. Hakim (1989b) has called for the 'destigmatisation' of self-employed people in analyses of income and expenditure data. She concluded that although estimates of unrecorded work and income derived from FES appear reasonable 'they rely on strong assumptions about behaviour patterns that may well prove unfounded, especially where they involve assumptions about where black economy work is most common' (p.16). The state of methodology currently allows us neither to pinpoint with any accuracy the reasons for underestimation of earnings nor to allocate proportions of global estimates to particular occupations or income levels, much less to individuals. Meager et al. (1994) suggest that higher earning self-employed people are generally likely to have more incentive to under-report their incomes than those at lower income levels. This argument receives some support from comparative research on the spatial distribution of informal economic activity, which finds that the most extensive activity takes place in more affluent regions with relatively high levels of employment (Windebank and Williams, 1994). The picture, according to this research, is similar across Europe to that in the USA, where Waldinger and Lapp concluded:

> Informal activities are not in fact principally associated with low-income, low status groups. Rather, the distribution of opportunities for underground income generation reflects the unequal distribution of opportunities for income generation of all types. (Waldinger and Lapp, 1993, p.7)

If this is true of self-employment in the UK, even average levels of under-reporting of the magnitude estimated by Pissarides and Weber would have the effect of widening further the dispersal of incomes already noted among the self-employed, without shifting significantly the position of lower income self-employed people in the overall income distribution. Clearly under-reporting of income by self-employed people does take place and should not be ignored, but if earnings data from a variety of sources tend to produce a consistent pattern then the trends observed need not be discounted for this reason alone.

Nevertheless, doubts about the accuracy of reported incomes are reinforced by other problems in the collection of data, including the relatively low rate of response recorded by self-employed people in household surveys.

Differential response rates

Non-response by self-employed people has been recognised as an important deficiency of household datasets since the 1970s (Stark, 1978; Atkinson and Micklewright, 1983). Special exercises to test response rates by comparison with census data have shown marked variations according to a number of characteristics including age, sex, household type, educational qualifications and country of birth, but one of the largest variations is by employment type. In a 1971 census check, for example, the response rate in the Family Expenditure Survey among self-employed people with employees was estimated as 56 per cent, and among self-employed people working on their own as 63 per cent, compared with around 72 per cent for employees (Kemsley et al., 1980). Redpath (1986) reported a similar matching exercise using 1981 census data, which again showed a significantly higher degree of non-response among households headed by a self-employed person. There are no published reports of more recent response rate estimates in FES, but there seems little reason to expect that the pattern has changed. In a recent and comprehensive analysis of self-employed earnings, using the first wave of the British Household Panel Study, Meager et al. (1994) found that 44 per cent of self-employed respondents failed to supply information on their incomes, compared with 13 per cent of employees.

Differential response rates give rise to a number of problems. First, it is common practice to gross up survey data to population estimates by using a set of weightings which are adjusted for different types of household according to their representation in the survey. This is done in the Households Below Average Income Series (HBAI), based on the FES, by allocating different weights for different types of benefit unit. Within each category non-respondents are in effect allocated the mean characteristics of those who did respond. The self-employed have a comparatively low response rate and they are also highly heterogeneous, so weights based on average household characteristics could perhaps give rise to greater margins of error for this group than for others.

The relatively high level of non-response by self-employed people also tends to support the assumption that they are inclined to conceal information about their finances. However, what is called non-response may not always be simply an indication of non-co-operativeness. It can also reflect inability to provide income data in the form prescribed by the research questionnaire, as well as problems of disentangling personal and business expenditure. This can be illustrated with reference to the General Household Survey (GHS), which unlike FES, treats failure to complete any component of the income schedule as a total non-response. The GHS has 50 questions concerning income, providing many opportunities for 'non-response'. By inserting test questions into the first quarter of the 1990-91 GHS, Foster and Lound (1993) found that the response rate for self-employed people increased from 76 per cent to 93 per cent (closer to that of employees) if they were asked to estimate their gross income as a broad weekly and annual amount. They also checked to what extent this information was consistent with figures generated by the normal GHS question schedule. Half the estimates were of the same order as the more systematic data, one-third were higher and the rest produced a lower figure. The authors attributed most of the differences to the greater variability of self-employed earnings over short periods and the different time parameters set by the two sets of questions, especially where respondents had recently undergone a change of circumstances.

For FES, partly completed schedules are acceptable. The main question in FES on which estimation of self-employed earnings is based asks for the net business profit or loss in the last 12 months for which information is available. People unable to answer this are then asked about sums of money drawn from the business to provide some estimate of earnings (the use of drawings as a proxy for profits is discussed below).

An examination of the answers to these questions (Kemsley et al., 1980) showed that in 1978 a substantial proportion of self-employed people were unable to answer them. Nineteen per cent could not supply a profit figure, 15 per cent had to supply an estimate and 20 per cent apparently did not know the date of their relevant business year. Respondents were often willing to have interviewers approach their accountants for figures, but this was not always possible. A similar picture emerges from Meager et al.'s BHPS analysis (1994). Almost two-thirds of those not responding said they did not know how much they earned. Although some may have been, in effect, refusing to answer, it is not clear why they should have done so when the option of direct refusal was also available.

It may be that some of the general level of non-response to surveys is linked to this so-called 'item non-response' and thus the response rate by self-employed people might improve if survey questions on income were made easier. This could, as the GHS experiment indicates, be at the expense of precision, though it is arguable that current survey data on self-employed incomes are hardly that precise.

Time-lags

Earnings figures from self-employed people in FES are acceptable from any business year ending during the 12 months prior to interview. This introduces substantial time-lags into the data, which might vary for different types of occupation. People with established businesses, for example, who are used to waiting for professionally-produced annual accounts would be particularly likely to present data relating to prior periods. Newer businesses may not yet have generated data for a 12-month period, and income covering less than a year is acceptable if a business is newly established. Income from self-employment can be highly variable across short periods, however. Trade or business cycles, for example the agricultural year, can generate quite different cash flows according to the stage reached, and data from a short period can be an unreliable indicator of business income (Boden and Corden, 1994).

This means that the periods of time to which self-employed income data in FES refer vary considerably. The longer these time-lags, the more uncertain it becomes that the profit figures provide an accurate picture of the current financial situation of the business. Since the detailed questions about earnings asked of employees in FES refer to the period of time covered by the most recent or usual payment of wages or salary, time-lags are rarely an issue and the data are likely to offer a more reliable indication of the current household situation.

The way in which analysts deal with time-lags depends on the purpose of analysis. In producing the published FES reports the Central Statistical Office (CSO) does not update self-employed earnings but presents them as reported. For the purposes of tax/benefit modelling, Atkinson et al. (1986) updated reported self-employed incomes using national accounts data for the calendar year corresponding to the income survey. They created a monthly index of self-employment income per head by dividing the national accounts figure for self-employed income by the estimated number of self-employed people and interpolating a monthly value. For each observation, the factor used to update corresponded to the mid-point of the period to which the recorded self-employment income related. The accuracy of this method clearly depends on the extent to which the national accounts figures themselves are correct. It also requires all self-employed respondents to be ascribed an earnings-updating factor corresponding to the average - an assumption which may be necessary but which is in practice rather unrealistic.

For the Households Below Average Income series (HBAI), DSS statisticians use a different method of updating, based on the movements in average earnings figures collated from industry surveys. Before 1986, self-employed people were ascribed the average earnings change in the industry in which they worked, but because FES no longer codes the information on industry types the data are now averaged across all industries.

Clearly some method of updating self-employed earnings is essential and both of the above methods have their merits. In aggregate we might expect to see self-employed earnings rise roughly in line with those of employees over a given stage of the business cycle. However, in the case of individuals or small groups there seems little reason to expect great accuracy from either of these approaches. In the HBAI method, for example, people recording business losses for a period ending four years before they are interviewed will be assumed to have had losses rising in line with the rise in average earnings over this period. This is logically consistent within the overall approach, but in practice some of those making losses might be expected to have recovered during a period when earnings are rising faster and vice versa. For individuals, changes in earnings from year to year will depend on a range of factors including inflation, interest rates and the market for products or services in their particular occupations.

In order to assess the extent to which time-lags might be distorting estimated incomes for the self-employed, we re-analysed FES data for 1990/1991. The two years were combined to provide greater numbers of self-employed respondents and to reduce sampling errors. The sample included 2,285 people with some self-employed earnings, of whom 1,898 were self-employed in their main job. In all, 52 per cent of respondents who were self-employed in their main job reported an end date for the accounting year applying to their earnings in the same calendar year as the survey. For a further 39 per cent this end date fell in the year before. Nine per cent gave a date falling two or more years before the survey. In all, 14 per cent of the sample reported earnings for a period of less than one full year. This analysis suggests that updating may not in fact present so great a problem. If we look at those reporting losses (193 or 10.2 per cent of the two year sample), we find that a slightly higher percentage (11 per cent) were reporting earnings from earlier years, and most of those reporting earnings from two or more years earlier also had losses in the higher ranges. The analysis does not reveal why more of those recording losses should be reporting on accounting periods before the year of the survey, and the numbers involved at this level of analysis are too small to draw reliable conclusions. Some speculative pointers come from other qualitative evidence. We found that some people whose businesses were making a loss were reluctant to pursue their accountants for figures. One reason was that they were hoping to postpone payment of the accountants' fees, which they felt they could not afford. Secondly, they were sometimes reluctant to let accountants, banks or other official bodies realise the extent of their financial problems, since keeping businesses going often depended on the continuing support and confidence of these other parties.

It may be that those recording losses would have continued to lose money in subsequent years, but if not, the effect of the updating process would have been to exaggerate the level of recorded losses. People recording nil profits (just over five per cent of people self-employed in their main job) would continue, in the updating process, to show nil profits. Even these figures may be uncertain, however, because of the way earnings of self-employed people are constructed in surveys such as FES.

The concept of earnings and the measurement of profit

Measuring earnings from self-employment is essentially an accounting exercise. Accounting methods are, however, socially constructed and reflect the context in which they are to be used. Within the UK a wide diversity of measures of earnings is in use, reflecting the different needs of, for example, business and commerce, fiscal policy and practice and social security requirements (Boden and Corden, 1994). What is measured in a survey questionnaire reflects merely the nature of the information requested and the technical rules constructed by analysts to deal with the information. While measures of earnings for employees are also subject to some conventions which have changed over time, they present relatively few problems compared to those of the self-employed.

The approach taken in the FES is, in principle, close to that adopted by the Inland Revenue. This looks primarily for net profit (or loss) after deducting expenses and wages but before deducting income tax, national insurance contributions or personal drawings. Some respondents will rely on figures from profit and loss accounts drawn up using traditional commercial accountancy measures. However, accounts vary in how they present such information. Items of income and expenditure may be treated differently according to different accountancy practices, or by the type of trade or business, and figures emerging as net profits in business accounts may reflect different computations. Without careful examination by people with accountancy skills, and incorporation of other relevant sources of information such as balance sheets, neither the interviewer nor the analyst is likely to achieve consistent, comparable income measures across a range of self-employed businesses.

In any case, tax assessment methodology has developed to provide an historical measure of what has happened in a business and may not capture a contemporary measure of income. Those respondents who have just started in business, or those with incomes below tax thresholds may not yet have needed to engage with concepts of annual net profit, and may find it hard, or impossible, to supply information in the form required. FES accepts data about earnings from people self-employed for less than a year at the time of the interview, as we have seen, but doubts have arisen about the reliability of declared income from those self-employed for short periods (Department of Social Security, 1991b). Examination of FES data since 1986 for the HBAI consultative group showed a relatively high proportion of people self-employed for three months or less reporting incomes which if projected for a full year would be over £20,000. This is not surprising, since people starting new businesses may well be over-optimistic, or may have felt the need to organise their finances so as to generate business confidence and secure loan investments. As these projections were felt to be unrealistic, households where a member has been self-employed for less than two months are now excluded from HBAI estimates (Department of Social Security, 1993a). Exclusion of these short-term self-employed had the effect of increasing real income growth of the bottom decile of the income distribution by about half of one per cent.

The use of drawings as a proxy for profits

The approach adopted for FES by the Central Statistical Office (CSO) in the case of respondents who report nil profit or losses, or cannot provide a profit figure, is to ask about personal drawings from the business. These are then used as a proxy for profit. If there is no figure for drawings at this stage, they are automatically imputed, using household expenditure minus income from other sources. Until the mid-1980s, respondents unable to answer questions about either profit, loss or drawings from the business were then asked for an annual turnover figure - turnover in this context being the gross cash inflow into a business from its trading activities. From the turnover figure notional profit was imputed, using gross annual household expenditure along with standard Inland Revenue 'profit margin' estimates for different kinds of business. There are no longer questions about turnover in the FES, however.

The argument for the use of drawings is that if people are taking money from a business to live on which will show up as consumption elsewhere in the survey, the amount taken may be a better representation of their current living standards than a loss figure which may merely represent a technical accounting exercise. To some extent our research tends to support this argument. In small enterprises people tend to draw out what they feel they need to live on, but the amounts are frequently determined by their access to overdraft finance. Where businesses are secured against substantial property or where it is traditional for long-term income fluctuation to be supported by overdraft and debt finance, such as in farming businesses, people may be able to rely on higher drawings than in small unsecured enterprises. This can be true even where the secured businesses are running losses much greater than the unsecured enterprises. However, there are also loss-making situations in which drawings essential to meet household needs may be adding to a burden of debt which becomes insupportable.

The FES does not ask questions about money owed or borrowed, or about the run down of previous savings. A few items of information are collected which may provide some clues about indebtedness, such as payment made to service loans, but these data are generally regarded as unreliable. Without more systematic information it is impossible to distinguish between the routine use of debt finance and that which may be associated with a crisis - where taking the drawings to represent ongoing income may produce a highly distorted picture of household circumstances.

Also, using drawings as a proxy for profit has meant that people reporting small losses can be assigned larger incomes than those reporting a small pre-tax profit. This question was examined in the DSS 'stocktaking' exercise on HBAI (Department of Social Security, 1991b). The consultative group recommended a change of approach and loss figures are now accepted in HBAI in order to produce a more consistent income measure. The number of people reporting losses in FES has risen substantially during the 1980s, so this change is partly responsible for the reported shift in the proportion of people in the bottom deciles in households headed by a self-employed person. Overall, government statisticians estimated that the effect of accepting losses has been to reduce estimates of income growth between 1979 and 1989/90 by an average of one percentage point before housing costs for the whole population and two percentage points for the bottom income decile (Department of Social Security, 1992).

Taking losses as the measure of earnings does not, however, remove the problem of establishing an income figure from the gross profit or loss submitted by respondents. Some of these difficulties were highlighted in our conceptual study of earnings assessment procedures (Boden and Corden, 1994) and they are discussed briefly here.

The derivation of profit by accountancy techniques

Estimates of earnings by self-employed people are most commonly taken from profit and loss accounts. In the first wave of the British Household Panel Study, for example, just over 70 per cent of self-employed respondents said they drew up such accounts (Taylor, 1992). Annual profit and loss figures quoted by interviewees are generally drawn up according to traditional rules of accruals-based commercial accountancy. What is represented by this technique is an historic picture of the profitability of the business, usually drawn up to meet the requirements of the Inland Revenue. Accountancy is an art rather than a science and accountants take different approaches according to the information available to them, the resources of the business, the nature of the trade or occupation, and the level of remuneration expected for professional services. If an interviewer takes the final profit or loss figure from business accounts offered by respondents, then the analyst has to accept a range of different measures resulting from a variety of treatments.

For example, documents prepared by accountants for established farmers in our study had been based on account books detailing sales and income, drawn up on a weekly basis. The documentation was substantial, itemising stock sales, receipt of government subsidies, and payments for feed, veterinary bills, equipment repairs and casual wages. By contrast, the profit and loss account prepared by an ice cream vendor's accountant had been based solely on the invoices for ice cream purchased for resale. The accountant simply applied a reasonable mark-up rate to derive a takings figure, then estimated expenses.

Items to be allowed as expenses in estimating profit may be a matter of judgement, based on the accountant's professional experience. A man working in the entertainment industry successfully claimed substantial dentistry costs as an expense against tax (to maintain his appearance), as well as licence and rental payments for his televisions (to follow developments in his field of work). These were not allowed as business expenses in an application for family credit. Which of these procedures should we regard as leading to a better measure of income?

A survey researcher cannot interrogate business accounts to ensure consistency in situations like this. Interviewers are not accountants and many would find it hard to understand the figures. This is especially likely to be the case where profits have been ploughed back into in the business and earnings data would have to be extracted from a balance sheet. We might indeed ask whether researchers should attempt any standardisation, since what is offered is the figure construed by an accountant whose own professional specialism is measurement of income. However, in accepting their figures we should not suppose that they necessarily provide a single, 'true' picture of profit.

This problem is compounded when we take in estimates of earnings which are not based on professionally-produced profit and loss accounts. Few of the established business people in our sample attempted to produce accounts to satisfy Inland Revenue without the advice of an accountant or book-keeper, but people who had only recently started in business, or whose finances appeared straightforward, had often got by without accountancy help. When applying for family credit, most attempted to supply cash flow information since they were unable to offer a profit and loss account. This was acceptable for social security purposes, but in fact the measures of income produced by cash flow accounting and accruals-based accounting can produce quite different results. This is especially the case where there are marked seasonal patterns or trade cycles. A market gardener, for example, received most of his income during the summer and autumn when he sold his plants and vegetables. Most of his expenditure was incurred in the winter and spring, on heating greenhouses and on buying seed and equipment. Cash flow statements for winter months gave much lower net earnings figures than those for the summer.

FES accepts profit figures covering less than a year if the business is newly established. Such figures may well reflect cash flows, rather than accruals-based profit or loss figures, and there are no further questions in the schedule to assess the representativeness of the months submitted. Using accruals-based measures alongside cash-flow measures can lead to major inconsistencies (Boden and Corden, 1994). We have already seen that a proportion of earnings figures in the FES from newly established businesses appeared to be over-estimated. The reverse can also be true, with cash flow for the first months producing a depressed earnings measure. For example, in our study a man establishing a small business repairing musical instruments incurred substantial expenses during the first six months for advertising and promotional work, setting up a workshop, and purchasing small instrument parts. Income figures collected at the end of the first six months would have suggested a loss-making situation, since it was not until the second six months that work started to come in. From then on the business would have shown climbing profitability, depending on which month the interviewer arrived. Our analysis of FES data showed that just over ten per cent of all the individual self-employed earnings periods in FES for 1990/1991 were for six months or less. If this is true of the self-employed population as a whole, some 300,000 people could be affected.

These simple illustrations from interviews with family credit applicants show some of the conceptual problems in accepting a variety of indicators of self-employed earnings in a household survey. While it may be possible to include more self-employed people within the survey by allowing information to be provided in a number of ways, response rates are likely to be increased at the expense of comparability and consistency of data. The difficulties in assessing a figure for gross profits are further compounded, where a net income figure is required, by the treatment of income tax.

The treatment of income tax

The collection and treatment of information on tax payments in household surveys are subject to a number of technical problems. They stem mostly from mismatches between the time periods covered by the profit reported and the payments made to Inland Revenue. This is most likely to affect businesses with variable profitability from year to year, and those where business is building up or in decline.

There are arguments for using tax liability imputed from the profits declared rather than tax payments actually made. This is the approach currently used for assessing self-employed incomes for means-tested social security benefits. The HBAI stocktaking report examined this problem too and concluded that imputation would simply substitute one set of anomalies for another. It was decided that the case for imputing tax for the self-employed was not strong enough to justify the additional complexity this would introduce to the analysis (Department of Social Security, 1991b). What is important to remember is that under the present system of collecting information for FES, situations arise where people report having paid no tax, but have self-employment profits above the tax threshold: conversely, others report substantial tax payments, apparently on the basis of low pre-tax profits. This can be perfectly legitimate, but it is yet another element in the confusing picture of self-employed earnings derived from household surveys, and one which contributes to assumptions of substantial under-reporting of income.

To summarise, income data on self-employment derived from household surveys are subject to a complex set of technical difficulties. Making use of these data requires adjustments and assumptions, with margins of error which are likely to be many times greater than those applying to earnings of employees or people not in the workforce. This is not to say that the data are worthless and cannot be used. Rather, we would argue that they should be used in a critical way which recognises the limitations and seeks to improve the methodology of collection and analysis. Indeed it is only by the use of such sources of data and discussion of improvements in methodology that self-employed people can be brought back 'in from the cold' where until recently they have languished. In this light, the next section reviews the evidence which does exist on the incomes of self-employed people to see how far it supports the picture developed in earlier chapters.

The incomes of self-employed people

Information on self-employed incomes has been derived from a number of sources, including the General Household Survey (GHS), the Social Change and Economic Life Survey (SCELI), the Inland Revenue's Survey of Personal Incomes (SPI), the Family Expenditure Survey (FES) and, most recently, the

British Household Panel Study (BHPS). This section summarises and discusses the results of recent research using these sources.

The first study, by Curran et al. (1987), was based on the 1980 GHS. It thus provides a useful benchmark for measuring the trend over the decade. They found, not surprisingly, that men tended to earn more than women whether they were employees, self-employed sole traders or people with small businesses employing others. The latter category also tended to be better off than those without employees. The distributional picture, however, was different for those with or without employees. Both groups were over-represented in the bottom category of people with gross earnings of less than £50 per week, with over three-fifths of sole traders and nearly half of employers falling into this group as opposed to only one in six of employees. However, while very few of the sole traders fell into the top bracket of those earning £200 per week or more, the proportion of employers in this category was twice as high as for employees. This suggests that even before the expansion of self-employment in the 1980s, the incomes of self-employed people were widely dispersed, with a disproportionate representation in the upper tail of the income distribution number of people (mainly men) with employees .

A similar picture comes from the Social Change and Economic Life study, which surveyed 6,000 households in six local labour markets in 1986 (Rubery et al., 1993). Unlike the GHS study, which was based on gross individual incomes, this study used household income, so the differences between men and women are less marked. Nevertheless, the same pattern can be observed of wide dispersion of self-employed incomes, with the small business proprietors with employees over-represented in the highest income group.

The most recent data from the Inland Revenue's Survey of Personal Incomes (SPI), based on individual tax returns, indicates that some 36 per cent of all gross personal incomes from self-employment in 1991 were assessed at less than £5,000 (Board of Inland Revenue, 1994). A further 28 per cent were between £5,000 and £10,000. Considering that the SPI is based on tax returns, one might expect under-reporting to be a particular problem. Even taking this into account, however, the results are striking. While people with self-employed earnings often have other sources of income, some of which are substantial, their mean total gross market income was still only just over £9,000, including other employment earnings, investment income and pensions. Further up the income scale the proportion of income derived from self-employed earnings increases. At the top end, six per cent of individuals (211,000) had an estimated mean income of nearly £55,000 from self-employment, which made up an average of 86 per cent of their total taxable market incomes.

Perhaps the key source of data on household incomes and income distribution in Great Britain up to now has been the Family Expenditure Survey, which covers around 7,000 households annually and has also been the main source of information on the financial circumstances of the self-employed. It is also, however, the survey in which the problems with self-employment income have been most apparent.

One analysis of FES data which highlighted the apparently low incomes of self-employed people was by Hakim (1989b). She found that self-employed people as a whole were more than twice as likely as employees to have reported earnings below the thresholds at which income tax and national insurance contributions are payable. This was true for both men and women, and for full- and part-time workers. Since there is a substantial overlap between part-time and female self-employment, the percentage of self-employed women with earnings below the threshold was particularly high, at 48.8 per cent in 1985/6 (two years' data merged) compared to 12.1 per cent of women employees. Another analysis for 1986/7, using somewhat different parameters, produced broadly the same results. Analysis of the 1990/91 FES shows that the picture has not changed substantially except that, if anything, even more self-employed people had earnings below the thresholds. Table 3.1 shows our analysis of merged FES data for 1990 and 1991. Just under a quarter of all respondents who were self-employed in their main job had total gross self-employed earnings below the personal tax threshold and just over a fifth were below the threshold for Class 2 contributions. Over half of all self-employed women fell below both the thresholds.

The Family Expenditure Survey is also, as we have seen, the basis for the main official source of information on income distribution in the UK - the Households Below Average Income series published by the Department of Social Security. The HBAI provides a cross-sectional analysis of the patterns of disposable incomes of individuals, who are assigned the equivalised total income of the household to which they belong. Recent reports in the series have highlighted the growing numbers of self-employed people falling into the lowest deciles of the income distribution. This often results from zero or negative incomes, but, as the report covering the period 1979-1990/91 states:

> ... the average expenditure of individuals from households reporting zero or negative incomes was higher than the population as a whole. This finding lends further weight to previous concerns about the extent to which income information from the self-employed gives a fair indication of their actual standard of living. (Department of Social Security, 1993a, p.26)

Table 3.1
Self-employed people with earnings below the tax and national insurance thresholds, Great Britain, 1990-91

	Below tax threshold	*Below National Insurance threshold*
	%	%
Men	15.0	12.7
Women	54.7	50.1
All self-employed	24.6	21.8

Base: 1,895

Note: The analysis differs slightly from that of Hakim's estimates for 1985/6, in that the Class 2 NI threshold is used rather than whether respondents were recorded as having zero contributions. Also the measure of income used is that of gross main income from self-employment plus any secondary earnings from other self-employed work. Hakim's analysis included income from any other subsidiary work, which in some cases where self-employed people have additional work as employees, might bring some above the thresholds. We follow Hakim's earlier analysis, however, in using only the lower, personal tax threshold and not attempting to incorporate the married man's or additional tax allowances (see the note to Hakim, 1989b, Table 3).

The income tax thresholds were as follows: 1990 - £57.79 per week, 1991 - £63.37 per week. Class 2 NI thresholds were: 1990 - £50.00 per week, 1991 - £55.77 per week.

However, although the numbers may have grown (reflecting the general increase in self-employment) the proportionate shift is less than dramatic. In 1979 the self-employed made up six per cent of the total population and ten per cent of those in the bottom decile, both before and after housing costs. By 1990/1991 the self-employed made up ten per cent of the population and 15 per cent of the bottom decile of incomes before housing costs. Thus the ratio of over-representation actually dropped slightly, from 1.67 to 1.5 over the decade. It was only after allowing for housing costs, as a result of which they made up 18 per cent of the lowest decile, that the over-representation of the self-employed in the bottom decile increased to 1.8. Perhaps more significantly the self-employed were the only group with working status who continued to be over-represented in the bottom decile. Most households at this income level were headed by an unemployed person. There was also an apparent shift down the income distribution on the part of the self-employed, with the percentage with incomes below 40 per cent of the average after housing costs doubling between 1979 and 1990/91 from seven to 14 per cent.

It is the group in the lowest deciles reporting zero or negative incomes which has attracted the most attention. As we have seen, many of the households with nil or negative incomes in the bottom deciles also report equivalised expenditures above the average for the population as a whole, and although the HBAI reports are properly cautious about the interpretation of such findings they tend to be cited as evidence of under-reporting of earnings by the self-employed.

FES data have also been used in three recent detailed analyses of income inequality trends, by Jenkins (1994, 1995) and Goodman and Webb (1994). Jenkins' studies are particularly important in their assessment of the factors contributing to the growing inequality of incomes over the period from 1971 to 1990/91. Jenkins follows the same approach to FES data as the DSS in the HBAI series, but uses 'shift share' and 'decomposition' analyses to relate the aggregate changes to movements within population and employment groups. He shows that between 1981 and 1986 (when self-employment growth was at its fastest) widening dispersion of self-employment incomes was an important force contributing to the general pattern of growing inequality. In relation to the distribution of self-employed earnings, Jenkins notes:

> ...inspection reveals significant shifts in concentration towards both tails of the distribution: in 1999/91 there were relatively more people with either very low (or zero) recorded income, or with very high incomes. (1994, p.23)

He also observes:

> ... preliminary explorations suggest that the growth in inequality of self-employment income between 1981 and 1986 is a combination of inequality growth amongst those in traditional self-employment, for whom inequality is relatively low, and increases in inequality amongst those in newer areas such as banking, finance and insurance, a group smaller in size but growing, and which has relatively high inequality. (1995, p.21)

Jenkins's analyses are further reinforced by that of Goodman and Webb (1994), who built up a time series of the components of income distribution from 1961 to 1991, using FES data. They show that the proportion of families with self-employed earners in the bottom decile income group has grown steadily, with the sharpest increase since 1980. In 1980 these families represented 5.7 per cent of the lowest income group and by 1991 they made up just over 13 per cent. At the other end of the spectrum, the self-employed also increased their representation in the highest income group, but to a lesser extent. The fall-back in self-employment in the recent recession also seems to have had a detectable impact on this group. Broadly the same pattern is found for individuals as for family units. Goodman and Webb also note an increase in the numbers of self-employed people reporting nil profits or losses, while echoing the caveat already made in the HBAI reports that many of these families reported expenditure levels at or above the average. They conclude:

> ...whilst the number of people with self-employment income has risen sharply, total self-employment income has not risen nearly so rapidly. This suggests that the nature of self-employment may itself be changing with the 'new' self-employment covering many lower income activities.' (p.56)

One group of low-income self-employed people Goodman and Webb point to as an example are those who started work with help from the Enterprise Allowance Scheme. Between 1983 and 1988 around 300,000 people started small enterprises with the help of EAS payments (NAO, 1988). An evaluation of the scheme two years after its national launch (Allen and Hunn, 1985) found that among the 61 per cent of businesses surviving, median pre-tax profits were only about £100 per week. There was only slight growth in profits compared with those recorded in earlier surveys. Also, the most common reason given by those who had closed down their businesses was insufficient profit. Participants in the EAS were all coming out of periods of unemployment and were likely to be among those with relatively low incomes from their businesses, at least in the early years. Nevertheless, these findings add to the broad picture of a substantial sector within self-employment where rewards are likely to be very modest.

The most detailed study focusing specifically on the incomes of the self-employed is that of Meager et al. (1994), using the British Household Panel Study (BHPS), and their findings are worth summarising. The study was based on interviews with 10,000 individuals conducted in autumn 1991, in which employment status was based on respondents' own classification of their work. As was mentioned earlier, 44 per cent of self-employed respondents failed to provide details of their incomes. Frequency tables produced in the survey handbook indicate that those with profit and loss accounts found it more difficult to provide this information than those without. Only 51 per cent of those with accounts gave an earnings figure, as opposed to 71 per cent of the other group (Taylor, 1992). However, there appeared to be few significant differences between those providing income figures and those not, except for some variation by industrial sector.

The results support the picture which has been built up from the previous studies. First, the distribution of labour income is more dispersed for the self-employed as a whole than for employees. Secondly, the level of income is lower than for employees at the bottom end of the income distribution and higher at the upper end. In the bottom decile, for example, mean self-employed earnings are only 70 per cent of those of employees, while in the top decile they are a third higher. Income profiles differ substantially, however, by gender. Self-employed women are much more likely than men in either employment status or employee women to have very low incomes and less likely to have very high incomes. This can partly be explained by women's greater propensity to carry out part-time self-employment (which was discussed in the last chapter), but it is also a function of relative hourly earnings. Analysis of hourly earnings also reveals that there is a group of the self-employed, both men and women, on particularly low incomes which cannot be explained by short working hours. As we saw in the previous chapter, self-employed people as whole tend to work longer hours than their employed counterparts. In later chapters we show how these indications of low hourly earnings identified by Meager et al. (1994) are supported by analysis of the family credit administrative data and by our qualitative interviews.

Meager et al. also carried out a multivariate analysis using logistic regression to identify the extent to which self-employment *per se* influences an individual's likelihood of occupying a particular location in the income distribution, as opposed to other factors such as age, gender, hours of work, occupation and qualification levels. They conclude:

> Multivariate analysis shows that self-employed people have more than three times the odds of appearing in the lowest income decile than an equivalent employee. Even once an estimate for under-reporting of self-employed incomes is included, the odds of a self-employed person falling into the lowest decile group remains higher than those of their employee counterparts. (p.63)

The study goes on to compare the level and source of non-labour income of employees and self-employed people. Here the self-employed are better off than employees on average, with the main differential sources of non-labour income for self-employed men being income from pensions and investments and for women from benefits and investments. Receipt of higher levels of pension and investment income can partly be attributed to the older age profile of the self-employed. Sample sizes are small at this level of analysis, but the findings suggest that self-employed women are more likely to be receiving benefit income because of their relatively low earnings. However, while the inclusion of non-labour income acts to reduce the income gap between the self-employed and employees, it does not change the overall pattern of income dispersal.

A final analysis of the BHPS data looks at the income distribution among those recently entering self-employment, including the overlapping groups of younger people, women, people previously unemployed, those without family backgrounds in small business, subcontractors and people working in the service sector. Small sample sizes make this element of the analysis less conclusive, but the indications are that other things being equal, the effect of the growth of the 'new' self-employment during the 1980s has been to increase income inequality, both within self-employment itself and in the wider population.

Conclusions

The evidence discussed in this chapter points to two perhaps somewhat contradictory conclusions. First, that we have to be cautious about the interpretation of income data on the self-employed derived from surveys because of a range of technical and substantive difficulties or inconsistencies in how they are collected and processed. This also means that we should not accept uncritically some of the widespread assumptions about the levels of under-reporting of income by self-employed people. Secondly, in spite of the problems we have outlined, the consistency of the patterns identified in the survey evidence we have discussed suggests that as well as a group of high earners among those with small businesses, there is also a substantial group among the self-employed with particularly low incomes. Over the period since self-employment began to grow, this group has expanded, widening the already dispersed income distribution among self-employed people and contributing to general income inequality. Some uncertainty remains, however, about the living standards enjoyed by some of the households in the lowest income deciles as their expenditure levels are suggestive of greater affluence.

It is among this lower income group that the self-employed family credit population can be found and we now move on to focus on this population. The next chapter provides the results of analysis of administrative data on family credit recipients, looking at their characteristics and their earnings and comparing them with those of employed recipients.

4 Who are the low income self-employed?

Although the conceptualisation and measurement of incomes from self-employment remains problematic, the general picture drawn in the previous chapter was one of an increasing number of self-employed people who are relatively poor, in comparison both with their employee counterparts, and with others working in self-employed occupations. They were being joined, throughout the 1980s it seems, by a disproportionate section of those in the 'new' forms of self-employment, including women, people previously unemployed and young people.

It was one of the aims of our research to explore some of the factors leading to this concentration of people working on their own account for apparently very low rewards. The focus of interest was families with children, people whom we might expect to be especially keen to maintain living standards and for whom very low incomes might lead fairly quickly to financial problems.

We hoped to discover how people in one group of such families - those who claimed family credit - managed to combine business activities, or other forms of self-employed work which brought such a little in the way of financial return, with bringing up their children.

One way of beginning to understand more about this group is to look at their characteristics. The administrative statistics collected by the Benefits Agency in order to decide claims and pay benefit provide a profile of the family credit population, with information on family type and size, regional and occupational distribution, hours of work, earnings and other sources of income, and continuity of claims. Secondary analysis of this dataset therefore gives us a preliminary overview of the circumstances of self-employed families claiming family credit in comparison with employee recipients. The information on recipients' incomes also allows us to locate these groups of families within the earnings profiles discussed in the previous chapter and to begin to address the question raised earlier of why self-employed families receive so much more benefit on average than those with employed earners.

The basis of the statistical analysis

Tabulations of family credit statistics produced for publication in the Department's statistical returns are based on a five per cent sample of claims in payment on a particular day each month, extracted from the main database held by the Family Credit Unit at North Fylde. As a source of information, the sample has limitations. The data are collected primarily for the administration of benefit delivery, rather than for research. This means that they include information only on claims in payment and not on applications. There is also no information on tenure or housing costs. Some aspects of considerable interest, such as how gross profits have been calculated, cannot be pursued in these data. There are also a number of areas where information is incomplete or is known to be subject to errors. These gaps and uncertainties in the data normally relate to variables which are not strictly essential for the adjudication process, such as occupational classifications. The five per cent extracts go back to April 1988, when family credit was introduced to replace family income supplement (FIS), but some of the early information is incomplete and the sample data cannot be regarded as fully accurate before July 1989 (Department of Social Security, 1990).

The analysis reported here is based on both a cross-sectional 'snapshot' of claims in payment at a particular date, mainly March or April 1991, and a longitudinal examination of the duration of claims by different employment and household types. April 1991 was chosen as the main date for cross-sectional analysis because although data were available for some months after this, they would not yet have been corrected to take into account backdated awards resulting from reviews, appeals and other adjustments. Appendix A includes further technical and methodological details on the dataset itself and on the analysis. Another team of researchers has also made use of these administrative data, concentrating on longitudinal analysis to explore factors influencing the duration of benefit claims (Ashworth and Walker, 1992). Their findings offer a further perspective on the dynamics of the family credit population.

A profile of the family credit population

In April 1991 there were approximately 341,000 families receiving benefit, of whom 53,000 received their main market earnings from self-employment (Table 4.1).

Table 4.1
Analysis of caseload and numbers of children per family by employment status and family type, 30 April 1991

	All families	*Couples main earner:*			*Single main earner:*		
		Male	Female	Total	Male	Female	Total
Employees							
Number of cases (thousands)	288	136	31	167	4	118	122
Number of children (thousands)	603	345	63	408	7	189	196
Average number of children per family	2.1	2.5	2.1	2.4	1.8	1.6	1.6
Self-employed							
Number of cases (thousands)	53	40	4	44	1	8	9
Number of children (thousands)	121	97	8	105	2	13	15
Average number of children per family	2.3	2.5	2.1	2.4	1.5	1.7	1.6
Total							
Number of cases (thousands)	341	176	35	211	5	126	131
Number of children (thousands)	724	443	70	513	9	202	211
Average number of children per family	2.1	2.5	2.1	2.1	1.7	1.6	1.6

Source: SPRU analysis of five per cent administrative sample
Note: Figures are rounded to nearest thousand.

The majority of claimants in April 1991 were couples with the man as the main earner[1], though a substantial proportion (37 per cent) were lone parents. Analysis of the total sample of recipients since 1988 also shows a similar pattern, suggesting that the distributional pattern among family types has not changed significantly. However, this impression conceals a sharp increase which has taken place in the (still relatively small) number of couples with a woman main earner, and which has been mainly at the expense of male-earner couples.

In April 1991 there were 53,000 families whose main or only earner was self-employed, representing nearly 16 per cent of all recipients. While the number of family credit recipients with main earnings from self-employment has grown since the introduction of the benefit in 1988, their share of the overall caseload has also not changed to any significant degree, as Table 4.2 shows.

The table shows that there was a large increase between 1983 and 1984 in both the absolute number of self-employed recipients and their share of the total claimant population. As we saw earlier, this was the period when self-employment was increasing most rapidly. The number of self-employed recipient families also increased sharply between the last year of family income supplement and the first year of family credit. However, it fell as a proportion of the caseload because of an even larger percentage increase among employed families. This can largely be attributed to the broader criteria of eligibility for family credit compared to those of FIS. Since 1988 the proportion of recipient families with a self-employed earner has remained virtually the same each year, with only small fluctuations by family type.

Table 4.2
Percentage of family credit and family income supplement recipients with awards based on incomes from self-employment, by family type, 1981-1991

	Couples main earner:		*Single main earner:*		*All families*	
	Male	Female	Male	Female	%	Numbers
Family Income Supplement						
1981		13	14	2	8	8,000
1982		14	21	2	9	13,000
1983		15	22	3	10	19,000
1984	21	5	26	3	14	27,000
1985	22	8	28	4	15	27,000
1986	22	9	28	3	15	29,000
1987	24	10	25	4	16	35,000
1988	24	8	28	4	17	36,000
Family Credit						
1989	21	11	25	7	15	44,000
1990	21	10	25	6	15	46,000
1991	23	11	26	6	16	53,000

Sources: DSS social security statistics, 1981-1991

Notes: a. Figures refer to claims in payment at a specific date in March or April of the relevant year.

b. Before 1984 figures were not given separately for male and female earner couples.

It has been suggested that the self-employed may be disproportionately represented among family credit recipients, compared with their presence in the labour force as a whole. In spring 1991, 13.2 per cent of all those in employment were self-employed (Department of Employment, 1993). However, taking into account the availability of family credit only to those with dependent children, the difference may only be apparent. As we saw in Chapter Two, self-employed people are older on average than other employed people and more likely to be married. Published analyses do not record the percentage of families with dependent children where the main earnings are from self-employment, but by analysing General Household Survey data for 1989 we found that 15 per cent of the 5,100 working heads of households with dependent children found in the GHS were self-employed. In 1991, family credit was available only to those families with an earner working at least 24 hours per week, so a more precise comparison should be made with those families with at least one adult working these hours. The definition of hours worked used in the GHS is not exactly the same as that in the family credit database, but it provides a reasonably accurate estimate of the population from which family credit recipients are drawn. We found that 18 per cent of family units in the GHS had dependent children and a main earner working in self-employment for at least 24 hours a week. Given the concentration of low earnings among the self-employed, highlighted in the previous chapter, we might speculate that, if anything, self-employed families may be somewhat under-represented as family credit recipients. The question of whether take-up might be particularly low among self-employed families is considered further in Chapter Six.

As in the workforce generally, men in the family credit claimant population were more likely to be self-employed than women, and families receiving benefit on the basis of women's self-employed earnings remained a small minority. In spite of the relatively large increase in couples with a woman main earner, these families only made up just under seven per cent of the self-employed recipients. Just over three-quarters of all self-employed recipient families in April 1991 were couples with a male main earner and a further 15 per cent were lone mothers (Figure 4.1).

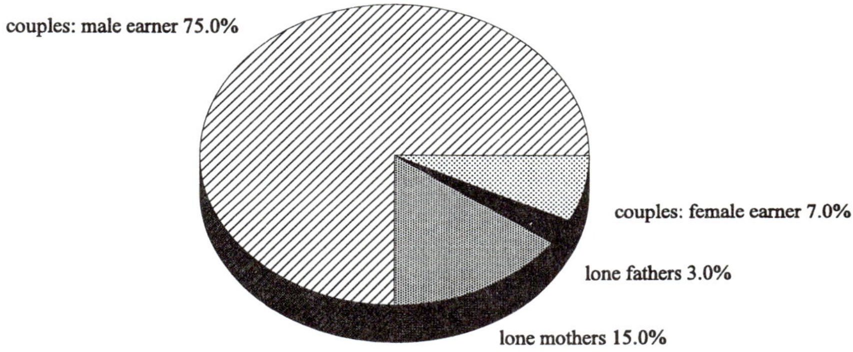

Figure 4.1 Self-employed family credit recipients, April 1991, by family type

The proportion of recipient families with awards based on self-employment varied by family type. Fifty-two per cent of all recipients in April 1991 were couples with a male main earner and 23 per cent of these were self-employed. Lone mothers were the second largest group of recipients but only six per cent of these were self-employed. We saw earlier that although some studies have found relatively high levels of involvement in small businesses among divorced and separated women, surveys of lone parents suggest that self-employment is fairly unusual among lone mothers at least. If, as some qualitative research suggests, working at home is one way in which women on their own with children manage to combine employment and child care, then either relatively few are eligible for family credit, or there is low take-up among this group.

The rate of self-employment among lone fathers in the family credit population was the highest of all the family types, at 26 per cent. However, because of the small numbers involved they still made up only three per cent of all self-employed recipients. Given that men are generally more likely than women to have access to various opportunities for working on their own account, it seems possible that the high self-employment rate among lone fathers can at least partly be explained by men's need to maintain their sense of themselves as workers while also being available to look after their children.

Occupational status

As would be expected, the family credit population as a whole is disproportionately drawn from lower paid occupational groups. Over a quarter in April 1991 were in work which was classified as in catering, cleaning, hairdressing and other personal services. Other important sectors included manufacturing, clerical work and transport. In their analysis of duration on benefit, Ashworth and Walker (1992) found that over time there had been some changes in the proportion of recipients from different occupational sectors, notably a fall in the number of manual workers (predominantly male) and an increase in the catering and cleaning industries (which traditionally rely on female staff). These changes are partly explained by varying propensities within different groups to renew existing claims or to make new applications. Ashworth and Walker also noted that the absolute monthly number of new claims from self-employed people has not fluctuated significantly since 1989, unlike those from employees - one reason why the former have maintained their share of a growing caseload. This observation is consistent with the picture outlined earlier in the book of high turnover in self-employment and of a sector facing considerable financial difficulties in the recession of the late 1980s.

Occupational categories are known to be imprecise where self-employed people are concerned. A high proportion of self-employed people tend to categorise themselves as managers rather than by their actual business activity - presumably because they see the running of a business of whatever size as a managerial activity. The occupational data in the family credit records are also thought not to be fully accurate. It is, nevertheless, of interest to compare the profile of lower income families receiving family credit against that of self-employed people as a whole. Figure 4.2 shows the occupational distribution of self-employed men and women in 1989 compared with that for family credit recipients in 1991. Separate years are compared because an occupational breakdown by gender is not available from the Labour Force Survey for 1991. Some changes may therefore have taken place in the intervening years.

As would be expected, there were fewer professional men in the family credit group than in the self-employed population as a whole, though it is interesting to note that women professionals were proportionately more common. Family credit recipients, both male and female, were concentrated in the catering, cleaning, hairdressing and other personal service occupations to a much higher degree than among the self-employed as a whole, reflecting the low earnings derived from this work. One point to remember about all such cross-sectional analyses, as Ashworth and Walker (1992) have pointed out, is that there is a tendency for long-term family credit recipients to accumulate in the system and thus distort the characteristics of a sample taken at one point in time. This would apply to occupations as much as to any other characteristics and might be expected to boost the proportions found in the lower earning sectors. A fifth of all family credit recipients with a male self-employed earner appeared to be found in the transport and storage occupations - four times the proportion of the self-employed as a whole. This group would include road haulage operators and taxi-drivers - both occupations identified by the Family Credit Unit to the researchers as groups which often pose administrative problems in assessment of earnings.

The proportions of self-employed people working in the construction and agricultural industries are of particular interest. The construction industry experienced the highest numerical growth in self-employment of any industry in the last decade. At its peak in 1990 some 31 per cent of all self-employed men worked in this industry and this figure still stood at 29 per cent in 1991. However, the proportion of self-employed family credit recipients working in construction in April 1991 was only five per cent. Similarly, only three per cent of self-employed family credit recipients were involved in agriculture, fishing and related work, although over half of all people engaged in this work are self-employed and nine per cent of all self-employment in 1991 was in this sector. Farmers and fishermen are two other groups which have presented administrative problems in terms of earnings assessment. They are occupational groups which have well-organised unions and trade federations to represent their interests, and their geographical concentration in certain areas has also led to energetic political representation on their behalf. According to administrative statistics, it appears that there were less than 2,000 families engaged in farming or fishing and receiving family credit in April 1991 on the basis of self-employed earnings. In terms of policy making, however, they have been a relatively influential group, bringing into focus issues of administration and procedure to which the DSS has felt it was appropriate to pay special attention.

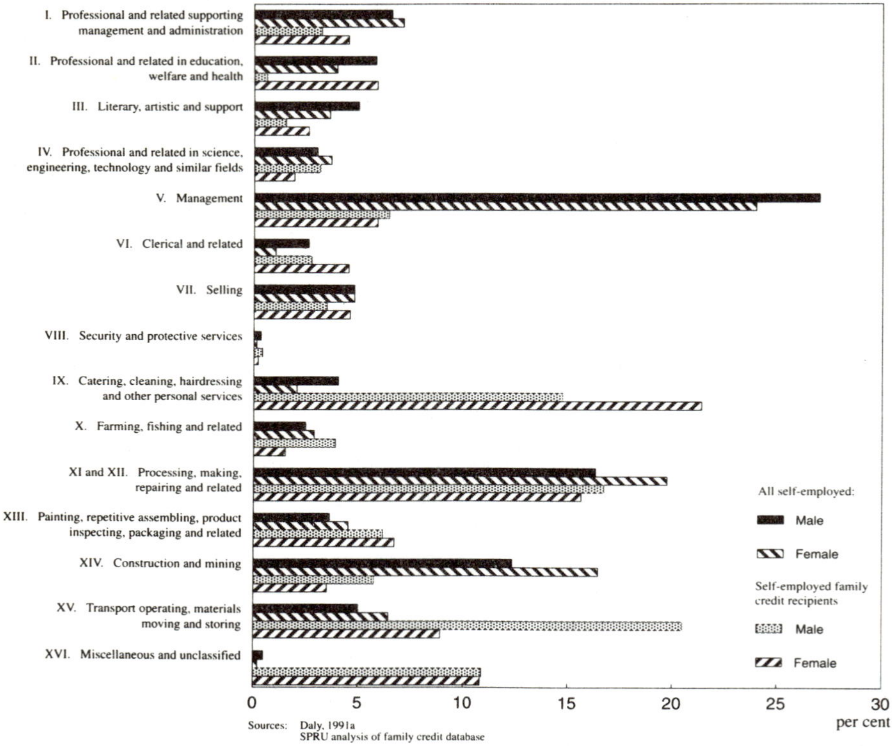

Figure 4.2 Occupational distribution of self-employed men and women, 1989 and recipients of family credit with self-employed earnings, by sex of main earner, 1991

Sources: Daly, 1991a
SPRU analysis of family credit database

Geographical distribution

Regionally, family credit recipients were distributed in a pattern that broadly reflected the distribution of the workforce as a whole, except that they were noticeably under-represented in the South East and somewhat over-represented in the Northern regions. This is likely to reflect regional earnings differentials. Self-employed recipients were even less likely to be in the South East and compared to employed recipients were found in higher concentrations in Wales and the South West. Again this is not surprising as these two regions have among the highest rates of self-employment. It is also more likely that small businesses will succeed and prosper in areas of greater prosperity, such as the South East, and thus less of those involved may need to claim family credit. On the other hand, there is evidence that self-employment growth and business start-up can be a phenomenon of both growth and recession (Daly, 1991b). There is, however, no way of knowing from the analysis of family credit data whether the regional variations reflect differential earnings or varying levels of take-up, although there have been suggestions that take-up of means-tested benefits in general may be higher in the North (Borooah et al., 1991).

Continuity of claims

One aspect of family credit claims which is of considerable policy interest is the length of time different groups of recipients stay on benefit and their relative propensity to come back on to benefit after a period without it. Our analysis showed that in the family credit population as a whole, there is a fairly high turnover rate. Looking just at families in receipt of benefit at the end of April 1991, it can be seen that 48 per cent in all were in their first six-month spell of claiming and two-thirds had been receiving family credit for one year or less (Table 4.3). This suggests that for many families the benefit represents one-off support. There was, nevertheless, a substantial core of long-term recipients. Fifteen per cent of all families, including the same proportion of self-employed families, had been receiving family credit for over two years.

Table 4.3

Percentage of family credit recipients of given family type and employment status with different lengths of time in continuous receipt of benefit: 30 April 1991

		< 6 months	*6 months - 1 year*	*1 - 1.5 years*	*1.5 -2 years*	*2 - 2.5 years*	*2.5 - 3 years*
Couples: male earner	Self-employed	44	18	12	9	5	11
	Employed	48	18	10	8	5	10
Couples: female earner	Self-employed	67	18	9	4	2	1
	Employed	74	14	6	3	2	2
Lone parents: male	Self-employed	42	25	12	12	2	8
	Employed	54	14	11	8	9	4
Lone parents: female	Self-employed	41	22	10	9	8	9
	Employed	40	20	12	10	9	9
All self-employed		45	19	12	9	5	10
All employed		48	18	11	8	6	9
All families		48	19	11	8	6	9
Sample numbers		8,095	3,156	1,839	1,417	1,023	1,528

Nine per cent appeared to have been claiming family credit ever since it was introduced. As we see later, transferring from family income supplement to family credit in 1988, and relying on these benefits for long periods during child-rearing years, was an experience described by families in various kinds of self-employment. A similar picture emerges from the distribution of spells of claiming among all those who received benefit between 1988 and 1991. Nearly 48 per cent had one six-month spell only, and a further 21 per cent had just two spells, while at the other extreme just under nine per cent had been in continuous receipt for three years or more. Ashworth and Walker's (1992) more detailed analysis of claiming spells reached the same broad conclusion.

Table 4.3 suggests that there were some small differences in lengths of claiming between employee and self-employed families. Analysis by type of award also indicated that those of self-employed families were slightly more likely to be 'renewals' and less likely to be 'repeats' than those of employees, although there is some doubt about the precision of these categories. Ashworth and Walker's (1992) analysis of the whole claimant sample between 1989 and 1991 further showed that the average duration of a first 'spell' of family credit receipt among self-employed claimants was 20 months, three months longer than public sector employees. This compared with a nine-month differential in second spells.

One possible explanation for self-employed recipients' greater likelihood of staying on benefit may be that having gone through what can sometimes be a lengthy and difficult process of establishing entitlement, they could be more inclined to renew an existing claim. They may, for example, be more aware of the time when a claim is due again, having had to establish the period of time covered by their accounts. Another reason might be the higher average value of family credit awards to the self-employed than those to employee families - it may take longer for self-employed families to move towards higher earnings because they have further to go. We shall see, in Chapter Six, that very long periods of entitlement were not unusual among the self-employed families, and that some businesses and ways of working were simply not viable without financial support over many years.

However, the differences in claiming periods between employed and self-employed families were not so great as between different types of family. Female-earner couples - both employees and self-employed - stand out in this respect in having shorter spells. This is not surprising since their numbers increased sharply between 1989 and 1991. Employed lone mothers had significantly longer spells on benefit than other groups, mainly because they were most likely to renew their claims.

So far, this chapter has shown that while there are some differences in the general profile of employed and self-employed families receiving family credit, these differences are in themselves not so marked as to suggest a clear distinction between them. Nevertheless, self-employed family credit recipients have tended to receive substantially higher levels of awards, on average, than employees. This was also true of recipients of family income supplement (Corden, 1987) and it has continued each year since family credit was introduced (Table 4.4).

Table 4.4
Mean levels of weekly family credit award, 30 April 1989-91, by employment status and family type

Year and employment type	*All families*	*Couples*		*Single*	
		main earner:		*main earner:*	
		Male	Female	Male	Female
	£	£		£	
1989					
Employed	23.20	20.50	28.30	19.80	25.90
Self-employed	36.30	36.30	35.90	36.20	39.80
1990					
Employed	25.40	22.60	29.90	22.90	28.10
Self-employed	39.20	38.80	39.10	39.90	40.80
1991					
Employed	27.97	24.61	32.83	22.74	30.75
Self-employed	44.27	44.50	40.59	43.45	44.91

Self-employed families in all family types received higher awards than employees in each of the years. In April 1991 the difference was over £16 on average. The greatest mean differentials were among male single parents (£21 per week) and couples with a male main earner (£20 per week). The distribution of weekly family credit payments is such that as the value of the award increases the percentage of employed families receiving payments decreases. For self-employed recipients, by contrast, the slope goes in the opposite direction (Table 4.5). Forty-three per cent of all self-employed families received £50 per week or more in April 1991 as opposed to only 14 per cent of employed recipients.

Table 4.5
The distribution of weekly family credit awards at 30 April 1991, by employment status; numbers and percentages

	Employment type					
Weekly credit	Employed	%	Self-employed	%	Total	%
< £10.00	2775	(19)	186	(7)	2961	(17)
£10.00 - 19.99	3004	(21)	228	(9)	3232	(19)
£20.00 - 29.99	2682	(19)	291	(11)	2973	(17)
£30.00 - 39.99	2252	(16)	297	(11)	2549	(15)
£40.00 - 49.99	1745	(12)	489	(19)	2234	(13)
£50.00 - 59.99	1115	(8)	587	(22)	1702	(10)
£60.00 or more	845	(6)	562	(21)	1407	(8)
N	14,418	(100)	2,640	(100)	17,058	(100)

A similar picture emerges from examination of the numbers of families receiving maximum awards. Family credit is structured so that there is a maximum amount payable for each family type, made up of a fixed adult credit and an additional sum based on the number and ages of children. Forty-four per cent of all self-employed families (12,000) received 90 per cent or more of their maximum award in March 1991[2], compared with only 11 per cent of employed families (31,000). Proportionately, the family types most likely to receive maximum awards among the self-employed were lone parents: female (54 per cent) and male (50 per cent). For employed families, lone mothers were again the most likely to receive maximum awards (15 per cent), but here the next largest group was couples with a woman main earner (11 per cent). Why were the low-income self-employed families receiving so much more financial support?

There are a number of hypotheses that might explain the discrepancy:

- the method of assessing earnings may favour the self-employed
- the self-employed may supply inaccurate details of their earnings, resulting in unrealistically high awards

- self-employed families may have more and older children than those who are employed, thus increasing average award levels

- average main earnings of employed families may be boosted by income from other sources to a greater extent than for self-employed families, thus reducing family credit awards

- high award self-employed earners may be working shorter hours than the average for employees and thus may be earning less

- self-employed families may simply have lower earnings on average than those of employees.

The first two hypotheses are not testable directly by analysis of administrative statistics, though we have already discussed a range of problems with measuring self-employed earnings, including the possibility that they may be under-reported. We looked at these two issues in different ways, and discuss the approaches in later chapters. What can usefully be tested by the present analysis are the remaining hypotheses, namely that the differences in award levels can be explained by differences in family composition, working hours or income from other sources, or a combination of all three. Here, we summarise the results of tests carried out to assess the relative contribution of these different factors.

Household composition

Only two aspects of household composition have any direct bearing on the level of family credit award - the numbers and ages of dependent children in the household. The age of parents does not affect award levels, though it is likely to be linked to family composition.

We have seen previously that there was little difference in mean numbers of children between employed and self-employed families (Table 4.1). There were, nevertheless, some differences in family composition between the two groups, which would have an impact on the levels of awards. For example, self-employed recipient families were less likely than employed families to have only one child (29 per cent to 37 per cent). There was almost no difference between the proportion of each group who had two children (both around 35 per cent), but 36 per cent of the self-employed had three or more children, compared with 27 per cent of employees. A further crucial factor is the age of children. Since self-employed families tend to be older, it might be expected that they would also have older children. The self-employed did, as a whole, have slightly more children than employed families in combinations which included older children. This would have had a small upward effect on the maximum levels of family credit available to the self-employed, compared to employees. However, awards were still much higher for the self-employed when the numbers and ages of children and types of family were held constant. For example, couples with a self-employed male earner who had one child under 11 years of age received an average family credit payment of £32 - almost twice the average payment for similar families where the main earner was employed. Differences of this order were repeated for many other family types (Table 4.6).

Table 4.6
Family credit awards to self-employed families as a ratio of awards to employed families, 30 April 1991, controlling for numbers and ages of children, by family type

Numbers and ages of children	*Couples*		*Lone parents*
	main earner:		
	Male	Female	
One under 11	1.3	1.5	1.5
One 11-15	2.0	1.3	1.5
One 16-17	2.0	*1.2	1.5
Two under 11	1.9	1.3	1.4
Two 11-15	2.4	*1.0	1.5
One 11-15 and one under 11	1.9	1.3	1.5
One 16-17 + one 11-15	1.6	!1.2	*1.8
Three under 11	1.8	1.1	1.4
Two 11-15 + one under 11	1.9	*1.4	1.2
Four under 11	1.8	!1.4	!1.4

Notes: 1. * ratio based on 6-10 cases
! ratio based on 5 cases or less
2. Some family types are not included because of insufficient cases.

Even controlling for differences in the numbers and ages of children, large discrepancies remained between the average levels of award received by self-employed and employed families. These discrepancies were smallest for most family types among couples with a female main earner and widest among couples with a male main earner. For those male earner couples with two children between 11 and 15 years, average weekly payments were two and half times as large for the self-employed as the employed. This suggests that differences in household composition can only be a minor contributor to the discrepancies in award levels between employed and self-employed recipients.

Working hours

The hypothesis on working hours is that self-employed people could have had lower average earnings because relatively more of them worked closer to the minimum qualifying 24 hours per week[3]. This assumes a fairly direct relationship between hours worked and remuneration received, which may be a reasonable assumption for most lower paid employees but is less clear for the self-employed. Table 4.7 shows the mean number of hours worked by employed and self-employed main earners, by family type[4]. It should be noted that while working hours of employee claimants are generally subject to confirmation by employers, the Family Credit Unit has no means of independently verifying the number of hours worked by self-employed claimants. Self-employed claimants are often unable to offer precise figures for working hours and the recorded figures may include estimates made by adjudication officers. However, our qualitative interviews suggest that although there can be ambiguities in what constitutes working time for some self-employed people, family credit recipients are as likely to under-estimate as to over-estimate their working hours.

Table 4.7
Mean hours worked by family credit recipients at 30 April 1991, by employment status and family type

		Couples		*Single*	
		main earner:		*main earner:*	
	All families	Male	Female	Male	Female
Employees	36	40	33	38	32
Self-employed	41	42	37	37	35
All families	36	40	33	38	32

Note: Mean hours have been rounded to the nearest whole hour

On average, women earners worked fewer hours than men in all family types and lone mothers worked the shortest hours of all. Self-employed people in all family types except male lone parents worked longer hours than employees. This is consistent with patterns of working time among the self-employed as a whole. The range of hours worked by self-employed people as a whole was greater than that of employees. Nevertheless, proportionately fewer self-employed recipients worked the minimum 24 hours per week than employees, but twice as many worked 40 hours or more. This does not support the hypothesis that shorter working hours contribute to the difference in award levels. The longer working hours among self-employed recipients were evident among women as well as men: self-employed lone mothers were nearly three times as likely to be working 40 hours or more per week as their employed counterparts.

For employees, awards declined as hours of work increased in a pattern consistent with a direct relationship between hours worked and remuneration received. For the self-employed, however, awards fluctuated and followed somewhat different patterns for different family types, but overall they remained stable or increased as hours of work increased. This suggests that earnings for the self-employed tend to bear little relation to their recorded hours of work.

Income from sources other than main earnings

If neither family composition nor the number of hours worked can account in any major way for differences in family credit payments to the employed and self-employed, a further possibility is that awards are differentially affected by the sources and levels of total family income. Family credit assessments are based not only on the net earnings of the main earner, but also on a range of other sources of income. These include the net earnings (if any) of partners, the net earnings of any non-dependent children, most other social security benefits received (except for income support, child benefit and one parent benefit), maintenance, rent, tips and benefits in kind, and any tariff income derived from savings over £3,000. If self-employed recipient families tend to have lower average levels of additional assessable income than employee families, this could help to explain the differences in average awards.

Meager et al.'s (1994) analysis of income data from the British Household Panel Study found that contrary to this hypothesis the self-employed tended to have higher levels of income from other sources than other people. This was also true of the self-employed family credit recipients. Table 4.8 below decomposes average total net incomes for employed and self-employed families into the constituent elements. It is clear that income sources other than main earnings played an insignificant part in the composition of average total incomes.

The self-employed consistently showed lower average net earnings and lower total net incomes than the employed. For example, self-employed male earner couples had net earnings, on average, amounting to only 58 per cent of those of equivalent employees. Similarly their total average net income was only £67 per week compared with £112 per week for couples with an employed male main earner. The gap between the self-employed and the employed in all other family types narrowed somewhat when taking into account other earnings and income, as in the income distribution within the population as a whole.

The small amounts of additional income involved make average figures somewhat misleading. In fact the extra incomes from particular sources tended to accrue to small numbers of recipient families. For example, only eight per cent of all the two-parent families had any recorded earnings from partners, but nearly two-thirds of these were self-employed - mainly families with a male earner. As we shall see in the next chapter, these are likely to be mainly either spouse partnerships or situations where the spouse was formally recorded as an employee of the business for tax purposes.

Table 4.8
Mean levels of net income derived from different sources of families receiving family credit at 30 April 1991, by employment status and family type: £ per week

Sources	*Couples main earner:*				*Single main earner:*				*All families*		
	Male		Female		Male		Female				
	Employed	Self-employed	Employed	Self-employed	Employed	Self-employed	Employed	Self-employed	Employed	Self-employed	All
Net earnings	109.94	64.06	87.95	58.72	108.44	63.69	87.51	51.93	98.43	61.87	92.77
Net earnings of partner	0.64	0.34	0.62	7.66	not applicable				0.64	6.83	1.60
Benefits	0.46	0.92	7.91	7.93	0	2.17	1.29	1.38	1.18	1.50	1.23
Maintenance	0.36	0.78	0.55	1.05	0.12	0.96	5.22	8.76	2.36	1.99	2.30
Other sources	0.41	0.54	0.51	2.14	0.65	1.10	0.24	0.25	0.35	0.62	0.39
Total net income	111.81	66.64	97.54	77.50	109.21	67.92	94.26	62.32	102.96	72.81	98.29

The other main sources of income were maintenance or alimony - accruing to 12 per cent of all recipient families, of whom 84 per cent were lone parents - and other social security benefits. The receipt of benefits is of some interest, since it throws some light on the circumstances of the couples with a woman main earner. Only three per cent of all cases in the sample were recorded as having assessable income from other social security benefits and more than four-fifths of these were employed families - mostly female-earner couples, with benefits accruing largely to their partners. The main benefit received was unemployment benefit, which accounted for more than half the cases where a benefit was in payment. Almost 90 per cent of the families receiving unemployment benefit were couples with a female main earner. Altogether, women with husbands or partners receiving unemployment benefit made up 15 per cent of all couples with female main earners.

The remaining income sources included tariff income from savings, earnings of dependent children, benefits in kind, rent, tips, and 'other'. The last category would include income such as occupational pensions. However, these items were insignificant as a factor affecting the level of family credit awards. There were, for example, only 131 cases in the entire sample recorded as having tariff income from savings. The average amount accruing to these families was £5.85 per week, with a difference of only 20p between employed and self-employed recipients, though a relatively high proportion of recipients were self-employed. Altogether less than 1.5 per cent of recipients in April 1991 were recorded as having any savings, of whom almost a quarter were self-employed. The mean amount for the self-employed families was £3,773, as against £3,035 for employees.

Overall, income from all sources other than main earnings made up only a small proportion of average total household income for most family types, though it made up a higher proportion for the self-employed than for employed families (Table 4.9).

Table 4.9
Mean percentage of total assessable household income of family credit recipients derived from net main earnings, by family type and employment status, April 1991

Family type		Employment status		
		All families %	Employed %	Self-employed %
Couples -	male earner	95.2	97.9	85.4
-	female earner	90.3	91.8	77.3
Lone parents -	male	98.0	99.3	94.3
-	female	93.5	94.3	80.8
All families		94.1	95.6	84.4

Families with women main earners as a whole, and self-employed families in particular, tended to derive a substantially larger proportion of total income from other sources. This is likely to reflect both the relatively low earning power of women and also the greater likelihood of male partners being entitled to national insurance benefits. Self-employed couples with a woman main earner, for example, derived nearly a quarter of total assessable income from sources mainly involving benefits accruing to their husbands or partners, such as unemployment, invalidity and sickness benefits, and partners' earnings. Lone mothers also derived almost one-fifth of total net income from other sources, particularly maintenance.

In spite of the particular circumstances of families with women main earners, however, Table 4.9 shows that it is the level of the main earnings which was the primary determinant of total income and thus of the awards of family credit, for both self-employed and employed recipients.

The earnings of family credit recipients

A comparison of gross main earnings in employed and self-employed families receiving benefit in April 1991 provides the clearest demonstration of the differences between the two groups. Table 4.10 presents average gross earnings, by employment and family type.

Table 4.10
Mean gross main earnings of family credit recipients, April 1991, by employment and family type: £ per week

	Couples		*Single*		*All families*
	main earner:		main earner:		
	Male	Female	Male	Female	
Employed	131.15	104.40	129.13	99.58	115.39
Self-employed	70.88	67.85	69.63	56.48	68.49
All families	117.48	100.54	113.62	96.58	108.13

Self-employed families as a whole had earnings of only 59 per cent of those of employees. This pattern was repeated, with only small variations, across all family types. Families with female main earners, both couples and lone parents, had lower mean earnings than those with male earners, reflecting women's lower earning power. The gap between earnings from employment and self-employment was also somewhat narrower for women. This is partly explained by the relatively shorter working hours of employed women earners compared to men. For these employed women, as we have seen, the length of the working week has a fairly direct relationship with levels of pay, which is not necessarily the case for self-employed women.

The administrative statistics record just over nine per cent of self-employed families as having nil earnings. Where self-employed family credit applicants can show that they have made losses from their business or enterprise over the assessment period, these can be set against any profits made. Where losses equal or exceed profits earnings are counted as nil. It is likely that most or all of those recorded as having nil earnings will be families with business losses. It may be argued that this approach creates an artificial picture of people's day-to-day incomes and expenditure, since they must have access to some money for living expenses. However, qualitative evidence suggests that people with business losses are often forced to draw on savings or sustain large bank overdrafts in order to meet living expenses. To record them as having nil earnings is not necessarily to paint an unrealistic picture of their circumstances, though this question is explored in greater detail in Chapter Seven.

Figures 4.3 and 4.4 show the distributional pattern of gross main earnings and of total net income (as assessed for family credit) once all sources of income are included and tax and national insurance deducted. It is evident that self-employed earnings are concentrated much further down the distribution than those of employees, and that even though the effect of including other sources is to boost the percentage of self-employed families with net incomes in the range of £75 - £150 per week, the difference between the two employment types remains.

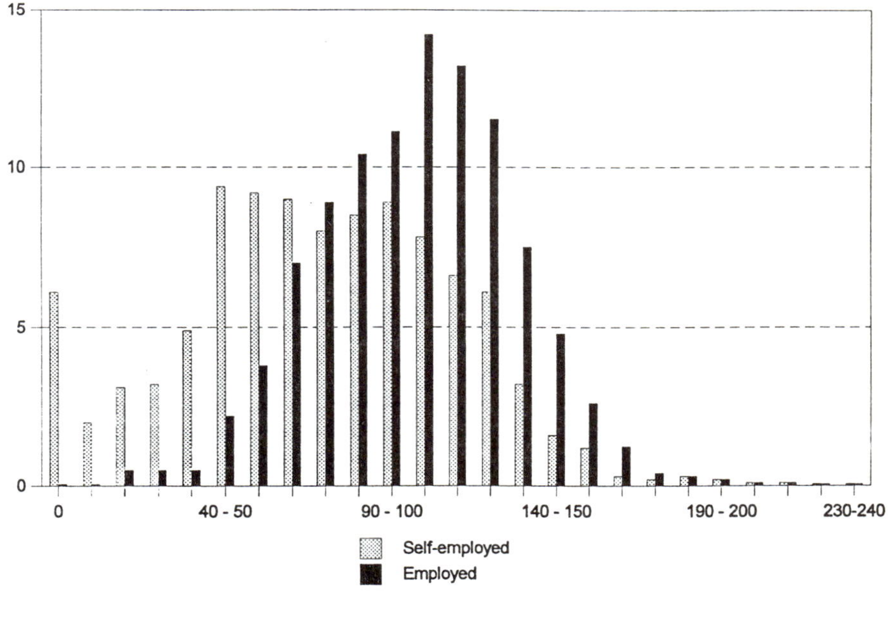

Figure 4.3 The distribution of gross main earnings, April 1991, by employment type: percentages of families with income falling into £10 banded ranges

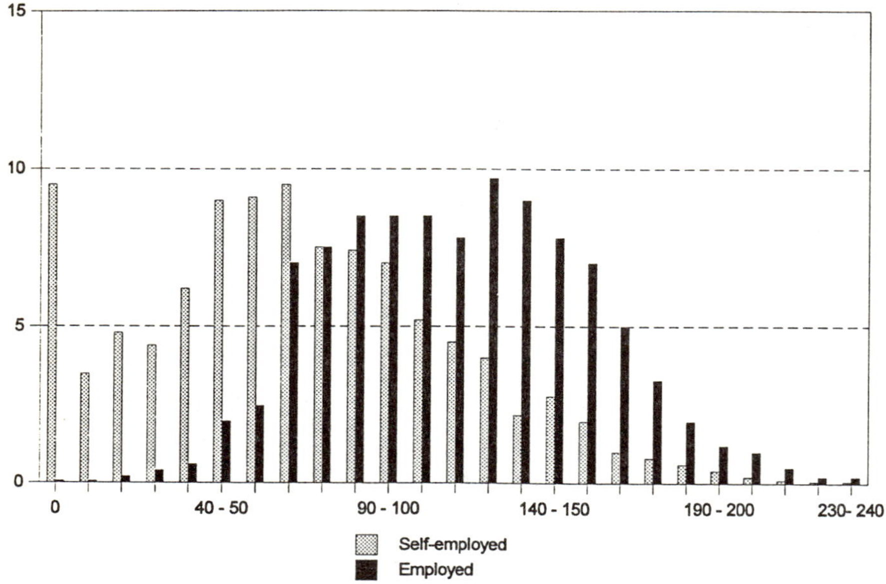

Figure 4.4 **The distribution of total net assessable income, April 1991, by employment type: percentages of families with income falling into £10 banded ranges**

Hourly rates of earnings

We have seen earlier that while slightly more self-employed main earners than employees were recorded as working around the (then) minimum requirement of 24 hours per week, a substantially greater proportion worked long hours. However, the long hours worked by many self-employed recipients of family credit do not necessarily result in high levels of earnings. This raises questions about the relative hourly rates of net earnings achieved by employed and self-employed earners. There are some limitations to a comparison of hourly rate between employed and self-employed earners. First, hours worked in self-employment are largely non-verifiable and may only be approximate estimates.

Secondly, while hourly rates for employees are based on gross earnings, the recorded gross earnings figures for self-employed applicants take into account allowable business expenses and other adjustments, and are often constructed as averages from business profit figures which may fluctuate considerably over the time period used. These factors make an 'hourly rate' something of an artificial construct for self-employed family credit recipients. Nevertheless, the gross earnings are those used by the Family Credit Unit to derive net earnings figures for the benefit calculation, so some comparison between the employed and self-employed may be useful.

Table 4.11 shows the mean hourly rates of employed and self-employed recipients of family credit in the main family types.

Table 4.11
Mean estimated hourly rates of gross earnings of family credit recipients at 30 April 1991, by employment and family type: £ per week

Employment type	*Couples* main earner:		*Single* main earner:		*All families*
	Male	Female	Male	Female	
	£		£		£
Employed	3.34	3.26	3.46	3.17	3.27
Self-employed	1.82	2.08	1.98	1.82	1.84

In all family types self-employed hourly rates were well below those of employees, but it is interesting to note that the highest average hourly rate in self-employment was achieved by women earners in couples. This is likely to be because of their generally shorter hours of work. Looking at the distribution of hourly rates, it appears that a high proportion of self-employed earners worked for net rates of under £2 per hour.

Fifty-eight per cent of self-employed recipients had hourly rates on this basis of under £2, as opposed to only eight per cent of employees. This picture was true across all family types, though self-employed lone mothers were concentrated particularly in the lowest band, with over a third earning less than £1 per hour net. More than two-thirds of employees had rates of £3 per hour or more, as against less than a fifth of the self-employed, though couples with self-employed female main earners were represented in greater proportion than any other family type in this earnings range.

Working in certain industries may be associated with long hours and low earnings, and hence low hourly rates. This may be true of both employed and self-employed workers. In some industries the self-employed do seem to work considerably longer hours than employees. In selling occupations, for example, they were four times as likely as employees to work more than 40 hours per week and twice as likely in managerial and clerical work, but less than twice as likely in catering, farming and materials processing. By contrast, employees were more likely to work long hours in construction and equally likely in transport.

The categories of selling and the broad grouping of occupations connected with making, assembling and repairing goods appeared to have the highest concentration of self-employed people working for very low hourly rates. It is also interesting to note that over three-fifths of those self-employed and classed as working in the professional and managerial group of occupations had hourly rates of under £2. Controlling for hourly rates results in very similar levels of earnings for both self-employed and employed recipients, which suggests that the long hours compensate in both cases for low hourly rates. A difference remains, however, for those with rates of less than £1 per hour, where the earnings of the self-employed were still about half those of the employed. The self-employed were also much more likely to have hourly rates at this level, as we have seen. This is one of the major reasons for the discrepancy between average levels of family credit awards for employed and self-employed families.

One possibility, for the self-employed in particular, is that the low rates of reward represent that period of time when a new business or line of work is being established and when returns are likely to be low compared to future profits. This might be the case especially for people moving out of unemployment into self-employment. Information is not kept in the family credit database on the previous employment circumstances of applicants, but it is possible to examine the length of time families with earners working for different hourly rates have been receiving family credit. The analysis does not in fact show that self-employed recipients with very low hourly rates were more likely than others to have been receiving family credit for shorter periods. Sixty-five per cent of those with hourly rates of under £1 in April 1991 had been receiving benefit for less than one year, but this was virtually the same percentage as amongst all the self-employed. More than two-thirds of employees were also in the same position. In fact those self-employed on higher rates of over £4 per hour were considerably more likely to be receiving benefit for a shorter period, though the numbers involved were small. Just over nine per cent of all the self-employed had been on family credit for over two years at an hourly rate of under £2 per week compared with only one per cent of the employed. However, 13 per cent of the self-employed families in the sample working for less than £1 per hour net had been on family credit for more than two years.

The combined effect of different factors on the level of family credit awards

In order to determine the relative effect of all the different factors examined above on the level of family credit awards, we carried out a multi-variate analysis using logistic regression. The bi-variate analyses have emphasised the difference in earnings between the employed and self-employed groups, although there are also differences with respect to family composition. This regression analysis aims to show how much of the difference in levels of family credit is due to differences in earnings and how much to differences in family composition. The results are set out in Table 4.12.

Column I of the table gives the regression equation for predicting the level of family credit. Substituting the mean values for the self-employed and employed groups gives the predicted values of family credit for each. The difference between these predicted values is 18.245 (the actual difference in levels of family credit between the two groups is 17.77). Column II sets out the contribution made by the difference in value for each variable to the overall prediction and this is set out as a percentage in Column III.

Table 4.12
Contribution of factors to difference in family credit for self-employed and employed families: regression analysis

Variable	I Regression coefficient	a Self-employed means	b Employed means	II Predicted difference (coefficient x (a-b)) (a-b)	III Percentage of predicted difference
EARNS	- 0.370	67.195	112.426	+16.735	+92
NCHAGE1	-22.215	0.179	0.223	+ 0.977	+ 5
NCHAGE2	-16.764	0.219	0.182	- 0.620	- 3
NCHAGE10	-17.864	0.066	0.106	+ 0.715	+ 4
NCHAGE11	-11.963	0.071	0.078	+ 0.084	+<1
NCHAGE3	- 9.033	0.101	0.077	- 0.217	- 1
FAMTYPE4	- 2.442	0.150	0.420	+ 0.659	+ 4
FAMTYPE2	- 1.758	0.065	0.102	+ 0.065	+<1
WKHRSW	- 0.004	381.276	343.140	- 0.153	100
Constant	83.196	*Predicted*	*difference*	*18.245*	*100*

Notes: All the coefficients are significant at the one per cent level; $R^2 = 0.70$; F = 4798 with 8 and 16397 degrees of freedom.

Variables included in regression analysis:
EARNS: Gross earnings of main earner in family unit
NCHAGE1: Dummy for one child aged 10 and under in family
NCHAGE2: Dummy for two children aged 10 and under in family
NCHAGE3: Dummy for three children aged 10 and under in family
NCHAGE10: Dummy for one child aged 11-15 in family
NCHAGE11: Dummy for one child aged 11-15 plus one child aged 10 and under in family
Base is all other combination of numbers and ages of children
FAMTYPE2: Dummy for couple with female main earner
FAMTYPE4: Dummy for female lone parent
Base is couple with male main earner
WKHRSW: Weekly hours worked.

The impact of family credit on total household incomes

One final piece of analysis examined the impact of family credit awards on the total net disposable income of employed and self-employed households. One of the key purposes in introducing family credit was to ensure that families with children would not be worse off in work than on income support. Our analysis tested the extent to which this purpose is being achieved. Again we used the sample of recipients at 31 March 1991 to avoid the problem of the year-end overlap in benefit rates, both in family credit and income support. The calculation may be expressed as a formula:

1. Net family income (NI) = net main earnings (as assessed for family credit) (NE) + net partners' earnings + those benefits which are taken into account (B) + maintenance (M) + notional tariff income (T) + other assessable income (OT). This is the sum on which the family credit assessment is based.

2. Total net disposable income (TI) = NI + the family credit award (FC) + child benefit (and one parent benefit if received) (CB).

3. Income support payable (IS) = the relevant adult rate (AR) + the family premium (and one parent premium if payable) (P) + the child rates payable depending in the number and ages of dependent children (C).

This can be written as:

$$NI = NE + B + M + T + OT$$
$$TI = NI + FC + CB$$
$$IS = AR + P + C$$

We then calculated a ratio (R) of net resources relative to income support rates, expressed as:

$$R = TI/IS$$

It should be noted that the calculation omits housing costs. Housing costs make a considerable difference to families' disposable incomes, but since the family credit database contains no information on tenure or housing costs, this factor had to be left out of the calculation. Among the whole population self-employed people are more likely than employees to be owner-occupiers. It is not known what proportion of those receiving family credit are home-owners or have mortgages to pay, but since income support can cover mortgage payments whereas family credit does not, some recipients with mortgages whose total income is below, or only just above, income support levels could be relatively worse off. This should not apply to tenants because they would be entitled to full housing benefit and 80 per cent community charge rebates if their incomes were as low as income support levels.

There was also no information available on whether any of the families involved might be entitled to additional premia for disability, so these were similarly ignored for the purposes of the calculation. It is unlikely that this omission could make any major difference to the outcome overall, though its effect would be to exaggerate the total incomes of any families with disabled members relative to their income support entitlement.

The results, which are presented below in Table 4.13, show that for the majority of recipients family credit does appear to lift their incomes well above income support levels - a finding supported by the survey of low-income families carried out by Marsh and McKay (1993). Lone-parent recipients in particular had mean total incomes of twice their income support entitlements. However, just over ten per cent of all self-employed families (or around 5,000 families grossed-up) had total net incomes (as assessed for family credit) of less than their income support entitlement. Nine out of ten were couples with male main earners. By contrast, only 0.2 per cent of employed families were in this position[5].

Table 4.13

Total net family income of family credit recipients, at 31 March 1991, compared with income support levels: percentage distribution of recipients into banded ratios of income to IS rates

	Couples				*Single*				*All families*	
	main earner:				main earner:					
	Male		Female		Male		Female			
Banded ratio	Employed	Self-employed	Employed	Self-employed	Employed	Self-employed	Employed	Self-employed	Employed	Self-employed
< 1.00	<1	12	<1	10	1	-	-	2	<1	10
1.00 - 1.19	1	8	1	7	-	11	-	9	1	8
1.20 - 1.39	9	26	14	23	-	8	<1	7	6	22
1.40 - 1.59	70	48	75	49	1	6	1	11	41	42
1.60 or more	20	6	10	10	98	75	99	71	53	18
Mean ratio	1.5	1.3	1.5	1.4	2.0	1.8	2.0	1.7	1.7	1.4
n	6,456	1,914	1,421	163	183	64	5,827	378	13,887	2,519

Only ten lone parents in the sample fell into the category of having total income below income support levels. These can be accounted for by the fact that none of them was recorded as receiving one parent benefit. Almost all the families in the sample with total incomes below income support levels had recorded gross earnings of less than £25 per week and among them were many of those with nil earnings. What this suggests is that the family credit entitlement calculation is designed with an assumption that no one working for 24 hours per week is likely to be earning less than around £1 per hour. If, however, they do have such low earnings, as it appears that some self-employed families did according to the figures arrived at for the family credit assessment, they could find themselves worse off than if they were on income support. This did not happen for lone parents, with the rare exceptions mentioned above, because they received the couple rates of family credit, but were only entitled to single adult rates of income support.

Apart from those with incomes apparently below income support levels, there were also a substantial proportion with incomes only marginally higher. Forty per cent of self-employed recipients had incomes of less than 140 per cent of their income support entitlement, whereas for employees this was only seven per cent. In contrast, 53 per cent of employed families had incomes of more that 160 per cent of income support, as against only 18 per cent of the self-employed.

The conceptual review of the family credit assessment system (Boden and Corden, 1994) suggested that the earnings figure for self-employed people may not always represent amounts available for week-to-week expenditure. Losses in one period may be offset against profits in another and produce a nil earnings figure for the assessment period. Notional tax and national insurance deductions may also not cover, or be paid in, the period during which family credit is being paid. How families managed, when family credit and child benefit appeared to be virtually the only cash income available for household expenditures, is explored in later chapters.

Since April 1991 child benefit has been uprated and increased by £2 for the first child. Both this and subsequent uprating both of income support and family credit will have had an impact on the proportion of family credit recipients with incomes notionally below IS levels.

Discussion

This chapter has presented the results of a statistical analysis of administrative records drawn from the family credit database. While the number of family credit recipients with main earnings from self-employment grew after the introduction of the benefit in 1988, their share of the overall caseload did not change significantly. Nor was there much change in the proportion of different family types receiving benefit, except for a sharp increase in the number of couples with a woman main earner. Furthermore, the self-employed did not appear to be disproportionately represented among family credit recipients compared to their presence among working families generally.

Families with self-employed main earners were somewhat more likely to renew claims and to stay in continuous receipt of family credit than employed families, although the differences were greater between family types than by employment status. There were also variations in length of continuous awards according to occupations, but without any significant difference between the employed and self-employed.

The main difference between the two employment groups was in the average levels of family credit awards. In April 1991 families with self-employed earners received average awards well over half as great again as families with employed main earners. Similarly, in March 1991, proportionately four times as many self-employed as employed families were receiving near-maximum entitlements.

The analysis tested a number of possible explanations for this discrepancy, including differences in family composition, working hours, and levels of income from non-market sources. However, both bivariate and regression analysis showed that the driving force behind the discrepancy in average awards was the substantially different level of gross main earnings of the two employment groups, as assessed for family credit, where self-employed earners had on average barely more than half the earnings of employees. Both family composition and income from other sources had a small impact but the net effect was to narrow the gap in income between the employed and self-employed rather than to explain it. Working hours, on the other hand, had the opposite effect. As in the workforce generally, self-employed earners worked consistently longer hours on average than employees (though working hours for the self-employed are not subject to any external verification), and whereas for employees earnings tend to increase in line with working hours, for the self-employed no such linear relationship existed.

By creating a notional hourly rate of pay or earnings, according to the weekly working hours recorded for family credit, we found that most self-employed earners apparently worked for well under £2 per hour, whereas two-thirds of employees had rates of over £3 per hour. For the self-employed an hourly rate may be an artificial construct and may not always represent the amount of money available for day-to-day household expenditure - a question explored in later chapters.

We also found that some lone parents on family credit were losing out on income by not claiming one parent benefit. The estimated take-up rate for one parent benefit among these families was only 56 per cent. Without knowing the tenure and housing costs of the lone parents involved, it is not possible to estimate the net value of this unclaimed benefit, since many tenants would have found up to 80 per cent of the extra money clawed back through reduced housing and community charge benefit.

Whereas for the vast majority of families, family credit fulfilled one of its main purposes in lifting basic incomes in work above what they would be receiving out of work, the situation appeared to be significantly different for self-employed families. More than ten per cent of the self-employed families, mostly couples with male main earners, had total incomes, as assessed for family credit, below what they would have received on income support. Two-fifths had incomes below 140 per cent of income support, as opposed to only seven per cent of employed families.

This raises some fundamental questions about the role of family credit in relation to self-employment. It also raises questions about the backgrounds and motivations of the people involved, the living standards in which children are being brought up and why people go on trying to make a living by working on their own account for long periods for such modest returns.

These kinds of questions are more appropriately pursued by talking directly to parents, and looking carefully at the way they are combining work and family life. The administrative data tell us little about how the earnings figures were arrived at or about the living standards which families in these circumstances are able to maintain. The remaining chapters of the book address these issues, drawing on three waves of interviews with self-employed family credit recipients in their own homes, which were often also the base from which they worked. Chapter Five introduces the families we interviewed, looking at their routes into self-employment, the kinds of work they carried out and the way their working lives were organised.

Notes

1. All claimants of family credit in two-parent families are women. In the Government's original plans for revision of family income supplement following the 1984 Social Security Review, it was proposed that family credit should be paid to the employed person in the household - more commonly the man in two-parent families - through the wage packet. This proposal was, however, dropped in the light of strong representations from a wide range of interested organisations. The family credit assessment is

nevertheless based primarily on the main family earnings, generally that of the man in two-parent households. 'Main' earnings where both parents are working are determined first by reference to whether one parent rather than the other qualifies on the number of hours worked. If both qualify on these grounds, the main earner is whoever earns the most. In the event of both earning the same amount, as in a self-employed partnership, the main earner would be the claimant. Where one partner has earnings from self-employment, irrespective of whether they are the main earner, applications are assessed by a special self-employed section of the Family Credit Unit.

2. March 1991 was used here in preference to April in order to avoid problems with claims which straddled the date of annual uprating

3. At the time of this analysis claimants had to be working for a minimum of 24 hours per week to qualify. In April 1992 this was reduced to 16 hours.

4. Information on working hours is missing for 708 cases (or four per cent of the sample). We compared the profile of this group with the rest of the sample to check for any bias resulting from their exclusion. There were some differences between the two groups, though not so great as to suggest a remarkably different pattern of working hours. The only major difference was in the families' main earnings and consequently the level of family credit received. Mean gross earnings for the missing self-employed families were significantly lower, at £59.21 per week, than for the main group (£69.10), whereas for the employed the earnings of the missing families were higher than the main group, at £122.70 against £115.11. The numbers involved are not large enough to distort the analysis in any serious way, but these differences should be borne in mind.

5. It is possible that some of the cases on which this estimate is based are incorrectly estimated. There were, for example, a small number of discrepancies between the weekly credit awards recorded and our estimates of entitlement. These could be caused either by our ignorance of some pertinent information which is not recorded in the statistics, or by errors on the part of family credit staff. There were also some 200 cases where families had nil entries for child benefit, even though they had dependent children. This can happen in some circumstances: for example, where a family has recently entered or re-entered the country and an application for child benefit has not yet been processed, the Family Credit Unit may accept birth certificates as interim proof of having dependent children. There can also be cases where one parent has retained the child benefit book as part

of a separation arrangement even though the children mainly live with the other partner.

There were also a small number of other cases with child benefit amounts not equal to multiples of the child benefit rates, which appeared to be errors in data entry. However, these cases were a very small minority and we found a remarkably good match between our estimates of family credit entitlement and that awarded by the Family Credit Unit. Our estimates are, however, based on the information entered on the computer by adjudication officers. If there are errors, as indicated by the Chief Adjudication Officer (Department of Social Security, 1990c), these are likely to take place in decisions prior to data entry or in the keying in of data itself, rather than in the calculation of awards. Overall we are confident that our estimates present an accurate picture of the relationship between recipient families' incomes and their income support entitlements in March 1991.

5 The working lives of self-employed families

One of the advantages of the qualitative approach adopted in our study was that it enabled us to get beyond the general occupational or industrial groupings which are traditionally used to represent labour market participation by self-employed people, and observe the detail of their day-to-day activities and working lives. The rest of the book draws mainly on information derived from our qualitative interviews, in which there was rich material about work, family circumstances, attitudes to financial support and experiences of using social security. Findings, as in all qualitative studies, are intended to provide insights and amplify our understanding, especially about how families combined their work and family lives, and how they constructed and maintained their living standards on apparently such low incomes.

Overall, we conducted detailed research interviews with working parents in 73 families, including 16 lone-parent families. Interviews took place in three waves, in 1991, 1992 and 1993. These families were not representative of self-employed family credit recipients in a statistical sense. They were selected in different ways, to provide information about a number of areas of special interest for policy makers. Appendix B presents details of the selection of the study groups, and the methodology of the fieldwork and analysis of data. While not statistically representative of the self-employed family credit population, the characteristics of the families interviewed suggested that they were not atypical, at least of the sub-groups of the population to which they belonged. The changes in circumstances observed, in this group of recipient families, made it evident that this is, in any case, a volatile population, with lives which do not fit neatly into simple administrative categorisation. As expected, some of the families selected as current recipients of family credit had undergone changes in circumstances by the time of their interview, which meant that they were unlikely to be eligible again when their current award ended. A small number of families had been selected, anyway, because their last award had been unsuccessful. This did not always mean that they were ineligible; some had found it hard to demonstrate eligibility in the way required (Boden and Corden, 1994).

This chapter explores the working lives of the self-employed families. How people come to be self-employed in their particular occupations, and how they view their present situation, is likely to be influenced by their previous histories and we begin by looking at the routes by which people came to their current work. The picture was one of great heterogeneity, which we saw reflected in their family backgrounds, and their levels of skills and qualifications.

Routes to current self-employment

The occupations of the main or only self-employed breadwinner are shown in Table 5.1.

Looking at the patterns in the previous work histories of the main earners in the families, we identified three main groups. The first were people who had been in the same area of work, mostly as self-employed, for all or most of their working lives. These long-term self-employed people were mostly men doing manual work, or engaged in farming or fishing activities that had been a 'way of life' spanning generations. The second group included people who had made a career change into self-employment, either by choice or prompted by redundancy or unemployment, marital breakdown, financial problems or some other life event. Some of these fit the image of the would-be 'entrepreneur', though for others this title is misleading, given the nature of their work. Thirdly, there was a more amorphous group of people who had developed particular interests or skills into self-employed work, or taken on forms of activity like child minding which can only be carried out as self-employed.

Table 5.1
Occupations of main or only breadwinner at last application for family credit

Two-parent families		*Lone parents*	
Men	Women	Men	Women
Farmers and smallholders (8)	Child minders (3)	Gardener	Child minders (2)
Fishermen and fish processor (5)	Shopkeepers (2)	Plumber	Shopkeeper
Building and construction workers (5)	Craft retailer	Consultant	Agents and distributors (2)
Taxi drivers (5)	Food retailer		Professional consultant
Shopkeepers (4)	Hairdresser		Transport operative
Agents and consultants (3)	Educational business director		Potter
Carpet dealer			Baker
Scrap dealer			Homeworker
Motor mechanic			Clothing retailer
Cleaning contractor			Luxury goods retailers (2)
Insurance agent			
Musicians and instrument repairers (3)			
Potter			
Artist			
Entertainer			
Minister			
Therapist			
Hotelier			
Restaurant owner			
Ice cream salesman			
Food wholesalers (2)			

Distinctions between these groups are not always clear cut. Nevertheless, the three groups displayed certain differences in the trajectories of their working lives which are important for an understanding of their living standards.

Farming and fishing are both occupations with their own special features, and people doing this kind of work spoke of themselves as part of 'the fishing community' or explained that theirs was a 'way of life' rather than a form of work.

Men who joined their fathers to work on family farms after leaving school had eventually inherited the business, or taken over the family tenancy, and often hoped to hand it on to their own children. A couple running a smallholding had also worked together for 16 years gradually building up a business in which their teenage children were now also involved. The older farmers had built up their skills through experience and working alongside others doing the same work. Younger men, however, acknowledging that farming was a changing industry, had spent periods at agricultural college, or enrolled locally on short courses on book-keeping. This fits with findings from other studies (Daly, 1991a) that the proportion of self-employed people with no qualifications at all dropped steadily during the 1980s.

Fishermen had also started to learn their craft while at school, spending weekends as unpaid crew members of local fishing boats. For those who wanted to continue fishing after leaving school the main option was to become a 'share fisherman', joining the crew of a boat-owner to be paid according to a share of profits from the catch. Men who had worked on the boats for many years were experiencing increasingly frequent lay-off periods during which they were obliged to claim unemployment benefit, and were looking for new work. Family credit seemed no substitute for the security of a proper wage. One alternative to share fishing in larger boats is to work alone. This can be a risky business, and even small boats are expensive to buy. Only one man had bought his own small boat to try to earn a living fishing on his own. Despite the danger and the heavy loan repayments for his boat (nearly £300 each month) he reported great work satisfaction.

In industries related to farming and fishing, the trend has been for employers to increase workforce flexibility by redefining former employees as subcontractors. This had been the experience of a fish processor, previously made redundant by one of the firms for which he now did the same work, as a subcontracted worker. His current earnings fluctuated widely according to the work available, but on average he thought he earned less than he had as an employee.

> It's contract, you see, which covers their backs. They don't have to pay any tax, they don't have to pay any stamp. You just do it all yourself ... and there's no retainer, you see. There's no holiday pay, no retainer and it's up to you to be down there every hour you literally can when there's fish. ...

Most of the other people in the group we have called long-term self-employed were also male manual workers. These were people who had been in the same kind of work since leaving school, and thought of this as their 'occupation'. Older men had moved between unemployment and self-employment at different times. Younger men, just starting careers for which they had completed trade apprenticeships or other training, expected to work mostly as subcontractors, with short occasional periods of unemployment, a pattern recognised in previous research on family credit (Corden and Craig, 1991). Included here were builders, a painter and decorator, a plumber, a scrap dealer, a gardener, and a second-hand goods dealer. We might expect to find that earnings had remained relatively low for such families over a long period of time. The lone fathers in this group of manual workers had moved between employment and self-employment several times, but after the break-up of their marriages had set up on their own to fit working hours around their domestic situations. This is a pattern better known among women breadwinners.

The male manual workers shared a number of characteristics. All had parents or parents-in-law in manual occupations and came from working-class families. In terms of qualifications achieved or training undergone, most of this was technical and directly related to their current work, such as certificates or apprenticeships in plumbing and painting. Most were currently council tenants, while the few owner-occupiers lived in areas with some of the lowest house prices in the country. The couples among them maintained traditional household divisions of labour, with wives or partners looking after the children and doing only a few hours of paid work, if any. Most of the men had histories of relatively low-paid, often insecure work interspersed with periods of unemployment, and those just starting on their working lives recognised this as a pattern to expect. Most felt that they were earning less than in the past, and some could point to particular periods when higher earnings had allowed them to spend more money on household goods. The earning capacity of the lone fathers in this group had been affected by their child-care responsibilities.

For the fishermen and farmers, the trend had been downwards over some time. Farmers saw themselves as subject to external economic forces over which they had limited control. These included the selling price of their produce, which had remained the same or declined while costs had risen; the subsidy systems on which they depended, and, perhaps most importantly, the interest rates on loans. Owner-farmers in particular reported having been encouraged by banks or the Ministry of Agriculture to expand and improve their farms in the early 1980s, only to find that sharp increases in interest rates and reductions in subsidies had eaten away at their profits. The share fishermen described a long-term decline in earnings which was exacerbated by fishing quotas, and the subcontracted fish processor linked his declining earnings with reducing profitability in the fishing industry.

It was a change in people's behaviour that had reduced the profitability of an ice cream salesman. He had settled in the UK from a Mediterranean country, coming to join a group of his fellow countrymen who sold ice cream as a traditional way to make a living in this country. He had managed to buy a modest house, and family life had been financially secure when his children were younger. However, over a period of 15 years his earnings gradually declined as local people acquired refrigerators and freezers, and bought ice cream from supermarkets. The business currently brought in very little income, and, along with some of the farmers and fishing families, he had depended for many years on family credit and its predecessor, family income supplement.

The final member of the long-term self-employed was a lone mother whom, interestingly, we might consider as one of the best examples of an 'entrepreneur' among the family credit families. After school she had joined her parents on a market stall - an example perhaps, of the 'inheritance effect' noted by Carter and Cannon (1988a). Gradually expanding sales led to opening her own retail business, and eventually an associated manufacturing business. Caring for her first child, she explained, had been fitted in alongside her work. At one stage she had paid for child care in order to continue work but it had been more difficult to keep the manufacturing unit going when she had a second child. Scaling down the operation had meant lower turnover. However, she had already seen new opportunities opening up in a different market - hiring out equipment for use at home. Although her latest family credit application had been unsuccessful because she had been unable to provide information about earnings in the way required, this had not affected her long-term plans to continue working on her own account.

'Career changers'

As a second group, we identified people who came into self-employment by making a definite shift in their working careers. It is among this group that we might expect to find people with a history of higher earnings which may have allowed them to develop a relatively high standard of living - either during a previous period with an employer, or when businesses were prospering.

People who had taken decisions to make a career change by starting a business talked about their reasons largely in terms of routes taken at critical stages in their personal or employment histories. There were big contrasts in previous work histories. Those who had previously been unemployed, or lone parents claiming income support, were accustomed to low incomes. Others, however, had previously been well-paid employees. The group included families who described the shock of moving from dual-earner, high-income employment to business ventures that were initially prosperous, but then rapidly declined, bringing them to unexpected, low incomes.

Changing careers could mean a move into a new occupation altogether - a construction worker decided to try his hand at fishing, and a textile factory worker moved into taxi driving. Usually, however, people who moved into a new occupation had relatives or friends who had some experience or knowledge of that kind of work.

Alternatively, a move to self-employment had meant setting up in the same area of work in which people had previously been employees. Included here was a part-time sales assistant who decided to open a similar retail business in another area in the city, and two men with previously well-paid careers as employees who set up as consultants in specialist areas of their work. Which route people took depended on their particular interests, skills and the nature of their previous work, but the spur in many cases was the experience of being made redundant. There were several examples here of what MacDonald and Coffield (1991) described as 'push and pull' factors in self-employment. It was common for men to say that they had always had an aspiration to try self-employment: redundancy had merely brought forward the timing. Others, however, felt they had no alternative: unexpectedly made redundant from a factory job, a man with five children and no qualifications had seen taxi driving as the only available option.

Chapter Two pointed to a number of studies which have examined the role of redundancy in self-employment (Lee, 1985; Leece, 1990; Johnson and Roger,

1983). These studies concluded that people using the redundancy 'window' tended to be men in the 30-40 years age bracket, who set up one-person businesses in the service sector and generally earned less, at least in the early years, than they had previously received in wages or salaries. This picture fits most of the men in the study who had taken such a route. For example, one person currently struggling to build up his own clientele for a home-based agency had previously enjoyed a salary of nearly £30,000, along with a company car and private health insurance for his family.

The amounts people received in redundancy pay were small, mostly under £3,000. Those who had received larger sums had generally used most of it on living expenses and keeping up mortgage payments when unemployed, as it was unusual to be able to make a direct transition from employment straight into a new business venture. Although large redundancy payments were rarely available for investment, smaller amounts were used to provide some of the working capital required for the Enterprise Allowance Scheme. Nearly all those who had moved from unemployment by starting new businesses said they had considered joining the enterprise scheme. Those who had toyed with the idea of self-employment in the past had already come across the scheme. Decisions to try self-employment had not been triggered by suddenly finding out about enterprise allowance.

Reasons for not joining the Enterprise Allowance Scheme included the problem of finding £1,000 working capital, or not wanting 'to go on a course'. One man had been deterred by the problems he expected to experience in preparing written plans or figures for discussion. Another reason for not using enterprise allowance was that the timing of the schedules in local schemes did not fit opportunities available. For example, a woman planning to open a shop had found a suitable property and wanted to be established in time to benefit from summer trade, but found that the next local intake for the Enterprise Training Scheme was not scheduled until autumn. One or two people had already had an enterprise allowance in a previous venture that had proved unsuccessful, and knew that they were not entitled a second time round.

Availability of enterprise allowance and in-work benefits, including family credit, had been strong factors in some people's decisions. A lone mother whose cash flow plan and profit forecast for a modest retail venture anticipated only £300 profit for the first year said that she definitely would not have gone ahead if enterprise allowance had not been available to ensure some income each week. Recognition of eligibility for in-work benefits came later on when she stopped claiming income support and was advised to apply for family credit by DSS staff.

Redundancy was not the only way in which members of this group of career changers came to be self-employed. The hoteliers had watched several friends make substantial profits during the early 1980s after leaving secure well-paid jobs to buy hotels, and they saw no reason why they should not be as successful, although this would be a completely new area of work. Other couples who had left good jobs to run a craft industry and a restaurant decided to put into effect skills and experiences gained as employees. It was among the people who moved from well-paid jobs that aspirations of making good profits were identified as strong motivations for trying to work on their own. By contrast, a man used to low earnings when previously employed in the construction industry did not expect to make more money when he left his skilled job to join a friend in a small fishing enterprise. The invitation to join the boat came as a welcome opportunity to do something more interesting, and since fishing had been his father's occupation, he understood what to expect.

For the minister, self-employed status was determined by the structure of the church to which he belonged. The stipends in this church were based on tithes from the congregation and set fairly low. When he began training for the ministry, he knew that he would be formally self-employed and would probably have to supplement low earnings with in-work benefits.

Whatever the routes by which people started their businesses, few of the breadwinners in two-parent families who had previously worked as employees said that they currently earned as much as when employed, although some businesses had previously been much more profitable. Other businesses had been trading for several years but profit levels had always been low. The food distribution manager saw possibilities for higher earnings in the future, but the heavily front-loaded cost structure of taking on a franchise meant that the couple's income was substantially less than it had been in their previous work.

It was especially difficult for men in two-parent families to move out of long-term unemployment and establish a business that generated enough income to support a family. One man who was unable to offer prospective employers good references had eventually succumbed to what he felt was pressure from the DSS to move into work, by trying his hand at work as a roofing contractor, but the business had survived less than six months.

Other men mentioned 'push' factors associated with feelings of some disadvantage in the waged labour market - unavailability of jobs, long periods of unemployment, perceived lack of skills or training, a general feeling of disadvantage as a member of an ethnic minority group, or lack of confidence in being able to hold down a job as an employee due to poor health. These were all factors mentioned that had encouraged some to think about becoming self-employed and explore the options. When coupled with experiences of feeling pressure to find work from Employment Services offices, or reduced income support levels due to benefit control sanctions on people deemed to have left previous work 'voluntarily', self-employed work such as taxi driving could seem the only possible way forward.

> Social security were giving me a hard time about not being employed, and saying that I'd have to take any job that was offered to me.

The experiences of mothers offered perspectives on combining self-employment with family care. Some had started new self-employed work at least partly in response to husbands' ill health or as a consequence of marital breakdown. A woman whose husband's chronic ill health had led to his early retirement found few opportunities of work for herself in the local area. Thinking how to manage this new stage of life, with teenage children, led to her decision to 'make a job for herself' by opening a new shop. This seemed a sensible way to use a small amount of equity released from the sale of a previous family home. It also offered possibilities for some participation by her husband when he occasionally felt well enough to do light work.

The need to be available to care for a disabled child influenced one woman in deciding to build up a home-based business after marital breakdown. She managed to keep the business going, despite recurrent bouts of ill health herself, but felt certain that she could not have held down a job as an employee, even if doing similar work.

In general, the picture among the 'career changers' was of families experiencing drops in income, whether they went into self-employment by choice or as a result of losing a job. These income gaps were often long term and showed no immediate signs of closing. Some had been temporarily obscured by an initial period of profitability, occasionally even fairly high profitability, in which case the subsequent big drop had come as a particular shock. Some families had experienced such low profitability in self-employment that they had already given up and entered unemployment again, trailing business and personal debts. Only two families thought current earnings had overtaken previous wages as employees, though in neither case were these particularly high.

As we might expect from the heterogeneity of backgrounds and routes into self-employment, there was a broad range of qualifications and training among the career changers. Some certificates or training were directly related to current activities, including training in bible studies, engineering drawing, book-keeping, secretarial work and motor mechanics. High level academic and professional qualifications were held by some of those who had previously been well-paid employees. What was interesting was that those who appeared to be operating most successfully in terms of financial stability and gradual expansion had no formal qualifications and had learnt their trades by experience. A carpet seller was formerly employed as a mill worker; a contract cleaner and a sales consultant both emphasised experience and hard work as more important than qualifications. It did seem, however, that qualifications and training had helped some of the self-employed start up in their chosen fields. It could be especially difficult for unskilled men without training or qualifications to start a small business from long-term unemployment. We do not know, of course, what the outcome would be for some of those who had started new businesses very recently, among whom were some of the most highly qualified men.

'Developers'

The third group identified as having some different characteristics are described here as 'developers' - that is, they became self-employed by developing some long-term interest or enthusiasm into paid work. There is some overlap with the previous category since in some cases people changed their work careers in the process. What particularly distinguishes this group of families is the personal enthusiasm and commitment which allowed them to pursue their interests without expectations of great financial rewards. In some cases their work was also connected to a chosen lifestyle which did not prioritise the accumulation of household possessions, although this was not always the case. As families grew larger and growing children became more expensive, or when relationship breakdown brought women into the role of breadwinner, it could be a struggle to maintain living standards.

This group included a potter, two musicians, an entertainer, people with small retail outlets - for craft items and food produce, a motor mechanic, two newcomers to small-scale farming, and a proprietor of an educational business. Some of these families came from relatively privileged backgrounds, where an anti-materialistic stance could be supported to some extent by a cushion of family support, expectation of future inheritance, or an extensive network of young friends, experienced in surviving on low incomes.

This was not true of all of them. One of the musicians had experienced a long period of unemployment before his wife persuaded him to try earning a living as a musician. With several children, life had been a constant financial struggle for some time, but working at his music was clearly preferable to being unemployed. Both he and his wife were worried about the future but he was sustained by optimism and commitment to his work.

> At least I'm busy, I'm active, I'm always trying. And things could be good one day. I don't know, I mean I just keep hoping, keep working at it. I want to work.

It was among this group of 'developers' that we found some of the people with the highest levels of academic qualifications, both men and women. Previous research has shown that self-employed women without employees are more likely to come from non-manual or professional backgrounds; they also tend to be somewhat better educated, with higher qualifications than both female employees and male sole traders. Such differences have been ascribed to some of the difficulties women face when trying to start businesses on their own (Carter and Cannon, 1988a). Among the 'developers' we met, there were women with postgraduate degrees unrelated to their current self-employed work, as well as professional qualifications. One had spent a period abroad, learning about a specialist form of animal husbandry. There were also men with high levels of qualifications, both relevant to current work or in an unrelated field, sometimes associated with a previous career. Other men had no qualifications, including people who had been unable to hold down jobs as employees. One man felt greatly disadvantaged by the racism he met from a predominantly white community.

Patterns of previous earnings varied considerably. Two-parent families who had been dual earners in previous periods of employment had sometimes experienced big drops in income when they started trading. Other families, however, had moved out of unemployment, or low-paid work as employees, and were used to managing on a shoestring. It was clear that among the 'developers' there were families who could only sustain their chosen occupation by income supplementation, and for some families, this had been the pattern for many years.

What linked the families in this group was their enthusiasm and dedication to their work. Determined optimism, and satisfaction with a chosen way of life pervaded the interviews with the parents in these families; levels of energy and commitment were high. There was some frustration at being unable to achieve better returns, especially among families who were not cushioned by family support, or material circumstances derived from previous more prosperous times. There was little talk of giving up, however. Indeed, within this group were families who had kept their chosen work going for eight or nine years, while caring for children.

We have now described some of the main characteristics of the three groups of self-employed people we identified among the family credit recipient families. It is worth mentioning separately the circumstances of women who had taken up child minding.

Child minders

Child minders are a group known to have particularly low earnings. This is recognised in the special treatment accorded them in assessment for all income-related benefits, including family credit. Net earnings are taken as one-third of gross receipts, acknowledging the very low levels of earnings traditionally associated with this work which is mostly done by women, and the problem of trying to disaggregate expenses from normal household expenditure.

Child minding is an important occupation, despite the low financial rewards it attracts. The survey of low-income families conducted in 1991 by Marsh and McKay (1993) identified child minding as one of the five jobs in which women were most likely to be working. In one of the sampling exercises carried out for our research, a randomly selected group of 100 self-employed families receiving family credit produced no fewer than 13 child minders, suggesting that this is an important way in which women can work.

Child minding is also an occupation that is strategically important within social policy. Lone parents who want to work may need to make child care arrangements in order to do this. We know that most lone parents make informal arrangements with relatives or friends, but others depend on employing child minders. Two-parent families, too, may need child minding provision if both parents want to work. Recognition of the importance of the need for child care is reflected in special arrangements introduced in 1994 to allow costs of formal, registered child care to be set against earnings in assessment of income-related benefits. Social security rules thus privilege both the expense of child care for some working parents and the earnings of child minders who provide such care.

Among the child minders interviewed, there were both lone parents and women in two-parent families. For lone parents, child minding at home was one way of combining motherhood and paid work. It was an occupation that could be started, with almost no financial outlay, while a mother was claiming income support. It could gradually build to the point where the woman concerned passed the administrative benchmark of 24 hours weekly work (now 16 hours) when she assumed formal status as a self-employed worker. However, child minding was not always such a modest, home-based venture. It was also being undertaken on a semi-professional basis by a woman with formal child-care qualifications, who kept a separate part of her house for the children in her care. She kept a stock of equipment solely for the children's use, and used her car for her work when fetching children from school or taking them out.

Child minding is also seen as a suitable occupation by women in two-parent families. If husbands are made redundant, have poor health, or are themselves involved in trying to get a small business off the ground, the wife's child minding activities may become the family's main earnings. Two women had previously given up reasonably well-paid clerical jobs to bring up their own children. Although they were committed to staying at home until their children were at school, they intended to work when they could. Until their husbands lost their jobs, therefore, child minding represented a source of extra income to sustain a good standard of living. It was also an activity they enjoyed which kept them in touch with the world of work. For these families, family credit was an important stop-gap until such time as the men could get back to work, as one had indeed done by the time of the interview. Their way of life, home-ownership, household possessions and standard of living in general had thus until recently been based primarily on the husband's long-term employment, supplemented by the extra money from child minding.

Although we have given special attention to child minders, there is no reason for not including them among the three groups of self-employed earners we have identified. Those we interviewed could be apportioned between the 'career changers' and 'developers'. Thus, the semi-professional child minder had previously had a good job as a residential social worker before she decided that working from home would fit better with her own family responsibilities. She was a 'career changer' in the same sense as the other women we identified in this group. The other child minders were more appropriately thought of as 'developers' - having started an activity on a fairly small scale, which had then gradually been built up to become the family's main earnings, or assumed new importance when a husband stopped working - a pattern seen among women with other small-scale activities.

Already, the picture emerging from accounts of the parents' backgrounds and routes into self-employment is one of extreme heterogeneity. Some patterns can be seen, which are reflected, as we shall see later, in corresponding patterns in families' current living standards. We now look more closely at the work that people were doing, how this was organised and how it fitted domestic circumstances and family expectations.

In some families, a conceptual distinction between work and personal life seemed inappropriate. Domestic partners, children, relatives and even friends were drawn into what might be better described as a 'family undertaking' or 'way of life'. This was certainly not true in all families, however: some self-employed people fitted their work squarely within the traditional terminology of 'having a job'. Nor were all domestic partners directly involved in the self-employed work: indeed some had their own separate waged employment. It was common, however, in two-parent families, for there to be some participation by the domestic partner who was not officially the main self-employed breadwinner. Such participation might appear a relatively small-scale and modest contribution, but could be vital both in the early stages of an enterprise and in longer established businesses. A detailed look at the extent of this kind of participation offers an additional perspective on the invisibility of some of the work undertaken by women.

Most lone parents were women, and they faced particular problems in trying to combine paid work and caring for their children. We look here at the special role that self-employment could play in the lives of lone parents. Our interviews revealed other sets of personal circumstances in which self-employment has a special role. Being self-employed could be important in providing opportunities to work for people with disabilities or chronic ill health, and for other people with additional caring responsibilities.

We start by outlining the modes of business organisation in the work carried out by the self-employed families.

Business organisation

It is known that the majority of self-employed people operate as sole traders or employ only a few other people apart from spouses. This pattern was reflected among the families we studied. Only 14 of the 73 self-employed main breadwinners were in partnership with other people, and business partners were usually spouses or relatives. An exceptional situation was that of a lone parent who worked with several other craftspeople and took less than a fifth of the profits. Men in partnership with their brothers included a builder and a newsagent, and one farmer was working on a holding in which one of his parents was still formally registered as a business partner. Otherwise, business partnerships were between domestic partners, and were usually in businesses which had substantial capital investment or stock, such as the larger farms, the hotel, restaurant and the fishing boat owner's business. Spouse partnerships tended also to be favoured by Asian families. As we shall see later, establishing a formal business partnership between spouses in a family where self-employed work is undertaken can be a sensible arrangement for tax purposes and financial security, but may not always indicate active participation in work by both spouses.

Another arrangement which may be advantageous for tax purposes is for one spouse to be described formally as an employee of the self-employed person. Among the self-employed people we studied there were ten men who formally employed their spouses, and one woman whose husband was her employee. Participation by employed spouses varied considerably, ranging from active involvement in separate and specific areas of work to minimal contributions such as occasional answering of the telephone. Other women were hoping to become more involved in the future if their spouse's businesses grew sufficiently. The wider question of labour market participation by partners of the main earners is discussed later in the chapter.

An analysis of General Household Survey (GHS) data from the mid-1980s by Curran and Burrows (1989) suggested that many one-person enterprises did not grow beyond this size even after several years of operating. This was true in our study: several of the business enterprises had been running for five years or more without taking on any employees other than the trader's spouse, whose participation was sometimes notional. Most people attributed this to the low profit margins, which were never large enough to allow expansion. Others had no great ambitions to expand, as long as they could make enough to live on. There were also people who had previously employed larger workforces, but had since reduced them, either through declining profitability and a need to cut back wherever possible, as in the case of the hoteliers, or through preference for managing a smaller undertaking. The motor mechanic had previous experience of running a larger garage and did not want to go back to employing other people. The manufacturing retailer had decided that the higher turnover associated with running a larger workforce had not led to an increase in profitability, and was not worth the additional management required. At the time of our interviews relatively few of the self-employed businesses were employing other people apart from spouses. Only 13 currently had non-relatives on the payroll in some capacity, and as we shall see later in this chapter, most of the jobs created were on a part-time or casual basis.

Among those who worked entirely on their own were most of the self-employed people whose work did not fit into the traditional organisational concept of 'business'. The organisational structures within which the subcontractors worked were quite different from those running businesses on their own account. As we suggested in Chapter Two, in terms of control, autonomy and independence their circumstances were more like those of employees. Employers' use of subcontracted workers is known to be as common among very small businesses as among establishments with 25 or more employees (Hakim, 1988) and the subcontractors in our study were working for a variety of types of employers. A painter worked for a national building firm; an outworker for a local leather goods manufacturer; and a labourer for a three-man family building firm.

The circumstances of all the subcontracted workers illustrated the relative insecurity of their position in the peripheral workforce, the disadvantages of uneven earnings over which they had little control and their vulnerability in health and safety matters. Thus the earnings of a painter, who was paid 'per house', receiving pay cheques on a fortnightly basis, depended on the rate at which new houses were erected by the firm. He received no holiday or sick pay, and was not insured against personal accident on the building sites.

While acknowledging the insecurity and disadvantages of working in this way, subcontracted workers generally accepted these circumstances as 'part of the job'. The people concerned saw few other opportunities for employment. Indeed, some occupations are almost entirely organised within self-employed subcontracted frameworks. The decorator was a skilled and qualified man, and had always worked in this way. The only alternative for him was to start a business of his own, but being only 22 years old he did not feel ready to take on this responsibility. The outworker was highly experienced in part of a local work process that was traditionally organised, in her area, largely through women working at home.

In between the two distinct groups of 'business people' and subcontracted workers are two occupational groups of special interest in this study. Taxi driving is often a short-term occupation to which people, usually men, are attracted in between jobs or periods of unemployment. Child minding is an occupation which offers opportunities for earning money to people who want to work at home, predominantly women. As we mentioned earlier, the family credit population includes significant numbers of taxi drivers and child minders.

The taxi drivers shared some of the characteristics of employment circumstances that were a feature of the subcontractors' work. Their work and earnings were subject to control by the organisations for which they worked. Charges to passengers were set by the firms who rented the cabs or radio paging facilities while the supply of work depended on the taxi controllers or the demand at the taxi ranks in town. The only kind of flexibility and autonomy that is more characteristic of self-employed business people was in the hours they worked. However, not all drivers were able to work long hours when demand was high in order to make up for leaner weeks, as some shared the taxi rental with a second driver.

The unique blend of domestic and professional responsibilities that is typical of the work of many child minders is recognised by the special status of this occupation within social security arrangements. Later sections and chapters have much to say about the child minders' work.

Having emphasised the organisational differences between business and the work of those whom we might call in 'quasi self-employment', we go on to give some flavour of the scale of the work that was being undertaken.

The scale of the enterprises

The aim of this section is to provide some background to the scale of people's activities, and what they were doing. Such pictures form an essential basis for understanding the financial aspects of their work, and later details about living standards and quality of life. What was being achieved in the small businesses depended, among other things, on the kind of occupation involved, the level of input of energy and commitment, the number of people involved and the stage of business development and profitability reached.

It is important to stress the small scale of some of the undertakings that had been started as new businesses during the previous two years, especially by people moving out of unemployment. A man trying his hand at a farming enterprise had started with a few animals in space loaned in a friend's barn. A musician had stopped claiming income support and taken formal status as a self-employed person a few months before the interview without any definite prospect of paid work. Little had subsequently come his way and he spent his days practising, composing and visiting recording studios looking for work.

People who had taken part in the Enterprise Allowance Scheme had reached relatively higher levels of planning and business development when they stopped claiming out-of-work benefits: even so, most had started modestly. Some new shops opened during the previous two years in small, rented premises were still only carrying stock worth less than £500. People who had invested recent redundancy payments to start a new business had not had substantial amounts of money available, as mentioned earlier.

Working from home was one way of trying to establish a business without incurring additional costs of separate premises. People with larger houses, bought in more prosperous times, were able to keep one room specifically for business use. A consultant had been able to equip a living room as an office without too much constraint on family living space. Smaller houses could be reorganised for similar purposes if the family was small. With only one child now living at home, the instrument repairer's family could keep the back room in their council house for the man's tools and repair work. It was more difficult for people with larger families, however. The roofer, for example, stored his ladders and equipment in the small kitchen and hall, and made appointments for work on the family telephone in the living room. It could be hard to get a new business off the ground when the main bedroom had to double as a professional office - the only option available to a man with several teenage daughters and dependent adult relatives at home.

Seeing such early stages of business start-up underlined their fragility, and the potential financial risk for the families involved. Indeed, one or two sole traders had not gone much beyond early advertising and promotional work, combined with waiting at home for long periods for clients to telephone, before deciding the venture was no longer viable. The roofer's wife told us:

> My husband has not worked for two months - his last work was in September. He has posted leaflets, but there is still no one ringing for any work to be carried out.

By the time we met them, the roofer and a musician had returned to income support. Others, however, felt optimistic about their chances of establishing their businesses on a long-term basis. It helped to be able to bring skills and expertise acquired during a previous business career, or from similar work done previously for an employer. The instrument repairer had not expected to make much in his first year, as he had run a small business before, and knew the first years would be hard. A food wholesaler had only been in business for a few months at the time of the interview. He thought he had identified a market niche in wholesale distribution of a specialised product to local food shops. He was still building up his work, and had drawn on previous experience in the retail food business. In terms of projected annual turnover, his business was already among those considered by DSS to have specially high business receipts. It was interesting to find such an example of the high, and perhaps unrealistic, estimated turnovers reported by people starting up in business, which was noted in analysis of HBAI data (see Chapter Three). High turnover does not imply high profitability, however, as we see in the next chapter.

The food distribution business provided an interesting example of a form of self-employment which is on the increase (Felstead, 1991). The man involved was dependent on a franchising firm for his produce, for most of his capital investment (freezers and vehicles) and for much of the structure of his work, which involved keeping retail outlets in stock with the foods. He would take initiatives to build up his customer base, extend sales and improve service, and in this way his work differed from that of the labour-only subcontractors. However, in the early years much of the profit made in businesses like this is absorbed by the franchising firm itself. It would be some years before a range of bonus and incentive schemes came into operation to make profitable trading more likely for this person, as we see in Chapter Seven.

There were plenty of examples of people who had sustained over a long period relatively modest undertakings which generated little profit. Some families had adapted well to surviving on low incomes and had no plans for major development or expansion of business activities. These tended to be people who had developed some self-employed work out of a consuming personal interest, or chose a way of working which suited a particular life style. The ice cream salesman had been driving the same second-hand ice cream van around the same residential suburb for the past 17 years. The musician with a large family had rarely earned much more than he could have claimed in out-of-work benefits, but he had chosen to pursue his work, with income supplementation, since 1986.

Most of the businesses which had been established for three years or more were, as we would expect, much more complex undertakings. The 'survivors' from those who had started from scratch some years ago, and most of those ventures which had been taken over as going concerns, were now operating on a scale readily identifiable as 'business'. This had sometimes been associated with greater profitability during previous years, although all were currently generating only low incomes. Chapter Seven looks in detail at family incomes; here we are concerned with the scale of activity in the established businesses.

Throughout the book the emphasis is on the heterogeneity of the self-employed families and their work. They do not fall into neat categories. For purposes of description of the established businesses, however, we will present them in three groups of related activities - farming and fishing; sales; and services.

Farming and fishing

The most heavily capitalised businesses in the study were the established hill farms, each of which covered between 100 and 210 acres, with animal stock, farm buildings and equipment. The hill farms ran mainly sheep and cattle, with occasionally an additional small-scale special interest, such as breeding show animals. These were all family concerns. The families lived on the farms and were often the second or third generation to work the same holding.

More recent entrants to the farming community had managed to establish a specialist dairy and poultry venture, building on a previous leisure interest and looking carefully for market niches for products in specialist local outlets. Not all the agricultural businesses were based on animal production, however. A market garden, also a family concern, had been built up over 18 years. Products from the large heated greenhouses and a few acres of fruit and vegetables were sold directly from the gate and marketed locally to shops, catering firms and on a weekly market stall.

Others who referred to their self-employment as a 'way of life' were the fishing families. The only boat owner in this group fished alone along the shoreline, depending on help from his partner in landing the catch. The other fishermen were engaged in share fishing, a traditional arrangement for crewing deep-sea vessels. Share fishing can also be undertaken on a more modest scale. One of the share fishermen worked in a two-man boat belonging to a friend. Together they caught shellfish close to shore and in the harbour mouth.

Agriculture and fishing are both industries with large subcontracted workforces, as discussed already, and our study included two men who worked on this basis in subcontracted agricultural labouring and fish processing respectively.

Sales: retail and wholesale

We have seen how the availability of the Enterprise Allowance Scheme enabled people to start up small retail businesses. It is difficult to equip, stock and advertise a completely new retail venture, without substantial capital to invest or fall back on, especially in a competitive retail environment, or in an area of predominantly low-income households with limited spending power. Among the four women who had embarked on market stalls, small rented shops or retailing from home during the past two years, one had already given up and another had doubts about her viability. Most of the better established retail businesses had been taken over as going concerns, including the rented corner shops. Asian families were represented among these retail businesses.

The only person who had managed to build up a substantial retail business from small beginnings was the woman already described, who had started on a market stall and gradually expanded her retail clothing business into design and manufacture. An Asian couple who sold furnishings from a market stall were hopeful that they might expand the scale of their business in the future, but some of the retail businesses had been deliberately kept fairly small. The proprietor of a small shop selling second-hand goods explained the risks involved in this kind of dealing. He had been unable to arrange insurance of either stock or premises, and there was frequent vandalism and theft because of the location of the shop and the nature of the merchandise. He thought such a business was probably only viable on a small scale without massive investment in security precautions.

Professional and trade services

The remaining businesses which had got beyond the initial start-up stages of the first two years provided what we shall call here professional or trade services.

Substantial undertakings included a seaside hotel open all year round; a restaurant open all day until late evening, and an educational business. Again, we see a pattern of development as 'family concerns' involving both parents and often older children and other relatives among these established businesses with high levels of investment and heavy workloads. The pattern was repeated in the work of the entertainer and in a craft business. Although the latter two were more modest in terms of capitalization and annual turnover, both these businesses had been built up over several years and depended on participation by both partners. The entertainer's family took bookings for private parties and promotional or festival events in the local area. The craftspeople designed and made a range of ceramic items, marketed through craft fairs and private commissions. In a later section we look at the involvement of family members in these 'family concerns'.

One alternative for developing self-employed work, for those who are unable or do not want to make substantial capital investment or build up a workforce, is to take on subcontracted work. This was a pattern seen among some of the male manual workers. The builders and plumber had their own small firms, but operated with relatively small amounts of fixed capital and equipment, and boosted earnings by acting as subcontractors for other larger building firms. The gardener had work in individual private gardens, where the tools and equipment were mainly supplied by the householders, but he generally combined this kind of work with subcontracted agricultural labouring work which was seasonably available.

People offering a service from home included the artist, the therapist and the book-keeper. We saw earlier that it could be hard to find working space in a small family home. One solution was to lease a small business unit from the local authority, or use a room in a parent's house where there was more space available.

The child minders were all home based. We have explained earlier that the concept of 'business' sometimes seems inappropriate to describe the way child minders work. In our study, however, there was considerable range in the scale of activities among child minders. At one end was a settled family arrangement whereby a woman looked after a relative's daughter, for which she received a child-minding fee. At the other end was a woman who kept her own family activities distinct from her paid work, and thought of herself as a professional child-care worker. In between were women who combined their child minding with the care of their own young children, and who thought of their work in terms of extending the scale of their everyday domestic responsibilities.

> I wouldn't like to just stay at home and not do anything. I'm not that kind of person.

We have now described the main patterns in the organisation of work, and the range and scale of activities in the small businesses. There is an important distinction between work conducted in a traditional business setting, and work which is technically self-employed but more similar in circumstances to working for an employer. We shall see later that the distinction can affect people's attitudes about work and financial support, and can affect current and future social security entitlement. We have begun to see how some occupations are closely bound up with families' personal lives. The concept of a 'way of life', for example, has important implications for standards of living and quality of life, while at a practical level, unravelling business expenses from child-minding arrangements, for purposes of social security adjudication, is no easy task.

We have also seen that the scale of the venture did not automatically correspond with the length of time people had been engaged in the self-employed work. It suits some people to maintain very modest undertakings and low earnings over long periods of time, whereas those who can afford to take over an established business can be running a fairly complex undertaking, with a relatively high financial turnover, in the early months.

A further perspective on the working lives of self-employed people comes from looking at hours of work and the patterns of activity.

Patterns of work activity

At the time our research was conducted, family credit regulations required one parent to be working on average at least 24 hours weekly (now 16 hours). There seemed little doubt that in all the families at least one breadwinner had been working 24 hours at the time they applied for family credit. Even when starting from scratch, with no established business base, long hours of work could be necessary to get a new business ready, for example equipping and stocking new shops, or doing intensive promotional and advertising work to attract clients and customers to a new service.

The development of cyclical patterns of work was common. We would, of course, expect this in occupations that are clearly seasonally affected. The ice cream vendor, for example, worked long days throughout the summer months, but only a few hours a day during January and February. The roofer, on the other hand, found most opportunities for work during bad winter weather, when people discovered leaks in their roofs. All kinds of other occupations had cyclical patterns as well. The pattern of student terms determined the variable working hours of city taxi drivers and small shops in student areas. The entertainer's busiest weeks were during the summer and leading up to Christmas, when bookings came in for outdoor promotions and parties, respectively. A book-keeper experienced for herself the seasonal effects of other people's self-employed work: small local businesses wanted accounts prepared during December/January, or June, for tax assessment purposes and there was little work for her during July/August. Even the child minders' working hours dipped during holiday months, when working parents took their own holidays and did not need child care.

Another kind of cyclical pattern was a seasonal change in the nature of the work rather than the amount of activity. Farmers, hoteliers and market gardeners typically described working very long hours throughout the year, but on a range of activities varying according to the agricultural cycle or the holiday trade. Observation of these businesses suggested that 70-100 hour working weeks reported in family credit applications were not exaggerations. This amount of work is necessary when one man manages over 200 sheep, and herds of cattle and calves on hill pasture. Fishermen, when not at sea, could be fully engaged full time in mending nets and maintaining boats. However, they were experiencing increasingly frequent lay-off periods when they were obliged to claim unemployment benefit.

Not everybody worked long hours however. All our respondents were parents, some were lone parents. The need to combine paid work with family responsibilities and child care meant that hours of work were constrained in some families, as we shall see later on. For others, the breadwinner's ill health constrained the amount of activity. As we have seen, the choice of self-employment sometimes arose specifically from the flexibility it allowed for reduction of work when health was poor. Cyclical bouts of depressive illness led one woman to believe that she would have been unable to hold down a job as an employee; being self-employed enabled her to manage periods of relative inactivity. An older man was managing to get back to work after two years claiming invalidity benefit. His choice of self-employment in a home-based service was specifically 'to pace myself, because of the angina'.

What our interviews showed was a wide range in the hours of work being undertaken in the self-employed ventures, and a variety of cyclical patterns within the work, both in hours and kind of activity. There was not a wide range in resultant income however - all these families lived on incomes low enough to bring them within the scope of family credit. Entitlement to family credit is calculated on the basis of average weekly income. It is no easy task to translate the fluctuating income flows that match the cyclical and diversified patterns of activity just described into average weekly income (Boden and Corden, 1994). We look at this in greater detail in Chapter Six.

A more detailed understanding of the amount of work that was going into the self-employed ventures requires a closer look at the number of people involved. The following section looks at the divisions of responsibility for the work undertaken in the families where the main breadwinner was self-employed. Here we complement work recently undertaken by Wheelock and Baines (1994) who have looked closely at small businesses set up in Wearside during the 1980s. They pointed out that it is the entrepreneurial family, and not the individual, that explains the survival of some of these small businesses, seeking livelihoods at the margins of employment. They emphasised the importance of flexibility, in three 'labour circuits': the business labour circuit, (the self-employed business), the non-business wage labour circuit (additional paid work taken on by the business proprietor or spouse) and the domestic household labour circuit (household responsibilities and care). Among the small business enterprises in our own study, many of our findings are consistent with those of Wheelock and Baines. However, as emphasised in the previous section, self-employment at low income levels includes a range of occupations and activities far beyond the traditional concept of 'business'. Our analysis enables a rather different perspective, in terms of the labour market participation of spouses and partners.

Labour market participation of spouses and partners

Small, home-based businesses of the kind common among two-parent families in the family credit population often rely on substantial contributions from wives or partners. What this means is that the low profit levels generated by these enterprises are based on the work effort of not just one but two people, who might under other circumstances be bringing in two separate waged incomes. Of course, some of the women involved might not be able to take paid work or might choose not to do so. This intensive work effort is also commonly seen as an investment in the business which may pay off in later years, although, as we have seen, such a result cannot be guaranteed.

Where there is no possibility of spouses joining the self-employed breadwinner's work, such as partners of taxi drivers or self-employed construction workers, then family credit may substitute for a second wage. Some women in two-parent families talked about family credit as a source of income which enabled them to stay at home longer with young children rather than going out to work themselves. They knew they would eventually have to get jobs to supplement their partner's low earnings, but lack of job opportunities meant that it would have been hard to earn as much as they were getting with family credit, anyway.

Marsh and McKay (1993) have discussed these effects in terms of family credit providing an incentive for women not to work. However, analysis of administrative statistics suggests that there may, in fact, be greater attachment to the labour market among the spouses of self-employed men than those of employees. Only eight per cent of two-parent recipient families had any recorded earnings from partners, but nearly two-thirds of these were self-employed, and these were mainly families where the man was the main earner. Looking at the actual participation by women in the families in our study however, we see that they only occasionally had independent paid work of their own.

The study was designed to include a number of dual earners, as well as some families where the woman was the main earner, in order to help us understand the nature of the contribution made by partners both to the self-employed work and to the family income. As we might expect, the characteristics of participation were quite different for male and female partners in two-parent families, and we look first at the female-earner couples.

Female-earner couples

There were two distinct patterns among the couples where the woman was formally identified as the main self-employed breadwinner. The first pattern was one in which both spouses made substantial contributions to the business. They come close to being full, working partnerships, and the men, in practice, were the main business and financial organisers. There were specific reasons why the business was registered in the woman's name. For example, one shop was not registered in the man's name because he had substantial debts outstanding from a previous failed business.

The second pattern was one in which the men referred to themselves as unemployed, or unable to work through ill health. They were mostly trying to get back into work in their own right, or they were building up a role of their own in the business. A stall owner's husband, for example, had been unemployed for some time, but they had recently borrowed some money for him to open a shop which he planned to run as an extension to the stall. Two of the other husbands had found work again by the time the research interview took place, and both these families thought it unlikely that they would be staying on family credit for long. Only the husband of the proprietor of a small shop did not expect to work full time again, due to poor health.

The key point about all the female earner families is that they were primarily *dual* earners, or had been until overtaken by ill health. In all nine self-employed families the woman had habitually worked either full time or part time. They had only taken on the role of the main earner for family credit because their husbands had become unemployed, had become sick, or, where they worked together, because there were technical reasons why it was more appropriate for a business to be registered in the woman's name.

Where husbands were not closely involved in the self-employed work, they might help out in some way, by dealing with the accounts, for example, or helping with child care, but in most cases their participation was not likely to substitute for paid employment of their own if they could find it. We see here some possible association between the recent sharp increase in female-earner families receiving family credit noted in the analysis of administrative statistics and growth in male unemployment. If the pattern observed in this study is reflected more widely in the family credit population, we might expect to see many of these female-earner, self-employed families remaining on benefit for shorter periods on average than male-earner families, because those unemployed men who were fit were making determined efforts to find other work. Secondly, we might expect to find that living standards in some of these families reflected their recent or earlier status as dual earners. This expectation is tested in later chapters.

Male-earner couples

Female participation in work among the self-employed, male-earner families took one of four main forms. Women involved in their partner's business either contributed substantially and were classified as formal business partners or employees, or contributed but were not thus described. Women not involved in the business either had a job of their own or they did not. We can therefore plot schematically women's participation in the various enterprises or forms of self-employed work, as in Table 5.2 below.

Table 5.2
Work and participation in self-employed enterprises by spouses of 48 self-employed men

	Substantial contribution to enterprise	*No substantial contribution*
Spouse employed in business or business partner	farmers (4) hotelier restaurant owner smallholder potter entertainer fisherman shopkeepers (2) scrap dealer sales consultant minister artist cleaning contractor	insurance agent carpet dealer farmer consultant food wholesaler
Spouse not employed or business partner	fish processor builder instrument repairer ice cream salesman food wholesaler	taxi drivers (5) fishermen (3) subcontracted construction workers (3) shopkeepers (2) musicians (2) farmers (2) roofer motor mechanic therapist consultant

The matrix in Table 5.2 is inevitably an oversimplification, since the nature and level of women's contributions varied, but the broad picture can be summed up in this way. We can see that, as would be expected, women's involvement in the subcontracted and quasi self-employed work was less than in the 'businesses', and that being formally employed by a spouse, or his formal business partner, did mostly represent actual involvement. Contributions like book-keeping and secretarial assistance were common, but some women had definite separate spheres of work. Thus the dairy farmer tended the animals, did the milking and maintained the premises, while his wife was concerned with the dairy produce and marketing. The minister's wife ran women's circles and undertook counselling as part of joint pastoral duties. The wife of the entertainer made properties and costumes, dealt with bookings and herself appeared in the stage act. The artist's partner had her own portraiture and illustration work. Sometimes, the women's contributions were only on a temporary basis: the scrap dealer's partner drove the truck during a period when he was disqualified from driving.

Formal profit sharing, or amounts shown as spouses' wages on business accounts, had often been worked out by accountants to ensure the most favourable treatment under Inland Revenue and national insurance regulations. It was not unusual for there to be some uncertainty as to whether the woman was formally a partner or an employee. However, while there was some relationship between women's involvement and their classification as employees, this link did not extend to the amount or nature of the work contributed, and to the way that household finances were organised. Most wages recorded in accounts were notional 'paper transactions'. None of either the men or the women suggested that any actual payments were made to women for the work they carried out. The only woman who reported having personal control of a portion of profit was a farmer's wife who managed the letting of a holiday caravan on the farm land, and retained control of her profits.

The women whose work was not formally recognised, although making a substantial contribution, also had no direct income in their own right from the enterprise. In this group were women who did all their husbands' business accounts, as well as women who were essential in cleaning and preparing equipment, managing appointments, and dealing with clients. What was clear was that the capacity for second earnings among self-employed couples was substantially reduced in some cases by the need for partners to contribute to the business. Men often relied on women being at home to answer the telephones, place orders, deal with deliveries and keep paperwork in order, and such work was often invisible in the formal economy.

Among those women making no substantial contributions to spouses' self-employment, attitudes to paid work varied. One or two of the older women had poor health and did not expect to be able to work again. Only one woman was regularly working full time - a job taken on at a time when her husband was employed on a relatively high salary now provided essential earnings. A second woman had just secured a full-time job. Few other women had any paid work outside the business. Where they did, it was usually part time, and sometimes a few hours only - teaching a weekly dance class, or evening shop work.

Women cited their responsibility for their children as a primary reason for not having a paid job of their own. Some also pointed to the lack of jobs in which they could earn more than they currently received in family credit. Even for families with school age children it was difficult to arrange child care during school holidays. There were also some strong expressions of preferring not to work from women who stressed the importance of staying at home to look after their children. The comments of the motor mechanic's partner were typical:

> I've always believed that I should be here for them. Nothing against women going out to work or anything if they're in a position to afford child care, but I would rather just look after them myself. From a personal view, even if I had the money I still wouldn't, because I firmly believe that, you know, I've had the children and it's my responsibility to see them through the first years.

For women who have taken on a supportive role in business, such views may be partly a rationalisation of decisions which have given little opportunity for paid work of their own. This may be particularly true where the work takes men out of the house for long hours every week and simultaneously requires the woman's presence at home. Overall, we can see that current earnings from partners contributed little to the overall incomes of the self-employed families, though in some female-earner families the non-working partners were normally the main breadwinners. In families with self-employed businesses, women often contributed substantially to the work, without receiving any direct income in their own right. How much this affects the way expenditure decisions are made is examined in a later chapter. It is clear that women's opportunities to seek paid work outside the home were often limited by traditional gender divisions of labour which, while accepted by many of the women involved, may be reinforced by the demands of the self-employed enterprises. In this respect, there is a difference between our findings and those of Wheelock and Baines (1994). Their study of small businesses suggested greater sharing in the domestic division of labour within small business families. The difference in findings may be partly due to the different kinds of occupations represented among our families, including the subcontracted workers, the sea fishermen and the taxi drivers, who may have to work long and unpredictable hours away from home.

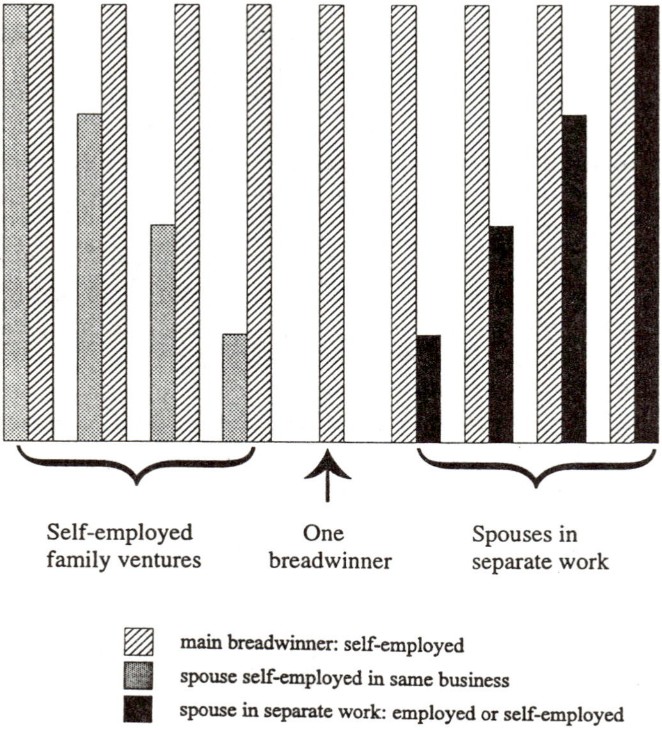

Figure 5.1 Schematic representation of spouses' labour market participation in two-parent families engaged in self-employment

The diversity of labour market participation by spouses of self-employed breadwinners described here can be thought of as a continuum of arrangements. A simple schematic representation is shown in Figure 5.1. At one end we see the full participation of both spouses in a joint business venture, either formally acknowledged or not. As we move along through lower amounts of spouse participation we arrive at those families where one parent is currently not doing paid work, either through ill health or unemployment, or choosing to concentrate on child care and family responsibilities. Moving along again through families where one parent is engaged part time in work other than the spouse's self-employment we come to the opposite end of the continuum. Here both parents each have their own substantial work commitment, either in separate self-employed work, or with one working as an employee.

There were examples in our study of families at various points along this continuum, but relatively few towards the right-hand side. We might expect this since our families came from the family credit population, and we would expect some of the families where the second earner had a full-time job as an employee to be floated out of eligibility for family credit. It is in the families to the left-hand side of the scheme where the 'invisible' work done by women is found. We have more to say in later sections about the role of benefits such as family credit in supporting families at different points along the continuum.

We turn now to lone parents. They do not have the same options for combining or sharing responsibilities for earning with a spouse. However, our study showed that being self-employed does offer special opportunities for lone parents to combine paid work with family responsibilities, and we look at these in the following section.

The role of self-employment for lone parents

It is known that women are likely to choose self-employment to fit in with personal and domestic circumstances. All the lone parents in our study, men and women, described the advantages of being self-employed while they were bringing up children. Working at home could seem the only possible way for some parents with toddlers or very young children to earn money, and it could still be an advantage with school-age children. Parents were at home when children were ill or on holiday, and child-care costs could be avoided to some extent.

Those lone parents who were not home based also stressed the advantages of flexibility in being self-employed. There were opportunities to fit work around school hours, and sometimes possibilities of taking young children to work, for example, lone parents in small retail units occasionally had their children on the premises.

Lone parents in isolated rural areas and areas of high unemployment said there were few opportunities for waged work anyway, especially work that could be fitted around children. In some local areas, employers based production on home-based, or subcontracted workforces, which were expected to be made up largely of women with children. By working as self-employed, lone parents said they were doing the only work available for women locally, or creating their own job opportunities.

To some extent these constraints are also faced by women in two-parent families when they have main responsibilities for child care and are also looking for work. However, women in two-parent families sometimes have the option of working in the evenings or at weekends when spouses are at home. It would be wrong to think that lone parents solved their child-care problems by being self-employed, however. Several reported having used child minders or baby-sitters at various stages, including those who worked at home.

Although they had come to self-employment as lone parents in different ways, as we saw in the previous chapter, both lone mothers and lone fathers stressed the general advantages of greater flexibility in being self-employed. As well as being able to have some control over work, there were some other interesting perspectives, of a rather different kind. One or two lone mothers who had never worked before, including previously married women, said that being self-employed was a way of regaining confidence. They felt they had little to offer employers, and were anxious about how they would cope in the early stages of trying to work. Self-employment had enabled them to pace themselves, and acquire skills and experience at their own rate. One mentioned being able to make mistakes in private, at an otherwise difficult stage in life. Even those whose small business ventures seemed likely to be non-viable, or had failed already, spoke of all they had learned in the process of setting up, and their growth in confidence for the future.

Another perspective came from women who had been carrying out some small-scale work on a self-employed basis when they lived with their husbands, and had been able to build this up into more substantial work when they became lone parents. They spoke of the element of stability this had brought to the turbulent period surrounding the break up of their marriage. They thought it would have been difficult to develop small jobs as employees into more substantial work in the same way without changing jobs - which would have been yet further upset at that time.

Despite the advantages seen in self-employment, our findings showed that it was hard for lone parents to start up completely new businesses from previous dependency on out-of-work benefits. Those who had tried and succeeded tended to be protected to some extent by housing and assets accumulated during previous times when at least one spouse, and sometimes two, had had better paid work. Lone mothers with young children and without special skills or expertise, who had been trying to set up small retail businesses after living on out-of-work benefits, were not protected by accumulated assets, and sometimes could not generate enough money for their needs, even with financial support from enterprise allowance and in-work benefits. The fragility of some of the self-employed ventures in which lone mothers were currently working, with apparently rather little chance of increasing profitability, suggested that these were likely to be transitional employment situations. Such women reported more financial independence, and greater satisfaction than they had experienced on out-of-work benefits. Some, however, were already looking beyond their small self-employed venture, to returning to education or training, or looking for a paid job when family circumstances allowed.

The only woman in the study group who had always been a lone parent and had kept her business going for several years, had started the venture before the birth of her children, and had a long history of self-employment. This was the only lone parent who talked generally about 'fitting her children into the work' rather than trying to fit work around children's needs, the usual reference point for the lone parents. 'Fitting the children into the work' was a more frequent observation among the self-employed couples who worked together in a demanding family concern.

Before moving on to consider the contribution of children to some of the self-employed ventures, we consider another aspect of self-employment - the opportunities found by people who have special caring responsibilities.

Families with extra caring responsibilities

All our families had responsibilities for caring for children. In the previous section we saw that some lone parents saw special advantages in being self-employed for people like themselves who had an extra share of responsibility. This was also the experience of other families who had to provide extra care, either for disabled children, or spouses or relatives with ill health. Self-employment meant that they had opportunities to work flexibly, to be at home while working or when required, or be within easy reach. The mother of a profoundly disabled teenager felt that it had only been possible for her to work because she could be self-employed. Her son would be going to live in a group home when he reached 18 years old: that would be the point, she felt, when other opportunities for employment would open up for her.

Another woman had taken over the role of family breadwinner after her husband left work on the grounds of ill health. Opening a shop close to home meant that she could be available when needed, and the business provided a sheltered environment where her husband could come occasionally to help, when he felt well. Small jobs taken home provided opportunities for him to engage in activities; this was all helpful to his mental health, and made family life easier. A two-parent family running a family business also mentioned the opportunities there were for a daughter with learning difficulties. There were many ways in which she could take part, meeting customers and taking messages, which were helping to build up her social skills.

There could be a thin line, however, for families with extra caring responsibilities, between the advantages of self-employment and the dangers if care became too heavy. Earnings could be constrained to the point at which businesses became non-viable. A couple whose son had become permanently disabled were finding it very hard to keep their business going and at the same time manage 24-hour care, and they were in considerable financial difficulty.

We have now looked at some of the divisions of work and responsibilities among self-employed parents, both two-parent and lone-parent families. In the final part of the chapter, we put another piece into the jigsaw. Our interviews suggested that the development and maintenance of some of these low-income, self-employed ventures depended on work input from children, relatives and even friends. Much of this work was done on an unpaid basis, and represents a further contribution to the economy that is largely invisible.

Additional work input

Children could make substantial contributions in some enterprises. What seemed tedious work to adults could seem quite fun to children. Distributing leaflets in a local area, errands on bicycles, or counting and arranging stock could be reliably delegated to quite young children and their friends. Other studies have shown that in farming families children are drawn into jobs and farm work from a very early age (Hutson, 1990). This was true of those farms and smallholdings in the study group where the farm was also the family home.

If children were really interested in their parents' work they could become an integral part of the undertaking. There could be firmly expressed expectations that children should help in the 'family business' and grow up taking part with their parents. One 15 year old son of a agricultural family was expected to work several hours weekly, without being paid. Such strong expectations of participation, or ideas expressed that pocket money had to be earned or children's help freely given, were usually justified by feelings that parents were teaching useful values in this way. Children were learning reliability and co-operation, and discovering themselves that 'money has to be worked for'. Parents explained that they were passing on their own values - that effort and hard work were valuable in themselves. One couple also said that working in the family business kept teenagers close to them, so that parents knew what they were doing - a useful control mechanism.

Where teenagers had been closely involved with the family business, it was apparent that parents' skills and interests had sometimes been directly passed on, to the extent that children were now making their own careers in similar occupations. Sons training to be chefs, or planning to go to horticultural college were following on in their fathers' occupations. It was just these kinds of links with parents' occupations, and the experience of working with self-employed parents that we saw reported by some of the new entrants to self-employment. The study demonstrated both how these family connections with self-employment are established, and how effective they can be in the propensity of people to try self-employment.

The involvement of older children in business offers another perspective on 'invisible work' within the general economy. Some received regular payments, while others were expected to participate willingly without direct reward, although sometimes 'helping out' was acknowledged in Christmas and birthday presents, or treats, depending on general business profitability.

As well as the involvement of children, relatives were drawn into the invisible economy surrounding some of the work. The self-employed people's own parents might give considerable help with practical do-it-yourself and conversion work on premises. Working siblings lent equipment or vehicles occasionally, and would come and help with different tasks on both a casual paid, or unpaid basis. In farming and fishing communities older men, who might have had official status as 'retired people' had they been employees, expected to go on using skills to help keep family concerns going.

People who had started completely new businesses from scratch had sometimes been surprised by the level of interest and active participation by friends and neighbours. One couple had described considerable input into their business at an early stage from their immediate neighbours, who wanted to be closely involved in some of the design and promotional work, and were happy to exchange skills and effort for friendship and hospitality.

Also mentioned by some was financial help. As we shall see later, generous money gifts would sometimes go into small businesses from the self-employed people's own parents, who wanted the ventures to succeed. Another way of helping was for parents to meet some of the domestic bills of the self-employed family, so that they did not have to draw on business accounts. The flow of money into businesses in the form of gifts from parents raises special problems for assessment of income for purposes of determining eligibility for means-tested benefits, and we return to this in the next chapter.

We have now looked at the family involvement in the self-employed work, and the informal help contributed by relatives and friends, and we conclude the chapter by considering the extent to which formal jobs for employees were being created.

Job creation for employees

Nationally, most self-employed people employ either nobody else or have between one and three employees (Campbell and Daly, 1992). We have already seen how in some businesses the spouse was the only formal employee. Some of the more complex businesses in our study had developed to the stage at which employees or subcontracted workers were taken on. In this section we consider how far these small businesses were creating job opportunities.

Excluding the 'employed' spouses, jobs that were currently provided by some of the self- employed people in our study group tended themselves to be within the 'peripheral economy' - part-time, temporary, casual or self-employed work. Small retail businesses employed people as sales assistants and cleaners: all these jobs were done by women and only one was full time. The larger farms took on subcontracted and casual labour in the summer months, or when there was a special job to do such as hay baling. Most of this work was undertaken by men.

Businesses which had once been more profitable had previously had larger workforces. The hoteliers had once employed several people including full-time waiting staff, and part-time chambermaids, washers-up and cleaners, but all had been asked to leave as business declined. In the year when they were interviewed they were relying on casual employees, including students and schoolboys, for part-time cleaning and waiting. Part-time cleaning work in the restaurant had also been cut down this year.

In the past the clothing retailer had a more substantial workforce when she employed three full-time women employees to make garments as well as managing two self-employed outworkers. She had recently scaled back this work, however, and now provided self-employed outwork to two women and employed a school-leaver for 30 hours per week. A leaflet distributor employed a varying number of other women on a casual *per diem* basis, and knew that some of these were other lone parents who were earning small amounts of money to top up their income support.

Few salaried full-time posts had been created for other people. One of the men providing a professional service had a full-time secretary who worked in his office. The educational business employed full-time and part-time staff. Regular wage costs are a substantial liability in a business with low profitability, and employed labour was one of the items cut back as far as possible if proprietors saw business declining. What this section has shown clearly is that in terms of job creation to boost the general economy there was only minimal contribution from these low-income, self-employed people. What jobs there were mostly fell into the traditional gendered labour market segmentation of manual work for male workers, and low-paid service jobs taken by people wanting to boost other sources of income - mainly women and students. There were only one or two examples of permanent jobs which had been created for skilled or trained people: some of these had not lasted long, or were currently vulnerable due to the low profitability of their employers. This is hardly a picture that encourages an idea of a thriving, booming enterprise economy. Rather it tends to confirm ideas about the marginalisation and increasing insecurity of some kinds of workers who are vulnerable to trade and seasonal fluctuations in the market, and dependent on the changing fortunes of small-scale enterprises, some of which are themselves hardly viable.

Summary

This chapter has given some idea of the backgrounds of the self-employed workers, the kind of work being undertaken and the way that this was organised. The picture increases our understanding of the heterogeneity of the low-income, self-employed population. It also points especially to the differences in working circumstances between those recognised as being 'in business' and those who are not businessmen or women, but work for themselves in some way. We have explored the different kinds of labour market participation in two-parent families, and we shall return to these different ways of sharing and combining work when we look at income supplementation in later chapters. Lone parents, and families with extra caring responsibilities, as well as breadwinners with poor health themselves, all saw advantages in being self-employed, in helping them fit work around personal circumstances. However, what may seem advantageous when things are going as planned can turn into problems fairly quickly at marginal profit levels, as we shall see in later chapters when we consider how these self-employed people made provision for financial security when they could not work, or faced retirement.

6 Claiming benefits

As has already been observed, research on self-employment has rarely addressed the issue of social security, and it is only comparatively recently that social security research has begun to pay attention to the self-employed. The relationship between self-employment and claiming benefits raises interesting conceptual issues, and implementing social security arrangements for self-employed people is by no means unproblematic, despite the little attention this has attracted. This chapter outlines the position of self-employed people in the British social security system and some comparisons are drawn with the position of self-employed people in social security systems in other European countries. The main entitlements to benefits of self-employed people in Britain are described, and the differential treatment they receive in respect of contributory and contingency benefits, in comparison with employees.

Reviewing the evidence of access to benefits for self-employed people in Britain shows how important are the main income-related benefits. The focus of the authors' research was family credit, and the chapter draws on empirical findings to explain how the families studied claimed and used family credit, and its role in their work and family lives.

Social insurance and self-employment

Social protection against the financial consequences of unemployment, invalidity, injury, old age and death in Britain developed in an incremental and piecemeal way out of the late nineteenth century patchwork of private, co-operative, employer, charitable, trade union and friendly society provision (Gilbert, 1966; Dilnot et al., 1984). These schemes offered only limited protection to the mass of the population and a combination of public concern, industrial unrest, and interest in the Bismarckian reforms in Germany led to the gradual adoption of the principle of generalised insurance. This was enshrined in the National Insurance Act of 1911, which introduced the first compulsory insurance against sickness and unemployment. In itself this was a very modest change, but it established the principle of social insurance which was to become the central theme of the Beveridge Report (Dilnot et al., 1984).

Self-employed people were regarded as relatively wealthy and capable of private provision, and as a result they were not covered by pre-World War II social insurance laws (Forde, 1979). Beveridge, however, did not automatically exclude self-employed people from all protection: one of his key principles was, after all, *comprehensiveness:*

> The fifth fundamental principle is that social insurance should be comprehensive, in respect of both the persons covered and of their needs. It should not leave either to national assistance or to voluntary insurance any risk so general or so uniform that social insurance can be justified. (Beveridge, 1942, para. 308)

Forde suggests that the inclusion of the self-employed in the basic insurance system lay not only in Beveridge's principle of comprehensiveness, but also in a relative deterioration in economic position of many self-employed people during the 1930s. Brown (1992) records that the Trades Union Congress was among those organisations whose evidence to the Beveridge inquiry recommended the inclusion of the self-employed in the post-war insurance plan. According to Brown, Beveridge had a good understanding of the range of incomes of the self-employed, and the occupations and work patterns of those in the lower income groups. Transitions between self-employment and working for an employer that were a feature of many lives, and concurrent combinations of the two ways of working were further arguments for establishing a single comprehensive scheme.

Nevertheless, Beveridge saw a clear distinction between employees, who would be covered for unemployment benefit, and the self-employed, who would not (paras. 314 - 315) - a distinction which has persisted to the present day. He recognised that this distinction was problematic for some special groups, including labour-only subcontractors and share fishermen (para. 314) - the latter being a group who still occupy a special place in the social security system.

Overall, however, the self-employed received relatively little detailed attention in the debate and legislation following the Beveridge Report. The traditional image of the self-employed as affluent and self-provisioning has persisted, leading to differential treatment in important areas of both contributory and non-contributory benefits.

Social protection of the self-employed in the European Union

It should be noted that the social protection available to the self-employed is not an issue of debate only in the UK. In Chapter Two we saw how self-employment had increased in a number of other European countries during the 1980s, though not to the same extent as in Britain. There have, nevertheless, been some of the same concerns about the levels of social protection available to the self-employed - partly because, as in Britain, it is increasingly being recognised that there are substantial groups of self-employed people who are financially vulnerable. In the European Union, the parameters of the debate have been framed by two independent but linked developments. One is the growth in all countries of the proportion of the workforces engaged in atypical or non-standard work (Cordova, 1986; Hinrichs, 1989; Konle-Seidl et al., 1990). There is evidence that in many countries the growth or resurgence of the more insecure and less rewarding forms of self-employment have similar origins to those of the parallel growths in part-time and temporary work.

Self-employment has also grown over a period when many countries have seen increases in long-term unemployment and when governments have promoted self-employment as an alternative method of job creation (Commission of the European Communities, 1988). Many of those involved may find themselves in the same lower bracket of the dual labour market, with consequent expectations of lower earnings and less legal and social security protection.

The second, associated development has been the political and economic drive towards the single European market. It has been argued that the single market is likely to sharpen further the trend towards flexible work patterns, but if the result is a growing proportion of workers without adequate social protection, markets may be distorted by the unevenness of the protection which exists in the different member countries. Thus the debate on social policy and comparative levels of social protection in Europe has focused to a large extent on the possible phenomenon of 'social dumping', whereby the competitive edge may be given to regimes with lower social and legal standards of protection. As a result, countries with higher standards may be forced to lower them to a common denominator (Bercusson, 1991; Ditch and Pickles, 1991). Many commentators have been unconvinced that such a scenario will be realised to any serious extent (for example, Bergman, 1991). Nevertheless, some of the sectors of work in which social dumping is more likely are those such as construction, where self-employment is prevalent but levels of legal and social protection relatively low. Whether justified or not, fears of the distorting effects of social dumping have arguably been as important in the development of the social dimension of the single market as concerns about poverty and inequality in Europe (Keithley, 1991).

Alongside the fear of social dumping has been the concern to facilitate free movement of workers in the Community. There has been considerable emphasis, for example, on developing mutual recognition of qualifications and on the cross-national market for skills in computing and new technology (Commission of the European Communities, 1990b). The possibilities of mobility in these professional areas in particular have highlighted some of the discrepancies which exist between countries in social insurance protection and which might act as an obstacle to free movement.

The question of self-employment has been addressed more directly in the development of Community law through Council Regulations. These regulations, enacted by virtue of Article 51 of the Treaty of Rome, are binding on the member countries and thus create a level of supra-national law. They do not, however, attempt to create an independent system of European social security. Instead, 'their objective is to secure the co-operation of national social security systems in situations with trans-national implications through co-ordination, all in the interests of an effective guarantee of the right to free movement' (Borchadt, 1989 p.59). With the growth of self-employment and the gradual, but uneven, assimilation of groups of self-employed people into national social security schemes, the entitlements of self-employed people migrating within the Community have assumed increasing importance. Case law on these regulations has gradually extended the concept of 'worker' in Article 51 to include self-employed people and other workers who may be 'assimilated' into the various national social security schemes (Forde, 1979; Lasok, 1982), though Lasok argued that even the broader definition still did not offer comprehensive coverage. Since then, further amendments have been put forward to consolidate the equal treatment of self-employed people and their families moving within the Community (Borchadt, 1989).

The most comprehensive examination of social security protection for the self-employed at a European level came in a conference organised by the European Commission in October 1993 (see Bercusson, 1993). While adding considerably to comparative knowledge about the subject, the contributions also showed, as a summary paper illustrates (Brown, 1994b), how diverse still are the approaches to social security for self-employed people in the different countries. They vary, for example, in whether self-employed people are covered by the same basic schemes as for employees or have their own, often sectorally-based schemes; in whether membership of such schemes is voluntary or compulsory; in whether the same levels of contributions and benefits apply to the self-employed as to employees; in whether they are included in particular schemes such as occupational injury protection; and in whether they have access to social assistance or other means-tested benefits. In general, the areas where the self-employed have the least protection across the member countries are for unemployment, where only two countries (Denmark and Luxembourg) include them in insurance schemes (and even here the definitions of unemployment are more limited than for ex-employees), short-term sickness and occupational injury. Broadly speaking, self-employed or ex-self-employed people have rather greater access to means-tested benefits, although the familiar problems exist in assessing their earnings. Also, a number of countries apart from the UK, including France, Ireland and the Netherlands, have schemes to assist low earners in the course of self-employment with the aim of avoiding business failure and consequent unemployment, though several of these schemes are aimed mainly at farmers.

The diversity of approaches observed in the member countries of the European Union reflects not only their different historical traditions, but also the heterogeneity of the self-employed populations which in itself represents one of the obstacles to extending social security provision. In this respect, the UK is fairly unusual in providing basic insurance-based and contingency entitlement for all self-employed people within the same national scheme as for employees.

Contributory and contingency benefits in the United Kingdom

Since Beveridge, self-employed people have remained within the same contributory insurance scheme as the employed, but the structure now provides for different contributions and different entitlements. Self-employed people pay flat-rate Class 2 contributions and additional Class 4 profit-related contributions on a band of income above and below specified thresholds. They are covered for flat-rate age pensions, survivors' benefits and the lower rated sickness and maternity benefits. They have restricted access to invalidity benefit. They continue to be excluded altogether from unemployment benefit (apart from share fishermen and volunteer development workers), and from the earnings-related pensions scheme (SERPS), both of which require Class 1 contributions. SERPS was introduced in 1978 and was probably the most significant change to social insurance since Beveridge. Among non-contributory contingency benefits, self-employed people are not entitled to industrial injury benefit, nor the employment-based schemes for statutory sick pay or statutory maternity pay. Brown (1992) traces the development of the current position of self-employed people within these schemes from the original post-war plan.

In recent years the partial exclusion of the self-employed from some of the most generous social security benefits has attracted criticism which has grown alongside the increasing recognition of their diverse circumstances. The exclusion from SERPS in particular has been seen as a major disadvantage (Lynes, 1989; Brown, 1990, 1992). Since self-employed people by definition have no employers, they can only have access to occupational pensions if they have acquired entitlement through earlier periods of employment. Tax concessions are available on premiums paid into private pension schemes, but these have a number of disadvantages compared to SERPS and occupational pensions. First, given the relatively low earnings of a substantial proportion of self-employed people, many may be unable to devote towards private premiums the large part of their income required. Secondly, individual pensions carry higher administrative costs then either SERPS or occupational schemes. Thirdly, private pension payments are not set by reference to final earnings but are 'money purchase' schemes dependent on the fluctuations of the investment markets and are generally not inflation proofed.

There is evidence that the number of self-employed people with private pension provision has been low. An insurance company survey conducted in 1984 found that half were not in private pension plans (Legal and General, 1985). Similarly, evidence submitted by the DHSS to the parliamentary Social Services Committee suggested that only 30 per cent of even those self-employed with earnings sufficient for them to pay national insurance contributions were claiming tax relief on retirement annuities (House of Commons, 1982). More recent analyses by Brown (1992), based on special tabulations provided by the Inland Revenue concerning retirement annuity tax relief, suggested that by 1987-88 the broad picture was that around 36 per cent of all self-employed people were contributing to a second pension, with slightly lower proportions of women covered than men. There was less likelihood of contributing to a private pension at lower income levels. Further special tabulations from the Survey of Personal Incomes, prepared for the authors by the Inland Revenue Statistics and Economic Office, indicated that the proportion of self-employed people making contributions was slowly increasing. In 1988-89, some 38 per cent of self-employed people were allowed retirement annuity relief or claimed tax relief for gross contributions to a personal pension, and in 1989-90, this was 38.5 per cent.

However, our analysis of administrative statistics from the family credit population showed that despite the general gradual increase in private retirement investment among the self-employed, it was unusual for low-income families with children to be making contributions. Only 17 per cent of those families claiming family credit whose main earnings came from self-employment were making payments towards private pensions. Average weekly contributions among those who did pay were £3.66.

This low level of private pension contribution can be set in the context of the eligibility of this group of low earners for tax relief on pensions premiums. Only 31 per cent of self-employed family credit recipients had some notional income tax deducted from gross earnings, and thus would have been eligible for any tax relief for pension investment.

Brown (1990, 1992) suggests that some of the failure to take out additional pensions or insurance may be temporary. Younger people, for example, are often not immediately concerned with their retirement. As employees they are obliged to make pensions contributions, but as self-employed people they can choose which priorities to meet. However, for the self-employed late decisions can lead to higher premiums or reduced payments, or both. Another possibility is that self-employed people may prefer to plough back any surplus funds into their businesses, hoping to use the eventual proceeds of sale to provide for their old age, or pass on the business to their children and be supported by them. Either way, these may be somewhat risky strategies.

Lynes (1989) has also criticised the exclusion of the self-employed from earnings-related pensions. He opposed the approach taken by the Labour Party, which has proposed that self-employed people should be able to join the earnings-related scheme voluntarily (Labour Party, 1990). This, Lynes argued, would be open to abuse, particularly if based on the best 20 years earnings, and would benefit most those among the self-employed who are already better off. Instead, he proposed an additional flat-rate pension based on the number of years people have been self-employed: this would benefit lower earners, would not require complex contracting-out and would be an appropriate return for a flat-rate contribution.

The Class 4 earnings-related contribution paid by the self-employed is often seen as particularly unfair, since payments are not related directly to entitlements to benefits. Self-employed people were excluded from the Graduated Pension scheme established in 1959, but have been required since 1975 to pay Class 4 earnings-related contributions, which are collected by the Inland Revenue and paid *en masse* to the social security fund without any personal identification of the contributors. The total contributions have to be set against the total of employees' *and employers*' contributions, and thus are set at a level which reflects the exclusion of self-employed people from both SERPS and other benefits (DHSS, 1980a).

The feeling among self-employed people that they are making contributions for little visible return may contribute to a certain resistance on their part to make the payments. The possibility of significant under-collection of Class 2 contributions from self-employed people operating outside the known economy was suggested by the findings from two Departmental reviews of national insurance contributions work in local offices in 1987 and 1989 (reported in NAO, 1991b).

According to a newspaper report (*The Guardian*, 1990), a leaked Department report on the collection of contributions and debts indicated that only around 57 per cent of the estimated total of national insurance contributions owed by self-employed people was currently being collected, and that the shortfall was around £250m per year. Examination of the Department's procedures for collecting and processing national insurance contributions (NAO, 1991b) pointed to administrative shortcomings as a possible reason for under-collection, in addition to the non-compliance and deliberate evasion that was assumed.

Our research discussions with self-employed family credit recipients threw some light on how they perceived and dealt with national insurance contributions. Non-payment did appear to be common, but there were a variety of reasons. These included lack of information, disputed assessments, delays caused by budgeting and cash flow problems, and competing priorities for family expenditure. The following chapter looks in more detail at some of the experiences described.

There is, of course, a significant number of self-employed people who are not required to pay national insurance contributions because their earnings fall below the lower limit on which contributions are due. Analysis by Hakim (1989b) of the 1985 Family Expenditure Survey (FES) estimated that seven per cent of full-time, and 52 per cent of part-time, self-employed people had earnings below the national insurance contribution threshold for Class 2 contributions. Our own analysis of the 1990/91 FES showed that just over one-fifth of all respondents who were self-employed in their main job had total gross self-employed earnings below this threshold. Analysis of family credit administrative statistics showed that, in April 1991, 37 per cent of self-employed recipients were estimated as not liable for national insurance contributions because earnings were below the threshold, currently set at £55.77 per week.

Such people are expected to apply for a certificate for Small Earnings Exception, and can elect to pay voluntary Class 3 contributions to count towards retirement pension or widow's benefits. However, levels of understanding of the links between contributions and pension rights among the families taking part in this study were often low. For some parents who should have been paying contributions, the reduction of accumulated arrears seemed less urgent when people were hazy about the implications of non-payment.

In general, governments have resisted the extension of benefits to the self-employed on grounds of cost and administrative practicality (Luckhaus, 1991).

For SERPS, the problem is said to lie in the difficulty of bringing together two different methods of levying and recording contributions. For unemployment benefit the objections are based more on the absence of methods of control and surveillance of self-employed people in order to make sure they are not working (Brown, 1992).

Similar problems have been identified as reasons for not including self-employed people within the industrial injuries scheme. The 1980 DHSS Discussion Document on Industrial Injuries Compensation concluded, first, that the necessity to exclude some categories of part-time self-employed work would create anomalies; secondly, the adjudication of claims would be difficult without verification that injuries took place in the course of work (DHSS, 1980b). In 1991 the Industrial Injuries Advisory Council believed that the recent growth in self-employment and the changing nature of self-employment were reasons for reconsidering the position of people who suffered disabling injuries at work. A consultation paper (DSS, 1991c) was issued, drawing widely on research conducted by Joan Brown. The paper considered possible ways of bringing self-employed people into the industrial injuries scheme, and suggested that a step-by-step approach might begin by including those who were self-employed in construction and agricultural industries.

In both these industries, it was suggested, self-employed people often work alongside and under the same safety conditions as employees. For example, subcontracted construction workers on building sites may work alongside employees of the building firm, doing the same work under the same conditions. Both these industries have a high proportion of the workforce working as self-employed - 45 per cent of construction workers in 1993, and 56 per cent of the agricultural workforce (see p.43). A further characteristic of both industries is a substantial incidence of industrial injury incurred by self-employed people. Sixty-five per cent of all major non-fatal injuries to self-employed people in Great Britain in 1988-89 were reported to be incurred by construction workers, and 11 per cent by agricultural workers (DSS, 1991c).

By including self-employed workers in construction and agriculture in the industrial injuries scheme, the paper argued, three-quarters of those with eligible injuries would be drawn in, representing some 29 per cent of all self-employed people, or nearly one million people. The paper went on to discuss procedural problems of implementing this first stage in a step-by-step approach. Additional costs, it was suggested, would be fairly modest.

The exclusion of the self-employed from statutory sick pay and statutory maternity pay appears to have resulted largely from the Government's decision in the early 1980s to save money in these areas by transferring their administration to employers, some of whom were already operating their own occupational schemes. Self-employed people are entitled to the lower-rated contributory sickness and maternity benefits, but as Luckhaus points out it is not clear why the employment status of individuals should in itself determine the level of protection available in cases of short-term sickness and pregnancy.

Brown discussed the apparently lower usage of the contributory short-term sickness benefit, and invalidity benefit by people who are self-employed. Data on take-up of these benefits by self-employed people is not easily accessible. However, analyses of special tabulations provided by the Department of Social Security led Brown (1992) to suggest that less than three per cent of spells of incapacity for which sickness benefit was claimed were due to self-employed people in 1988-89, although 12-13 per cent of the labour force were self-employed. Reasons suggested included not understanding entitlement to sickness benefit, as well as reluctance to take time off work.

If there is generally lower usage of the short-term contributory sickness benefit among self-employed people, this would be expected to be reflected in low proportions of people claiming invalidity benefit, a long-term benefit for incapacity for work which depends, among other eligibility criteria, on 28 weeks receipt of sickness benefit. Brown presented results from special tabulations provided by DSS which show that for years 1984-85, 1985-86 and 1988-89 between 5.6 and 6.9 per cent of intake of recipients were self-employed in their last job. During the same years 10-13 per cent of the overall labour force in Great Britain were self-employed. The DSS 1992 cross-sectional survey of invalidity benefit recipients confirmed that use of this benefit by people incapacitated for work during self-employment was still low. A few men (eight per cent) but hardly any women (two per cent) had been self-employed in their last job (Lonsdale et al., 1993).

There is much still to learn about the apparent low use of short-term sickness benefit and long-term incapacity benefit by self-employed people. It might be argued that those with poor health are unlikely to remain in self-employment for long, such that the self-employed population was generally healthier, with less need for financial support during periods of ill health. On the other hand, however, we know that those disabled people who do work are slightly more likely to be self-employed than the general working population (Prescott-Clarke, 1990). Other recent work has shown that people with ill health or disability may see particular advantages in working in a home environment and/or on their own account (Thomas, 1992). Our own interviews confirmed this, as described in the previous chapter.

Other possible explanations for the apparently lower use of sickness and incapacity benefit include insufficient contributions records, as already described, or factors recognised from previous research on non-take-up of benefits (Corden, 1995) such as non-recognition of eligibility and problems with application procedures or demonstration of incapacity for work. Another possibility is that some people may prefer to continue to try to keep things 'ticking over' despite ill health, in order not to lose business opportunities or contacts. Our research interviews provided illustrations of many such situations. In general, people were dismissive about the possibilities of claiming benefits while sick. A common view among those who were usually fairly healthy was that managing short periods of illness was part of being self-employed. 'You can't afford to be ill' and 'you have to soldier on' were typical expressions used. Indeed, being self-employed was itself a strong motivation to get better:

> You live on what you might have already, or you struggle. It concentrates the mind on whether you're really ill.

People whose health was not so good described a similar process of 'struggling through'. If spouses worked together, there was somebody who could keep business at least 'ticking over' until the sick partner felt better. Those who found short periods of ill health most difficult were people who worked on their own and depended on weekly cash earnings. Bouts of influenza for taxi drivers meant a hard week for their families. It was even more difficult for self-employed lone parents during bouts of illness. With sole responsibility for children and home they also had to try to maintain some earnings.

The possibility of claiming sickness benefit was rarely mentioned as an option for periods of ill health. Many knew they would not be entitled as a result of their contribution record. A shopkeeper, for example, received permanent medication for blood pressure and did have weeks when he was unable to open his shop. However, he had applied for a contributions exemption certificate for several years past and knew it was unlikely he could be eligible for sickness benefit.

Even those who had paid regular contributions were reluctant formally to take time off work. It seemed better to try to carry out even the smallest task, like answering the telephone or dealing with correspondence, in order to stay in touch with work. A formal declaration of illness in order to claim benefits might ensure a week's minimal income but increase problems in the longer term.

Those who had at some time during self-employment applied for benefits when sick usually remembered this as a problematic or frustrating experience. Fishermen, builders and farmers remembered arguments about their contributions records, or demonstrating that they were not working. Some had eventually gained some income support for a period of sickness, but remembered problems of assessing income.

It seems unlikely that the apparently low use of sickness and incapacity benefit means that self-employed people depend more on private insurance when sick. Various forms of private insurance policies have been developed to cater for the illness or accident protection needs of self-employed people, but these can be expensive, can reduce the amount of money available for pension premiums and can be vulnerable to fluctuations in net income in self-employment (Gaselee, 1983). In addition, some schemes identify high risk occupation groups among self-employed people, who are then charged extra premiums or excluded altogether (Brown, 1992).

Among the self-employed people we spoke to, hardly any were currently making payments for private health insurance. A fisherman and builder who had taken out private insurance both subsequently found that they were not covered for injuries they sustained, in spite of having paid substantial premia.

In summary, the self-employed continue to be excluded from a number of important areas of contributory and contingency benefits, partly on historical grounds of costs and administrative practicality. The potential disadvantages created by their exclusion from earnings-related pension provision have been pointed out (Lynes, 1989; Brown, 1990, 1992). Until recently little has been known about the impact of this differential treatment on the day-to-day lives of self-employed people with lower earnings. The depth interviews with family credit recipients provided some opportunities to look at these issues. Further aspects of effects on family living standards are presented in Chapter Seven.

In the absence of entitlement to some insurance and contingency benefits self-employed people may at times have to rely on one or more of the means-tested benefits, to all of which they are in principle entitled, subject to the same qualifying tests applied to all claimants. However, although they are subject to the same tests of income and capital, these tests are not necessarily applied in the same way. The next section looks at self-employment and means-tested benefits.

Self-employment and means-tested benefits

Self-employed people may claim all the main means-tested benefits - income support, family credit, housing benefit, council tax benefit (previously community charge benefit) and disability working allowance, as well as means-tested health service and educational benefits. Until recently, little has been known about the use of these benefits by people who are or have been self-employed, partly because official statistics do not always categorise people separately by their sources of earnings. Changes to the social security system over the last decade have meant that means-tested benefits have assumed a growing importance. With evidence showing large numbers of self-employed people with apparently very modest incomes, we might also expect a concomitant increase in the numbers using these benefits.

It is not easy to collate comparable quantitative data about the use of means-tested benefits by self-employed people, but Table 6.1 brings together some of the information available.

Table 6.1
Receipt of means-tested benefits by self-employed people in Great Britain

	No. self-employed recipients
Income support[a]	250,000 formerly or currently self-employed (April 1992) includes approx. 8,000 currently self-employed in part-time work (May 1992)
Housing benefit[b]	14,000 tenants not in receipt of income support (May 1992)
Community charge benefit[b]	35,000 tenants and owner-occupiers not in receipt of income support
Family credit[b]	68,200 (January 1993) represents 14.5 per cent all recipients
Disability working allowance[c]	approx. 796 (May 1993) represents approx. 25 per cent all recipients

Sources: a. NAO (1993)
b. DSS (1993b)
c. *Hansard* (1994) col. 786, 30 March combined with data from Rowlingson and Berthoud (1994)

Income support

People working part-time and earning very little could be entitled to income support if self-employment provides their main household income. Numbers at present appear to be small but to have increased substantially in the last few years. In May 1989, around 130,000 of all income support claimants received income from their own earnings in addition to their benefits and some 32,000 had a wife or dependant with earned income (DSS, 1993b, Table A2.23). However, according to figures supplied by the Department (Brown, 1992) only some 1,200 income support claimants had earnings from self-employment.

This suggested that most of those working in part-time self-employment either had earnings above the income support levels or additional sources of income in the household, although there may have been some non-take-up of income support, for example through lack of awareness of eligibility or preference for not claiming income support.

By May 1992, about 8,000 income support claimants were recorded as self-employed and undertaking part-time work for less than 16 hours weekly (NAO, 1993). This increase in absolute numbers and what appears to be a proportionate increase of self-employed people among the part-time earners claiming income support may reflect some new entries into part-time self-employment. The increase is specially interesting because effects of changes in the benefit regulations in April 1992 might have been expected to reduce numbers of part-time, self-employed, income support claimants. At that point, the hours requirement for eligibility for family credit was reduced from 24 to 16 hours work weekly, and income support was no longer available to anybody working more than 16 hours per week. We would expect some self-employed parents working between 16 and 24 hours to have been 'floated off' income support at this stage, onto family credit. Some people might have reduced hours of self-employed work in order to remain within the income support safety net. Establishing entitlement to income support under such circumstances might be problematic, however. In addition, apart from lone parents and people over 60 years of age, a formerly self-employed person has to be willing and available to accept a job as an employee. It may not be easy to try to keep a business together while claiming income support, in the hope of upturn in the trade.

In addition to the use made of income support by a relatively small number of people continuing to work in self-employment on a part-time basis, the benefit can be important for those whose self-employment is intermittent, whose business fails or who leave self-employment for some other reason, such as ill health. People who have not paid Class 1 contributions as an employee in relevant previous years have no entitlement to unemployment benefit, and gaps in contributions records may mean that income support is the only means of support available in periods of sickness. According to an enquiry by the National Audit Office (1993) approximately 13 per cent of income support recipients classified as unemployed in May 1992 were formerly self-employed.

It has not always been easy for those who have left self-employment to establish entitlement to income support. Demonstrating that trading has definitely ended, or that they are actively seeking employed work, may both be hard for some in the transitional period when people are winding up their affairs and facing a number of problems. Residual capital from the enterprise may take them over the capital limit for income support. Business assets can be disregarded for a period of time to allow for their sale, but the length of time taken for administrative decisions to be made about such matters may create problems for those who have no other source of income. Brown (1992) describes a variety of circumstances in which self-employed people had experienced problems and delays in establishing eligibility for income support, drawing on case records from Citizens Advice Bureaux.

Prior to Brown's analysis of problems reported by Citizens Advice Bureaux, little attention had been paid to the experience of people applying for income support when they were currently or formerly self-employed. The media spotlight occasionally focused on the situation of people whose self-employed activities provided no income but who had difficulty in establishing entitlement to benefit (for example, *The Guardian*, 1992). In the case reported (CIS\270\91), the Social Security Commissioners reinstated eligibility to income support for a writer who had earned nothing during an 18-month period. Although she had been spending more than 24 hours weekly at this work she had applied for numerous other jobs and was ready to take work if a suitable opportunity arose.

With continuing promotion of entrepreneurial activity, and expansion of subcontracting, franchising and other forms of quasi-self-employment, we can expect income support to continue to be an important source of support for some currently or formerly self-employed people.

Enquiry by the National Audit Office (NAO, 1993) into the quality of service provided by the Benefits Agency to this group of people showed a concentration of use of income support in Southern England. Fifty-seven per cent of self-employed and formerly self-employed income support recipients lived in London and South East, and South West regions, compared with 37 per cent of all those receiving income support. (Self-employment is generally more common in these parts of the country, as was shown in Chapter Two.)

A survey of around 1,000 self-employed and formerly self-employed people receiving income support was included in the NAO enquiry (MORI, 1993).

Around 22 per cent expressed overall dissatisfaction with the claim process. The main problems had been delay in processing applications and the attitude of staff. Criticisms of staff included their lack of understanding of the relevant rules, and having insufficient time to spend in discussion and negotiation. About one-fifth of claimants felt they had not been believed.

The NAO enquiry pointed to a widespread belief amongst self-employed people that they would have no entitlement to any financial support from social security if they stopped working, based on their disqualification from unemployment benefit. The availability of income support and the rules governing claims from self-employed people were not well understood. Among those who had claimed, delays were attributed to job search, expectations of changes in circumstances and misconceptions about the rules. Documentary evidence required in support of claims placed extra demands on some people. For example, in the survey for the NAO enquiry, half the professional people asked to provide annual accounts or company accounts found this hard, either because they did not have such evidence or payment was needed to obtain it (MORI, 1993). Such findings suggest that there is likely to be considerable non-take-up of income support among the self-employed population.

The Benefits Agency responded quickly to recommendations from the National Audit Office for improvements in quality of service to self-employed people. A handbook for income support staff dealing with self-employed and business cases (Benefits Agency, 1993) recommended training and procedural improvement in local offices, and improved liaison with the Contributions Agency. A number of initiatives led to improvements in the information and advice available both to the general public, and to staff dealing with claims from self-employed people.

It is difficult to monitor what is happening as a result of these efforts to improve the service. Official estimates of take-up of income support have always excluded the self-employed on the basis of lack of sufficiently detailed information available on income in the Family Expenditure Survey (Department of Social Security, 1994). Published government social security statistics do not identify separately income support claimants who were previously self-employed, or those with current earnings from self-employment.

The authors' research interviews with self-employed family credit recipients provided opportunities to discuss experiences of claiming income support. Some problems were reported by people who had claimed income support after recently leaving self-employment, or when unemployed while partners had small earnings from self-employment. A roofer, well-known in his local community, had mended guttering and broken tiles on neighbours' roofs free of charge, after he had closed down his business and registered as available for work in order to claim income support. He had also made good some guttering installed while running his business, which subsequently needed further attention. This led to accusations from his local office of working while claiming income support. Another couple remembered their anger about some of the suggestions made when the man claimed income support after his unemployment benefit ran out. He declared his wife's small earnings from her farming activities, at that stage still more of a hobby than a business enterprise. The man had been asked why the couple had not sold some of the assets from the small-scale farming (such as equipment and stock animals) in order to raise income.

Our research confirmed that the ways in which self-employed people were dealt with when they claimed income support led some to feel they were being asked inappropriate questions, or treated with suspicion. However, it was not always the case that income support claims had been problematic. An outworker in the leather industry occasionally experienced periods of several weeks when she received no work at all to do at home. As she was paid on a piece-work basis, when the supply of work dried up she needed to claim income support until factory output improved and the associated home-working processes were again required. She experienced no problems in claiming income support in the weeks when no work was delivered. This may have been associated with the fact that her pattern of working was common in the local area, where many women carried out such work at home for a few well-known 'employers'. She had 'pay slips' to demonstrate previous earnings, and her supervisory staff readily confirmed that work was not available. It is, of course, in the interests of employers who rely on the continued availability of this kind of experienced outworker in a manufacturing process to be helpful when workers need to turn to income support. In terms of assessing eligibility for income support, the outworker's situation would be easier to deal with than that of a person whose business appeared to have failed but who did not have available the relevant accounts or order books to demonstrate their circumstances.

As we show in the sections following, assessment of income from self-employment is a problem common to all means-tested benefits. What is a technical difficulty for policy makers who write the rules determining eligibility is also an administrative problem for those who assess entitlement, as well as a factor contributing to delay and non-take-up at the client level, and applications from ineligible people (Corden, 1995).

Housing benefit and council tax benefits

Housing benefit and council tax benefit are both available to people on low incomes, irrespective of whether there are dependent children. In this respect, eligibility criteria differ from those of family credit, the other main in-work means-tested benefit available to self-employed people. However, housing benefit is only available to meet rental costs, and a great majority of the self-employed are owner-occupiers. Another factor tending to reduce numbers of people entitled to housing benefit and council tax benefit is the inclusion of family credit and disability working allowance in the assessed income.

Nevertheless, DSS statistics show that considerable numbers of people depend on the means-tested benefits available to help people meet the costs of rented housing and local taxes. Changes in the housing benefit rules in recent years, and successive replacement of domestic rates by community charge and then council tax, mean that it is hard to follow trends.

By May 1989, some 17,700 claimants were receiving housing benefit (including rate rebates) in Great Britain, on the basis of self-employed earnings (DSS, 1991a). This figure did not include owner-occupiers in Scotland, where the community charge had just replaced domestic rates. Almost 37 per cent of the 17,700 were local authority tenants, and the rest were more or less equally divided among private tenants and owner-occupiers. Almost seven per cent were entitled to the lone parent premium in their housing benefit. A survey conducted for the National Audit Office (NOP, 1990) found that almost a third of self-employed family credit recipients also received housing benefit (including those in Scotland). Around 46,000 families received family credit on the basis of self-employed earnings in 1990, which meant that over 15,000 would also be receiving housing benefit. This suggested that the number of self-employed people without dependent children receiving housing benefit was relatively small, despite the fact that at that time the capital limit was set at £16,000, rather than £8,000, as for income support and family credit.

Domestic rates were replaced by the community charge in Scotland in 1989, and in England and Wales in 1990. Community charge benefit followed closely the previous arrangements for rebating rates in housing benefit, although there were no non-dependent deductions, and since 1991, no minimum benefit rule. People receiving income support were entitled to 80 per cent of their community charge liability. Those not in receipt of income support had their benefit assessed in a similar way to housing benefit. However, the maximum available was reduced by 15 per cent of any net income above the applicable amount.

The increased number of people liable to pay the community charge meant that community charge benefit had a larger potentially eligible population than housing benefit. By May 1992, 35,000 people not in receipt of income support and claiming community charge benefit had net income from self-employment. Our interviews with self-employed family credit recipients were carried out under the community charge regime, before its replacement by council tax.

As with all income-related benefits, take-up of housing benefit is incomplete. Self-employed people are excluded from official take-up estimates of housing benefit because information on incomes recorded in FES and used to calculate take-up is not in the right form to model eligibility of self-employed people. The latest government expenditure-based estimate of take-up by employees was in the range 91 - 95 per cent, in 1992 (Department of Social Security, 1995).

Unlike those for income support and family credit, applications for housing benefit and council tax benefit are dealt with at a local authority level. The current system for assessing self-employed incomes for housing and council tax benefits are based on similar principles as for family credit. There are some differences in what is to be included as income. For example, child benefit and one parent benefit are taken fully into account for housing benefit and council tax benefit but ignored for family credit, where the level of child credits is already set to take these benefits fully into account.

In terms of how housing benefit is administered, the tone of the housing benefit manual is less categorical and lays more emphasis on the importance of discretionary decision-making about self-employed income than does the guidance issued to family credit officers. The latter tends to focus more on obtaining information that can be dealt with in a more standardised way. Self-employment has not had a high profile as a problem area in housing benefit, unlike in family credit. This may be because individual housing benefit officers generally meet relatively few claimants in this category, or because the many other problems associated with the introduction and administration of housing benefit have received more attention. Also, the position of self-employed family credit recipients has excited interest partly because of the disparities in average awards received when compared with employees. With housing benefit, community charge benefit and now council tax benefit, it is not as easy to compare the value of awards, because rent levels differ between properties, community charges differed between local authorities, and council tax varies both by local authority area and the value of property.

In their discussions with housing benefit officers prior to the 1988 changes to the scheme, Walker et al. (1987) found that local authorities saw the assessment of self-employed incomes as a problematic area even though the number of cases was relatively small. There were widespread suspicions of dishonesty and officers saw the accounting figures provided as often misleading. Thus they had devised a range of *ad hoc* procedures in order to penetrate the information provided and would often engage in 'bluff' or 'horsetrading' to arrive at an agreed figure. More recently, the Association of Metropolitan Authorities reported problems with self-employment and housing and community charge benefits. A document tabled at a meeting of the Housing Benefit Standing Committee (Newcastle City Council Housing Department, 1991) raised several questions on regulations which were seen as either disadvantaging self-employed claimants compared to others, acting against employment initiatives, or being at odds with conventional accounting practice. While administration of housing and community charge benefits for self-employed people could be problematic, those applying for these benefits could also meet difficulties. Early research on perceptions of family credit (Corden and Craig, 1991) showed that self-employed people were among those who were confused about the interaction between family credit and housing benefit.

In this study of self-employed applicants for family credit nearly all the tenants had applied for housing benefit. There was little proper understanding of the interactions between family credit and housing benefit, however. Different claiming experiences and different outcomes from the two benefits meant it could be hard for people to understand that the assessment procedure is based on similar principles. For example, self-employed people whose Inland Revenue certificates had been accepted as evidence of earnings for housing benefit purposes, with few additional questions to answer, found it hard to understand why the family credit assessment could not also be made on that basis. As a result of experience of refusal of benefit, it was a common belief that families were entitled either to housing benefit or family credit but not both.

Most of the self-employed people interviewed were currently making some community charge payments. Only a very small number had decided on principle not to pay, although many families were in arrears. Most of those paying the tax had applied for community charge benefit. Among the very few who had never thought of applying was a couple for whom low income was a completely new experience. As they discussed how they felt about applying, now they had been reminded that people could apply for reductions, they said they disliked the idea of becoming even more dependent on benefits. Embarrassment, and the idea that applying locally for benefits might weaken business confidence, were the reasons given by another couple for deciding not to apply.

As with housing benefit, those who had applied for community charge benefit reported a variety of experiences. Some remembered that things had gone smoothly; others reported a frustrating experience, with too much administration. A common misunderstanding was, again, that it was an 'either/or situation' - getting family credit meant people were not entitled to anything else.

Only two people demonstrated that they understood exactly how family credit affected entitlement to housing benefit and community charge, both of whom were women. A lone mother had been angry to discover that when family credit was introduced, a higher award made her ineligible for housing and community charge benefits. She had preferred the previous situation when she claimed family income supplement - a lower weekly award but a higher housing benefit entitlement, which made her household budgeting easier to manage. The second woman had learned the hard way about the interaction. Not realising that receipt of a family credit award had to be declared as a change in circumstances for assessment of community charge benefit, she ended up having to pay back substantial arrears of community charge. This kind of experience had been reported earlier - people getting into financial difficulty when they accumulated rent arrears through overpayment of housing benefit (Corden and Craig, 1991).

The relative scarcity of research on the procedure for assessment of self-employed people at local authority level, and the accumulating evidence that self-employed applicants for housing benefit received variable treatment which could be problematic, led the authors to conduct an exploratory discussion with a small group of housing benefit officers from three northern local authority areas. The methodology and findings have been reported fully elsewhere (Corden et al., 1993). The findings demonstrated differing approaches to measuring self-employed income between housing benefit officers and family credit officers, and among housing benefit officers themselves. Although housing benefit officers saw themselves as working strictly within regulations, they felt they had considerable scope for deciding how to deal with individual self-employed people, acting on the basis of information provided. Local administration inevitably leads to differences in treatment between authorities. Although officers tried to work towards consistency within their own authority, they found that other authorities did things rather differently in some aspects of their work. The different socio-economic characteristics of their local areas also resulted in a differing range of expertise among staff, according to the types of self-employed occupations common in each area.

The outcome for individual self-employed people is that their income is likely to be assessed differently for different means-tested benefits. It is hardly surprising that claimants we spoke to had little understanding of the assessment of their earnings, and reported different requirements and procedures. Moreover, the interaction between family credit and housing benefit, and the different approaches to assessment, mean that there are likely to be complex individual 'better-off situations' for some self-employed applicants, involving the timing of applications and the way in which financial information is presented (Boden and Corden, 1994). It seems unlikely that claimants or advisers, or even researchers, can expect to make full assessments of possible entitlements in these cases. It follows that estimates of take-up of housing benefit by self-employed people, conducted by researchers without detailed understanding of local practice within individual housing benefit offices, must be approached carefully, and may not be especially useful.

Family credit

One of the policy concerns which prompted this research was the growth in numbers of self-employed families receiving family credit and the relatively high proportion of these families who received the maximum levels of payment. An earlier chapter explored the composition of incomes of self-employed families in the family credit population, and showed how different components of assessable income affected the comparative levels of awards.

In spite of the increase in self-employed recipients, it has been suggested that take-up of family credit among eligible self-employed families may be lower than that for the employed (Lynes, 1988, 1991). It is difficult to test this assumption since official take-up estimates deliberately exclude the self-employed because FES data on self-employed incomes is unsuitable for this purpose. Chapter Three explained the main problem areas in the collection of income data from self-employed people in household surveys.

Problems recognised in collecting income data from self-employed people for purposes of research and analysis are reflected in problems experienced by some self-employed people who are required to provide evidence of earnings for purposes of means-tested benefits. Lynes (1988, 1990) suggested a number of possible reasons why take-up among self-employed people might be low, including assumptions of non-eligibility by potential applicants, problems with the application process and inequities in the income assessment system. Previous work on unsuccessful applicants for family income supplement showed that some self-employed applicants had considerable difficulties with the presentation of their accounts for assessment (Corden, 1987). These problems could be critical for a business in decline which might fail before a benefit decision was reached, or where the business was running on very low profits. Early research on family credit suggested that failure to recognise eligibility might be a particular problem for self-employed people (Corden and Craig, 1991).

Brown (1989) suggested that the point of transfer between income support and family credit could be particularly risky for lone parents if there were delays in the assessment process. Difficulties experienced by the Family Credit Unit in dealing with some self-employed applications did lead to considerable delays in the years immediately following the introduction of family credit (NAO, 1991).

Brown's analysis of case reports from Citizens Advice Bureaux (Brown, 1992) threw some light on reasons for such delays. It could be hard to provide complicated financial information in the way required; a special problem for people for whom English was not their first language. Advice which might have been available from applicants' accountants was sometimes not sought due to reluctance to incur additional cost.

The survey of family credit recipients conducted in 1990 by NOP for the National Audit Office included 73 self-employed people. Of these, nearly a quarter reported some problems in understanding the leaflet or application forms, and the same proportion found it difficult to work out household income. Requests from the DSS for further information had caused problems for nearly a half, and over a third remembered that the time taken to get a decision had been problematic. Getting hold of leaflets or forms in the initial stages, or getting entitlement to family credit after decisions had been made had not, however, usually been difficult. In 1993 a Family Credit Helpline was launched to provide telephone advice about family credit. Most of our research interviews were conducted before this advice service became available.

Our detailed interviews provided opportunities to explore levels of understanding of the rules of this benefit, and to discuss experiences of the application process with both successful and unsuccessful applicants. Those who had received a family credit award explained how they used the money, and discussed the role of family credit in personal and business financial arrangements.

The application process

All the families interviewed had eventually applied for family credit, and most had been successful in their most recent attempt. Findings therefore help us to identify factors in the application process that were experienced as helpful and might be encouraging take-up. Accounts of delays and difficulties on the way to gaining an award, and experiences of unsuccessful applicants show us where people met problems. It is reasonable to project that similar problems may prevent applications from other self-employed people who do not manage to overcome them.

The number of applications made, of course, affects people's perceptions. Some families in the study group had claimed family credit and family income supplement continuously for several years. Each new claiming experience overlaid memories of previous experiences and the effect could be dilution as well as reinforcement of views. Their accounts differed from those of people for whom claiming family credit had been a new experience. What is presented here is thus a distillation of claiming experiences, described retrospectively by a group of claimants, most of whose recent applications had been successful. It is these memories that they take forward into their next applications for family credit, or other benefits as well - since people project experiences from claiming one benefit into expectations of claiming others (Corden and Craig, 1991). It will be these recollections or assumptions that may influence future labour market decisions - an important consideration in view of the volatility of some of the businesses. Additionally, it will be these recollections or assumptions that may be shared with other people including those who might claim family credit, and those who advise and help them or represent their views to policy makers.

Earlier studies have pointed to some of the barriers to recognition of eligibility for in-work benefits (Corden and Craig, 1991). In this study the main barriers identified, to recognition of eligibility for family credit, were:

- problems in self-identification as a 'worker'
  It could be difficult for people to recognise the point at which they crossed administrative bench-marks between being unemployed or out of the labour force and being formally self-employed.

- reduced expectations of availability of in-work benefits to self-employed people
  Low profitability, a normal business risk, had been assumed by some to be outside the province of social security provision.

- problems in conceptualising incomes
  Fluctuations in income, or the way in which financial data was recorded, could make it hard to think in terms of weekly earnings, to compare with eligibility criteria.

These barriers to recognition of eligibility were discussed at length in an earlier publication from the research (Boden and Corden, 1994). Factors that could break through such barriers included direct information or advice from friends or relatives, staff in Department of Employment or housing benefit offices, staff in Enterprise Allowance schemes, book-keepers and accountants.

Seeing advertisements about family credit at a time when people were worried about money could make them consider potential eligibility. Non-working wives mentioned informal discussions with other women in similar family situations as their source of influential information - a gender-related pattern that is known to be important in passing information about family credit among employee recipients (Corden and Craig, 1991).

Earlier research on family credit had suggested that dealing with applications for family credit was generally considered women's business among two-parent families with a male breadwinner who was an employee. Not only did the women deal with the application forms, but they also had a better grasp of the family credit rules (Corden, 1991). The pattern was not so clear in this group of self-employed people. Among couples, self-employed men were often more closely involved with applications than their employee counterparts in the earlier study. This was particularly the case if the man working in a small business also took the main responsibility for financial record keeping, and himself dealt with the Inland Revenue and VAT returns. Such men tended to see applications for family credit in terms of paper work associated with their business, and thus an extension of normal responsibilities. In those families where wives did not write English the man took the entire responsibility for the application procedure.

It was not the case that husbands always took the initiative in getting the form and starting the application however. As seen previously among employees (Corden and Craig, 1991) it was often the women in two-parent families, motivated by the need for housekeeping money, who brought home the form, started filling it in, asked for co-operation in supplying earnings information and monitored subsequent enquiries and their husband's response. Men were sometimes more doubtful about making applications than their partners and had to be persuaded to supply the information needed. Previous experiences of claiming out-of-work benefits put some men off. A taxi driver and his wife agreed that the man did not like dealing with social security matters. He was annoyed by the intrusion in his life, the time it took, the letters backwards and forwards, and the expense of the stationery and stamps on both sides. It was his partner's need for extra housekeeping money that made her persist in getting him to co-operate. On both occasions they had applied for family credit this caused domestic tension.

A construction worker and his wife also agreed that the woman had been the main source of energy in their application. He just did not believe that they would get anything. 'I was a bit dubious about all that free money. I couldn't see it happening myself'. He was persuaded to fill in forms and reply to extra questions, but the eventual refusal confirmed his views that it had been wasted effort. He was currently unemployed, and the couple were now united in their view that availability of family credit should be discounted in the search for work, because of the income risk associated with the uncertainty of outcome (see McLaughlin et al., 1989).

People in this study were those who, by definition, had overcome initial barriers in making application. Finding that this group included a number of couples who reported tension between them during the application procedures suggests that there are likely to be other couples who do not overcome such differences in attitudes, contributing to non-take-up among self-employed people. Different attitudes between partners were found among business people, subcontracted workers and taxi drivers, alike.

Those self-employed women in two-parent families who are sole earners, and those women who do the book-keeping and keep accounts for their self-employed husbands are in a stronger position in regard to making applications for family credit. They can themselves supply all the information about business activities and income that is necessary to support an application. Husbands only have to be asked to sign initial applications forms, or letters and replies that have been prepared by wives. This was acknowledged as an advantage by some women. A farmer's partner told us that since she prepared the farm accounts she could herself deal with the complete application process. While this was a lengthy business, and she had once experienced refusal as a result of not supplying information within time limits, it was still an advantage to deal with it on her own. 'He doesn't like all the bureaucracy and the form filling - they annoy him more than they do me.'

Other experiences of dealing with initial application forms, supplying information about earnings and responding to subsequent enquiries have been described in an earlier publication (Boden and Corden, 1994). In summary, there was strong criticism of the current form on which financial information was sought. The questions frequently seemed inappropriate, hard to answer and time consuming. There was variable use of accountancy help. Those who had accountants sometimes avoided approaching them for help with family credit because of embarrassment or reluctance to incur additional fees.

It could be difficult to supply financial information in the way required. Trying to telephone the administrative office in order to sort out supplementary enquiries, or to check on the progress of applications led to variable experiences. For some it had been easy to get through quickly to an appropriate person who could deal with the matter helpfully. Others, despite persistent attempts, had never been able to get through to the switchboard. Two families abandoned their applications in the face of perceived problems. A taxi driver had struggled with questions about business premises, goods and equipment on the supplementary form he was asked to submit. For a retailer, the level of financial detail required was too hard for her to manage on her own, and professionally prepared accounts were not yet available.

The main anxieties about the application process that some people retained, and which would accompany their next applications, were the problems associated with supplying information, and the possibility of refusal or delay in payment causing financial hardship. Some people also mentioned anxieties which they remembered from their first application, and these may well be relevant to other potential applicants approaching family credit for the first time. This study confirmed that the name of the benefit has been a problem for some self-employed people, for whom the word 'credit' has special business connotations. A couple, whose business had once been highly profitable, hesitated before applying for family credit.

> We got the impression that because it is called family credit it is going to be like a loan scheme and somehow or other you are going to have to pay all this back.

A further common anxiety had been the possibility of supplying incorrect information. Previous studies have shown that the risk of being thought to be giving misleading information can put people off applying for family credit (Corden and Craig, 1991). This may be a particularly significant barrier for some self-employed people if they are unsure how to supply financial information, or have had problems collating what is required, and feel they may not have got it right.

Difficulties experienced with applications may have a strong effect on people's attitudes and perceptions, and hence influence take-up. There is much to learn about the effectiveness of the administrative procedure by studying examples of delays and difficulties. We conclude, however, by looking at the small group of people who said they saw no problem in applying for family credit and were always satisfied with the procedure. One feature they shared was knowing about the availability of family credit and how to apply in advance of becoming eligible. Included here were lone mothers who had learnt about family credit while doing part-time work on income support and understood how to claim immediately they became eligible. Familiarity with financial reporting procedures was also a characteristic they shared - both lone mothers had accountancy training. Neither found it difficult to supply information about their business and income, and supplementary enquiries had not been hard to deal with. Another option chosen by people without accountancy expertise or familiarity with financial detail, was to supply 'approximate' or 'estimated' figures. When further enquiries were easy to deal with and processed quickly, this left people with the feeling that the application had been straightforward.

These findings from self-employed families who saw no problems attached to family credit showed how important it is that people on income support understand the availability of family credit, so that they apply as soon as they become eligible, avoiding the delays in benefit payments that cause financial problems. One message for policy making is that even if people have relatively low levels of financial expertise, when they understand how to give financial information and why supplementary questions are necessary, they manage the data satisfactorily. The aim must be to design forms and questions seeking information in ways that enable people with no accountancy expertise to approach the task with confidence, and provide what is required. There was immediate response from the DSS to these research findings about problems with the application procedure. A redesigned family credit pack included special information and provision for self-employed people, and new forms for use by self-employed people. Advertising campaigns now include special promotion to self-employed people. Other initiatives included extending 'fast track' application facilities for previously unemployed people to those moving into self-employment, and measures to improve staff training.

Understanding family credit rules

Making a successful claim for family credit did not mean that people had a good grasp of the basic rules. Levels of understanding of the basic structure of the benefit and the main eligibility criteria were generally low. As for the technical rules for assessment of earnings - no applicant fully understood the measure that had been applied, and a good proportion said they had no idea at all.

Those who were aware of the hours requirement (24 hours work weekly at the time of the interviews) tended to be lone parents whose working hours were restricted by child-care responsibilities - especially those who had purposely built up their hours of work in order to claim. Nobody worried about whether they fulfilled any hours requirement prior to application, although some had subsequently realised that time spent on thinking or waiting for telephone calls might not be interpreted as proper work by somebody who did not understand the nature of their occupation. Receipt of enterprise allowance helped to confirm in people's minds that what they were doing was work and could be counted as such. (These issues to do with conceptualisation of work are discussed further in an earlier publication (Boden and Corden, 1994).) More common than awareness or concern about an hours requirement was a lack of recognition that this was an issue of any importance. Many found it difficult to put a number of hours to the amount of work they did, anyway, and 'hours of work' was not a concept that meant much to them in these words.

More people understood that family credit was a benefit for people with children than had been aware of the hours rule. Those who saw the connection with children usually understood that the number of children had some effect but it was less widely appreciated that children's ages made a difference in the assessment of eligibility. Most confident that there was an age effect were parents of teenagers, especially those who had already experienced a drop in family credit when other older children left school, and those who had checked the rules on the application form as children approached school-leaving age.

Nobody in the study group had a full understanding of how their income had been computed for purposes of family credit. The few who felt confident that they had a fairly good grasp of the way their business receipts had been treated all either had some book-keeping training or were long-term claimants. Among those who believed they understood the rules fairly well were two couples who had won appeals against Family Credit Branch decisions at tribunals. Indeed one farmer and his wife had attended three tribunal hearings covering the same application, eventually winning their case.

Apart from this small group, most respondents had little idea how the information they supplied had been used to generate a figure for net earnings, and how deductions for tax, national insurance and private pensions had been made. Several people were surprised by the net earnings figure notified by the family credit branch when an award was made. A craftsman could not understand how his net earnings could be greater than his turnover. On the other hand both child minders were surprised that their earnings were apparently so low - they were both unaware of the special family credit rules for child minders.

When prompted, people thought it likely that there would be some mechanism for considering tax and national insurance contributions in their assessment for benefit but few could suggest how this worked. Those who were not currently paying national insurance contributions anyway, or had not yet made a tax return from their business, had not thought much about this aspect of family credit. But others who bought national insurance stamps had been puzzled that these payments had apparently not been taken into account, while people who had not yet paid any tax noticed that some kind of tax adjustment had been made when they were notified of their award. The researchers were asked several times whether family credit was taxed. (This information is available in the claim pack.)

Not everybody felt a need to understand how their earnings were computed. If people were satisfied with the amount of the award, or indeed pleasantly surprised to receive such large awards, they often did not mind that they did not understand how it had been worked out. A high degree of trust in the family credit decision-making process was expressed in these situations. Only one person, a shop proprietor, queried an award that was much higher than expected. Most of those who queried their assessments of earnings, as might be expected, had thought their award too low. Requests for copies of the computation led to attempts to discuss details with adjudication officers by correspondence or telephoning. There could be great dissatisfaction if the technical rules for treatment of various components of income and expenses showed divergence from those used for other purposes, such as tax. Such issues were discussed at length in the earlier publication (Boden and Corden, 1994).

Few people in the study group had much in the way of personal savings, as we see in Chapter Seven. Couples who had declared £3-4,000 savings on their application form understood how this had been dealt with, but there was some annoyance that including tariff income from savings in the assessment was a disincentive to build up savings. Those without savings found it hard to think what effect savings might have. The issue was sensitive for some, especially those people who had large personal overdrafts. There were one or two observations that if people had savings they should not be entitled to family credit, or would not need to apply anyway – similar feelings to those expressed by employee recipients in an earlier study (Corden and Craig, 1991).

Three women who received maintenance payments for children knew that this money counted in the family credit assessment. Not everyone knew how child benefit was treated – indeed, some appeared not to have thought about this before. It was a fairly common belief that rent or mortgage costs, or housing benefit affected family credit entitlement, but little understanding of how this worked in practice.

Not surprisingly, given the low level of understanding of the structure and basic rules of the benefit, few people interviewed could suggest to the researcher how measures of earnings and income were translated into size of awards, or reasons for refusal. The same small group who had the best understanding of how earnings were computed were the most confident that they could move from a net earnings figure to an amount of award. There was not the same distinction in levels of understanding about family credit according to gender, that was so strong in the earlier study of employee claimants (Corden and Craig, 1991). Those who had the best understanding included both men and women, and people with the least understanding were of each sex. Levels of understanding were associated more with responsibility for filling in forms and supplying further information, which was not clearly gender related. Lone fathers to whom the world of social security was relatively new had a particularly poor grasp of the rules. Indeed, one said he did not want to know much about family credit, as he hoped to be independent of it soon – a view shared with a husband who had a similar experience of a previous high salary.

Throughout these accounts of the application process and people's levels of understanding we have stressed the importance of remembering that most people in the group had been successful in their last application, and many were currently receiving the maximum award available for their type of family. Despite frustrations and annoyances on the way, and experience of previous refusals in some cases, most were receiving quite high awards when interviewed. Moreover, the group included some people who were long-term claimants, and had used family credit and family income supplement continuously over a number of years to support their self-employed ventures.

These characteristics may be significant when we consider the low levels of understanding of the benefit. Once awards have been made and people are pleased with the amount of money they receive, it may not seem so important to understand the basis on which their eligibility has been established. If people have re-applied continuously over a number of years and family credit has become a regular, reliable source of family income, then the grounds for eligibility may well have been forgotten, or no longer hold much interest. We have seen that the main areas of interest or anxiety were how to supply information about earnings in a way that was acceptable. People were concerned about how to answer questions, not why they were eligible. Such observations make it easier to understand an apparent paradox, that families who were long-term claimants, those to whom family credit was very important, and those who were pleased to receive high awards, often had little understanding of the basic rules of eligibility and structure of the benefit.

Among this group, interest in the family credit rules was renewed when results of applications were unexpected; when people were refused or when a previously high award suddenly dipped in a way that could not be matched with what was happening in their work. If information then seemed hard to get, or when supplied challenged their assumptions, dissatisfaction rose quickly.

It must be a cause for concern that this group of successful applicants was apparently poorly equipped for passing on information about family credit to other potential applicants. We know that information and help from recipients of family credit can be a powerful influence in triggering applications (Corden and Craig, 1991). However, few of the people interviewed in this study were in a position to provide much in the way of accurate basic information that might help another family (employed or self-employed) recognise eligibility, for example a simple explanation of the hours requirement, thresholds for capital, or children's age bands. This lack of general understanding of the benefit may help to explain another finding. The informal networks (friends and relatives) of the people running businesses appeared to contain high proportions of self-employed people. Indeed, several people interviewed said that nearly all their personal friends who worked were self-employed. Yet only a few business people had talked about family credit within these informal networks. It may be that self-employed people do not have many chances of getting authoritative help or information about family credit within their own informal networks because other self-employed people who receive family credit are not alert to the basic eligibility criteria, or in a position to pass on information. (There may also be avoidance of such discussion by business people, as we shall see later.)

If this is a general pattern, then exceptions are particularly interesting. The partner of a share fisherman had one of the highest levels of understanding of the benefit among the group. She offered some explanation of the 70 per cent taper, felt confident about the basic rules and had fairly accurate understanding of the treatment of different components of income. On a past occasion she had been successful in an appeal to a Tribunal, concerning the earnings to be taken into account in measuring income. She told us that 'family credit is fairly well known among fishing families'. The fishing industry is one occupational group in which there has been organised representation in respect of family credit, with media publicity in the national and trade papers (*The Scotsman*, 9 July, 1991). The guidance for assessment of earnings of share fishermen was adjusted in 1991. Our respondent was unaware of these national developments, but confirmed that family credit was a subject for discussion, and information sharing within her local community. In considering ways of increasing take-up among self-employed people, it may be useful to think about targeted approaches to particular occupational groups and professional associations.

Method of payment

Since managing businesses tends to require use of bank services, including cheques and other kinds of non-cash transactions, we might expect that self-employed people would be specially inclined to use the automatic credit transfer system to receive family credit.

However, this was not the case: only a small number of recipient families chose to have family credit paid into a bank or building society account. Some women who were sole earners, and some in two-parent families who had responsibility for managing family budgeting said that it was easier to have the various components of family income 'in the same place'. Another reason for preferring to have family credit paid into a bank account was privacy - a woman who lived in a small village did not want to be seen cashing an order book in the local post office. A lone father had chosen automatic credit transfer because he liked to use cheques and credit cards for family budgeting. In addition, 'this provided a way of maintaining some credibility with my bank manager; so he sees some money coming in regularly!' Most recipients, however, chose to draw family credit at the post office and most preferred to draw the benefit weekly.

In nearly all two-parent families who had order books, the woman drew the weekly cash and controlled its spending as part of her general overall responsibility for household budgeting – the pattern evident among employee recipients in the earlier study (Corden and Craig, 1991) and in other research on low-income households (Wilson, 1987; Pahl, 1989). If the man drew the benefit while at the post office on work-related business (buying postage stamps or national insurance stamps) he often handed it straight to his wife.

Use of family credit

The use of family credit in household financial management was one of the key issues discussed with self-employed families. Drawings from business income were usually kept to a minimum in order not to increase overdrafts. Even where larger bills were paid from business income, family credit and child benefit were often the main sources of ready cash for regular household expenditure. As such they played an important role in maintaining living standards. The following chapter looks closely at the families' overall living standards. Here we are concerned with the way they used family credit.

Because managing on a low income was a matter of constantly juggling sources of income and items of expenditure, the particular use of a specific sum of benefit did not always seem relevant to people. Family credit was often just another source of cash for use on whatever was needed that week. Nevertheless, a number of core items were mentioned regularly as the needs which respondents saw the benefit as contributing towards. Those most often mentioned were food and other weekly household shopping, children's clothes, nappies, rent and mortgage payments, fuel, catalogue payments, and school fares and dinners.

When use of family credit was specific it often figured as part of a carefully planned budget. To some extent this depended on the size of award - high awards sometimes seemed to 'match' regular expenses, and then it seemed sensible to earmark the benefit. One woman, for example, had found that her award was almost the same as her weekly fuel costs. She would cash the family credit each week, buy the fuel stamps needed, and use the small amount left over towards school dinners.

A particularly interesting issue is the use of family credit for business expenses, reported by a few people. This was usually done to ease cash flow when business bills had to be met, or immediate cash payments were necessary and family credit happened to be available. Expenses met in this way included petrol for business use, occasional small purchases of materials, repairs or advertising. At the hotel, the window cleaner had been paid by drawing family credit, and casual wages to other staff had occasionally been paid in this way. A consultant had settled an outstanding VAT bill using the lump-sum payment of family credit arrears.

A more regular use of family credit for business purposes was described by a farmer, the only man among the two-parent households who both drew and kept control of family credit. He made some of the money available for rent and food, but expected also to spend £10 weekly on petrol for the vehicle he needed for his work. There was then usually some left over, which was used to buy animals. The interview schedule in this study was not suitable for discovering how the woman felt about this use of family credit or her husband's similar control of child benefit. The extent to which she and the four children eventually benefited from the social security income invested in the business would depend on the extent to which he made any earnings available.

The partner of a scrap dealer also described how family credit might be needed to pay for essential repairs to the truck. It was apparently acceptable to her to pass the weekly benefit to her partner for this kind of expenditure, when needed, instead of using it for food. She recognised that, in the long term, the family depended on the man being able to go on trading.

The implications for families who use social security benefits for business expenses are interesting. The assessment for family credit treats as earnings any social security benefit that has been introduced into the business (Boden and Corden, 1994). Thus the regular use of family credit (or child benefit), or the use of lump-sum payments of arrears of family credit to settle business bills, could have the effect of inflating earnings for the next assessment of family credit, as well as reducing money available for household budgeting. Whether this effect does operate will depend on whether the transactions are apparent in the documentation made available for assessment of earnings. Accounts prepared professionally, which include a proprietor's capital account, are likely to make this use of benefit visible. It is not necessary for a benefit to be named in accounts for its use to be identified – benefits introduced may well appear in ledgers and accounts as 'cash introduced'. For example, normal commercial accounting techniques and their current interpretation in assessment for family credit make it likely that if somebody had settled a £500 VAT bill using family credit arrears, and submitted professionally-prepared business accounts for the next assessment of family credit, earnings would be assessed as £500 higher than if business income or overdraft had been used.

There was little evidence that payments for business expenses, made using family credit, would regularly be recorded as cash introduced into the business. For example, use of family credit to buy animals and petrol was not apparent from the information supplied on the forms submitted by the farmer, and was not treated as cash introduced. In such cases, while earnings were not inflated, if benefits were used for business payments this might have a marked impact on cash available for household expenditure.

It is important to remember that many of these families received a higher proportion of their income from benefits (and maintenance) than from earnings. What earnings there were often came unevenly. There were also a small number of businesses which technically produced no earnings, but were trading at a loss. Any withdrawals from bank accounts increased bank overdrafts for these families. The facility to draw family credit in cash was then even more important, providing a cash supply without incurring bank charges. It was especially frustrating not to be able to have access to this weekly cash while waiting a long time for adjudication decisions. Families who were confident about eligibility knew they would eventually get a lump sum for arrears, but what they wanted was a steady supply of weekly cash.

As in the overall family credit population, most of the self-employed people in this study group had relatively high awards. There were high levels of satisfaction at the amount of money received. It was common for the researchers to hear that family credit was 'a big help' or 'a very good thing', and that respondents were 'very pleased', 'quite satisfied' or 'really grateful'. One or two expressed even stronger feelings. Their benefit had seemed 'a lifesaver' and it was common for people to say that they 'could not manage without family credit' or 'it would be impossible to do this work without'. Only very few people in the study group were dissatisfied with the current levels of their awards. A farmer and his wife had received above £50 on each of two previous applications, but their last award had plummeted to under £2 despite yearly accounts which showed a business loss of over £8,000. The farmer was certain that a mistake had been made, had appealed, and was withholding his national insurance contributions as a demonstration of his dissatisfaction.

There was universal knowledge about the availability of free prescriptions and reduced dental charges among these families. People who wore spectacles also tended to know that charges were reduced using family credit. There was less certainty here about the mechanism, and people said it was difficult to work out in advance how much they would have to pay for glasses. This is the same finding as in an earlier study with employee families (Corden and Craig, 1991).

There was strong support for the availability of these passport benefits, and particular appreciation that people could have necessary dental treatment that they could not afford to pay for. Free prescriptions were a considerable help to people who needed regular medication for ulcers, angina, back pain, blood pressure and depression. Parents whose health was good, did not need spectacles and only went for occasional check-ups at the dentist still emphasised the value to low-income families of these benefits.

Among those who could have claimed passport benefits there was some sensitivity, and some non-take-up. This was mentioned, particularly, by people who knew personally the chemist counter staff, or the dentist's or optician's receptionists, and those who felt it was important to maintain business standing in local communities. If business people were seen to be in financial difficulty, local business confidence could drop – bills might be called in earlier, or bookings not confirmed. Some people were selectively sensitive in this respect. The same person who would use the passport facilities at the dentist and optician in the nearest market town where she did not know staff personally, chose to pay for her regular prescription because she was too embarrassed in her local village chemist.

One or two people mentioned their surprise and appreciation at some of the local services that were available at concessionary charges, using family credit order books, for example leisure facilities. There were disappointments about the passport facility, too. The mother of a disabled teenager had hoped that her maximum family credit award would be a passport to claiming fares to hospital to visit him during his long stays. Fares to take him and fetch him home were reimbursed, but not her £2 daily bus fare to visit him during a five-week stay. (Nor would this person have been entitled to any help from the social fund for this purpose.)

We have chosen to present in some detail findings about the claiming experience and use of family credit by self-employed families, since so little was known previously about this. We conclude this section on family credit by drawing together what we have learned so far about the role of the benefit for self-employed people.

The role of family credit

Other studies have demonstrated a number of roles for family credit in the waged economy. We know that the benefit can influence moves out of unemployment and help people to stay in low-waged work, can act as a 'stepping stone' for lone parents moving from part-time work and income support, and can help to prevent hardship among families with children

(Corden and Craig, 1991; Marsh and McKay, 1993). Similar roles were apparent among this group of self-employed people.

Incentives to work

Family credit did provide an opportunity for people to move off out-of-work benefits by trying to start a new business. Men and women breadwinners recognised the incentive of family credit in maintaining minimum living standards for their families while they tried to re-enter the world of work by working on their own account. Sometimes this incentive was seen alongside enterprise allowance and/or housing benefit as a package of support available, but for others, just the knowledge that family credit was available was sufficient.

It was not easy to assess the extent to which family credit was keeping people in work. Business owners tended to reject this idea, arguing that their personal characteristics and work satisfaction were more important than availability of benefit. Indeed, some had demonstrated this by staying in business despite previous refusals of family credit. Nevertheless, some of those who had been in the same business for several years agreed that it had probably only been possible to organise their lives in this way because of continuous availability of high levels of family credit. Those who had turned to taxi driving as an alternative to unemployment agreed that, when they had discovered how little they could earn each week, they would have had to return to income support to support their families if family credit had not been available.

A 'stepping stone' for lone parents

Our findings confirm that availability of family credit can help self-employed lone parents already working part-time to increase their hours of work and move off income support, in the same way as has been demonstrated for wage-earning lone parents in previous research (Corden and Craig, 1991; Marsh and McKay, 1993). The incentive came not only from knowing that they would be better off financially and progressing towards independence, but also from being able to avoid negative aspects of being an income support claimant, including particular problems of demonstrating self-employed earnings for the purpose of income support assessment. The transition from out-of-work to in-work benefits did not always go smoothly, however.

Women who were using family credit as a 'stepping stone' had chosen their self-employed occupation to fit around the care of their own young children, either when they lived with former partners or when they started small amounts of part-time work on income support. Their work was often home based and had started on a small scale, sometimes with little thought that it might eventually evolve into self-employed work as the sole family earnings. Family credit had helped to move them along the path.

Self-employment did offer advantages to some lone parents, compared with trying to work for an employer. They saw no opportunities for waged work that would fit in with their family commitments. By working as self-employed they created their own job opportunities, in which they had some control over the amount of work they did and the time of day at which they did it. Self-employment also enabled some lone parents to work at home, which could seem an advantage to people with young children, large families, special caring responsibilities or lack of confidence in working for an employer.

'Breaking the fall'

Marsh and McKay (1993) used the term 'parachute claimants', to describe people for whom family credit arrested the fall from dual earnings, when a couple's main breadwinner lost his job. The second earner could boost the lower income with family credit until the other parent returned to work.

There were some examples of this among the self-employed families in our study, but there were also other ways in which family credit could be said to 'break the fall'. Rapid decline in business profitability meant that some parents were desperate for regular sources of household income, while people whose profits had been steadily reducing over several years had been able to depend on increasing proportions of benefit in their family incomes, using family credit. Major business collapse usually meant that the amount of money available through family credit was too small, on the scale of expenditure required, to be the means whereby a business might be 'rescued'. What it offered was a means of family support while people waited for an upturn in profitability, or made other long-term decisions about future employment. One or two older parents were using family credit to 'coast down' towards retirement.

Substitution for a second wage

The parachute effect discussed above included situations where family credit had been used by couples to offset loss of one breadwinner's earnings. Other women talked about family credit as a source of income which enabled them to delay taking on the role of dual earner. Those women in two-parent families who preferred to be at home while their children were young explained that family credit meant that they could do this.

Some women had no possibility of joining their spouses in self-employment because of the nature of that work (for example, taxi driving, subcontracted construction work or fishing). They knew that they would eventually have to get part-time or full-time jobs to supplement their partners' low earnings. For the time being, family credit provided enough. Some of these women thought that they would not have been able to earn as much as their family credit award, anyway, because of the lack of job opportunities or their level of skills and experiences.

Preventing hardship

Marsh and McKay's (1993) analysis of the effects of family credit on families' relative material well-being raised a number of interesting issues. They constructed a seven-point index of relative financial and material stress, and scored the families surveyed in 1991, all low-income families with children. According to their rule-of-thumb measure of severe hardship - a score of three or more on the seven-point scale - 20 per cent of employee recipients in their study were in severe hardship, and 26 per cent of the self-employed. They argued, from their analysis, that claimant couples were only slightly better off than those out-of-work, while eligible non-claimant families appeared better off than the eligible claimants. They suggest a number of possible reasons for such findings, which are explored further in Chapter Seven.

In our study of self-employed families, the generally high family credit awards reflected very low earnings, and the report has explained in detail why earnings were so low in some families. It was common for families to receive more money from benefits than from earnings, and some were running businesses at a loss, with the only income properly available for family spending coming via benefits (or increased debt). The language in which they described family credit, for example, as a 'godsend', reflects their own assessments of the help available in this way. Some explained how they would have to cut down household expenses if their applications were refused. Another alternative mentioned might be to look for additional work, for example doing paid work at night in addition to daytime earnings from self-employment. People said this would be a strain on their own health, and family relationships.

There were, however, a number of families where it was hard to argue that family credit was preventing hardship that would otherwise accompany low earnings from self-employment. As we have already explained, it seemed likely that without family credit some of the businesses could not have existed anyway. In addition, the group included a small number of families who observed that their domestic circumstances must seem hard to equate with eligibility for family credit. The appearance of such households was of comfortable, well-furnished properties, high levels of consumer goods and assets, and good diet (from farm or country produce, or hotel or restaurant cooking). Living standards were being maintained by increasing overdrafts and loan commitments, use of assets acquired in more prosperous times and reliance on family help. Several families also described a wide network of contacts and support that was part of the life-style associated with certain occupations, or the personalities and interests of those who own their own business. The subsequent levels of participation in society, and the opportunities for the children in such families, suggested a 'richness of life' that had a poor fit with traditional ideas about financial hardship, poverty and exclusion as a result of low earnings, but had little to do with family credit.

When asked how they viewed their overall financial situation, families often pointed out that effects of their current low incomes were to some extent hidden, in large and increasing overdrafts and bank loans, in mortgage and rent arrears, in business debts. The resulting anxiety and financial distress could be a different experience, some suggested, from that of families who had always had low incomes, or did not have access to large amounts of credit. It was no less real, they emphasised; indeed it might be more acute, compounded by the possibility of financial disaster and the shock of discovering themselves in this position. The following chapter pursues these issues in a closer examination of living standards and quality of life.

Enabling care

Another role for family credit was seen by people who needed to combine paid work with caring responsibilities. We have already discussed how lone parents were helped to combine child care and self-employment. We have also seen how some women in two-parent families felt able to choose child care rather than paid work for longer than would otherwise be possible.

In addition, some parents saw a link between family credit, self-employment and the extra caring responsibilities they had on top of normal child-care responsibilities for younger children. Opportunities to work flexibly, to be at home while working or within easy reach were all advantages for people who helped care for family members with disability or chronic ill health. At the same time, earnings could be constrained by these responsibilities. Family credit was a way of enabling self-employment, maintaining flexibility while securing income. Self-employment enabled people to care for family members, and family credit helped them to be self-employed, as well as making up incomes reduced by constraints on the work they could do. All the pieces in this jigsaw were important.

Breadwinners who themselves had health problems that had a significant impact on the type and amount of work they could do, saw similar links. Work could be managed within a self-employed regime, and family credit both helped them be self-employed and compensated for their reduced earnings.

'Ready cash' for money management

While the roles for family credit in labour market decisions, opportunities and living standards that have so far been described were all important, so also were the practical ways the money could be used in budgeting strategies. The family credit awards provided regularity and security of a proportion of family income - a particular advantage when earnings were unpredictable or uneven. 'There's a lot of security in that regular payment.' Moreover, order books provided weekly cash. For people doing business mainly by cheque or credit card, finding cash for personal expenditure could otherwise be a real problem. The payments could help to prevent bank overdrafts increasing, thus avoiding additional expenditure in bank charges, easing relationships with bank managers, and reducing anxiety about the extent of debt. Some had found it helpful to use the benefit for business use, either in occasional emergencies, or on a regular basis to ease business cash flow or increase turnover.

These practical issues of money management were considered important across the whole group of people. Indeed, among those who had become used to depending on family credit or family income supplement over a number of years, these roles for the benefit were often the first that came to mind.

Job creation

Our study showed that with family credit and other in-work benefits (and enterprise allowance in some cases) people could 'make' work from their own skills and interests, and create new jobs for themselves where there were none before. This could be a risky process. Jobs so created sometimes did not last long, and could lead to unemployment and debt. But the process of job creation could be successful and some had managed to stay in such jobs for several years. Financial returns were modest but job satisfaction was high. The study suggested that, within the wider economy, family credit has some role in the process of job creation.

Such findings raise questions about the policy aims of family credit and how it fits into the wider economy. It was possible to stay in some of these newly created 'jobs' and support a family only because of the availability of in-work benefits, including family credit. Some might query whether it is a proper function of a social security benefit to maintain otherwise non-viable small business ventures over many years. Similarly, how far is it sensible for the availability of in-work benefits to encourage people into risky ventures which may end in debt and unemployment? We have more to say about this later on.

The findings also raise interesting questions about our current assumptions about 'work', and the terminology available for describing and categorising employment activity. Is 'a self-employed worker' an appropriate description for a person who is engaged for long hours over a period of several years in an unprofitable occupation and whose main income comes from social security benefits? This study provides some information and insights which help inform such debate. Respondents themselves found it difficult to discuss ideas of this kind. In general, they tended not to have a 'global view' of their position as self-employed people and many found it hard to talk about general issues of social security provision or their own position within the wider economy.

In terms of job creation for other people within the small businesses supported by family credit, the study showed that, although a number of jobs had been created, many of these were short-term, low-paid and without the security and rights associated with employee status. It is not possible to evaluate these job opportunities, however, without further investigation into the circumstances of those people who took the jobs, and what happened to them when the work ended.

This concludes the overview of the various roles that family credit plays in self-employed families. Some of these roles are familiar from earlier work, but our study of self-employed families has thrown into focus roles that have been less frequently articulated previously, and bring family credit into a wider economic perspective.

The section on family credit has included much material, since this benefit was the focus of our research. The chapter continues by looking at other means-tested benefits available to self-employed families.

Disability working allowance

The disability working allowance is a new in-work benefit for people with disabilities, introduced in April 1992. It is modelled on family credit and is available to disabled people with low earnings from either employment or self-employment. In Chapter Four we discussed the position of disabled people in the labour market. Many who want to work face severe disadvantages, and for them self-employment can be an important option. Traditionally, social security for disabled people was based largely on the premise that they do not work, and financial support was made available mainly through invalidity benefit (for those with appropriate contributions records), and severe disablement allowance and income support (for those without). Disabled people with children might be entitled to family credit if they worked for more than 24 hours a week (16 hours from April 1992). People with reduced earnings capacity through disability might retain entitlement to income support if they worked more than 24 hours weekly (the threshold for non-disabled people) but only the first £15 of weekly earnings was disregarded in the assessment for benefit. This structure of benefits meant that social security arrangements themselves could create disincentives for disabled people to try to enter work. First, there was little possibility of building on partial capacity for work via the benefit system. Secondly, disabled people were unable to experiment and test their capacity for work without losing entitlement to long-term incapacity benefits.

The disability working allowance was aimed at reducing these problems. The objective was to help disabled people with some capacity for work to take up or remain in work. Disability working allowance aims to supplement low earnings, from paid work or self-employment, so that disabled people whose earning capacity is reduced are not worse off financially than they would be on long-term incapacity benefit. Disability working allowance supplements low earnings at a higher rate than family credit, regardless of the presence of dependent children. Secondly, the benefit should help to remove one element of risk for people who would like to try working, but are unsure how they might manage or who expect that their capacity for work to fluctuate.

The original Government estimate was that disability working allowance would benefit some 50,000 people. This estimate was based on the OPCS disability surveys, and included those currently working who would become eligible (*Hansard*, 1991). There were no estimates of the number of disabled people likely to claim on the basis of self-employed earnings. However, given the importance of this type of work for people disadvantaged in the labour market it seemed reasonable to assume that their numbers would be substantial.

First findings from an evaluation of disability working allowance (Rowlingson and Berthoud, 1994) confirm that this benefit may be of special importance to self-employed people. One-quarter of the sample of workers receiving disability working allowance were found to be self-employed. So far, no further details about this group are available, but results are awaited with interest. The range of occupations and location of work will provide valuable insights into opportunities available for disabled workers. Evidence about the administrative procedure for assessing self-employed earnings of this group will also be of considerable interest, in view of the attention this has attracted in respect of family credit.

Overall, preliminary findings about disability working allowance have been somewhat disappointing. One conclusion was that although disability working allowance has helped a significant number of people it has not persuaded many disabled people to move into work. Among those who are eligible, only a small proportion are receiving disability working allowance. By March 1994 there were only 3,680 recipients (*Hansard*, 1994). Using the results of the evaluation survey, Rowlingson and Berthoud suggested that the level of take-up was almost certainly lower than a third, and likely to be between one-tenth and a quarter. They pointed to the problems in estimating take-up from the results of questions asked in an interview survey, problems that have been emphasised previously (Corden and Craig, 1991). In view of the proportions of self-employed people apparently within scope of this benefit, and the known problems of assessing earnings of self-employed people, there is likely to be room for considerable caution here.

Health and education benefits

People receiving income support or family credit are exempt from NHS charges for prescriptions, optical and dental charges, and a number of other health-related costs. Others are exempt through pregnancy, or a range of medical conditions. Those who would otherwise have to pay but still have low incomes can apply for partial help with some costs under the Low Income Scheme, administered by the Health Benefits Unit in Newcastle. The income assessment for entitlement for help with health charges is a modified version of that for income support. No systematic research has been carried out on this scheme and it is not known how many self-employed people apply, or whether there are problems with the way their incomes are assessed. A recent Citizens Advice Bureau report (NACAB, 1991b) suggested that there are considerable problems with the complexity of the scheme overall. Bureaux around the country receive around 200,000 enquiries each year on health issues, most of which are about these benefits.

Another area where the assessment of incomes from self-employment might arise as an issue is in local authority educational welfare benefits, including free school meals, school clothing grants and educational maintenance grants. Corden's (1985) study of take-up of family income supplement among clients of the educational welfare department in Cumbria found a number of cases where the local authority assessed the incomes of self-employed clients quite differently from the Family Income Supplement Unit, causing the clients some confusion. This is not surprising given the different nature of the two organisations, but it shows again how maintaining a variety of different means-tests can cause problems and inequities, particularly where self-employed incomes are concerned.

Enterprise Allowance/Business Start-Up Scheme

Though not a social security benefit, the Enterprise Allowance Scheme (EAS), called the Business Start-Up Scheme since 1991, has been a key element in the Government's promotion of job creation through individual enterprise. It aimed to smooth the transition from unemployment to self-employment by guaranteeing some basic income during the initial start-up phase. Brown (1992) points out that although not actually a social security benefit, EAS was linked to the benefit system by the requirement that participants were previously receiving a benefit for unemployment. She describes individual cases, drawn from Citizens Advice Bureaux reports, to illustrate the links between enterprise allowance and social security benefits.

The scheme was introduced in 1982 on a pilot basis and started nationally in 1983. Until April 1991 it provided a standard £40 per week for one year to people previously unemployed who wanted to start a small enterprise and had £1,000 capital available for investment. People joining the scheme were also offered information and guidance sessions on running a small business. In April 1991 responsibility for running the scheme passed to private sector Training and Enterprise Councils (TECs) which were given greater discretion about how to organise the programme. Participants might receive between £20 and £90 per week for a minimum of 26 and a maximum of 66 weeks. Similar initiatives have been pursued in a number of other countries. Demonstration projects in two States of the USA (Massachusetts and Washington) suggested that take-up was low, but most participants pursued their business for some time (OECD, 1993). The OECD review (1993) of studies in Australia, Iceland, United Kingdom and Denmark showed that it was hard to estimate the net employment effects of such schemes.

The EAS has been evaluated at various stages for its job creation effects by means of surveys of participants (Allen and Hunn, 1985; Department of Employment, 1986) and qualitative interviews (Gray and Stanworth, 1986). However, as with many specifically labour market-focused studies, little attention has been directed towards the role of any other social security benefits in helping to sustain the participant businesses. Corden and Craig's (1991) work on claimant perceptions of family credit found some evidence that the 'package' of enterprise allowance plus family credit had influenced respondents to move into self-employment, but only a very small number of those interviewed were self-employed. The way family credit administrative data is collected makes it difficult to identify how many recipients are also getting enterprise allowance/business start-up. Nor was it possible from any of the published data to tell how many EAS participants had dependent children and thus might also be eligible for family credit.

The same problem exists with housing benefit: local authorities tend not to keep any separate record of claimants where enterprise allowance/business start-up is in payment. However, the local authority paper referred to above (Newcastle City Council Housing Department, 1991) suggested that most self-employed housing benefit claimants were just starting up in business or within their first two years of operation. The paper argued that taking enterprise allowance into account as gross income was a discouragement to enterprise and compared this regulation to those covering training premiums, bonuses and career loans under the Department of Employment's Adult Employment Training Scheme, which are disregarded as income.

Between 1982 and 1988 more than 300,000 people participated in the scheme (NAO, 1988). The evaluation surveys show that the participants have been predominantly male, with around half under 35 years of age. Half were also unemployed for six months or more before joining the scheme. Most businesses set up were in the service sector, but the biggest single area of work was in construction, mostly small repairs. There is also some anecdotal evidence that in some sectors the EAS has encouraged the growth of labour-only subcontracting (Gray, 1987). One survey found that 61 per cent of those who completed the twelve-month term of enterprise allowance were still in business two years after the enterprise allowance payments had finished; four per cent were self-employed in another business and 18 per cent employed elsewhere (Department of Employment, 1986). According to the NAO, the overall survival rate three years into the scheme was 57 per cent of those who completed the twelve-month term of enterprise allowance receipt. The most vulnerable period for business appeared to be just after the allowance stops: two-thirds of business closures happened at or near this time. There are a number of reasons why this might happen, but one factor for people receiving family credit can be the loss of income without any consequent upward adjustment of benefit.

Survival rates appeared to be higher for men and those over 30, also for those with a part-time working partner, those who had been previously unemployed for only a short time and those who had larger sums to invest in the business at the start. The main reasons given for ceasing trading were too much local competition, a lack of demand for their product or service and cash-flow problems because of insufficient profits. Takings from the business were often low: after two years the median pre-tax weekly profit figure was under £100 and even this was skewed upwards by a small number of high earners.

The EAS is often judged by its effectiveness in reducing unemployment and its net cost to the Exchequer. The first of these is difficult to measure precisely because of the uncertain parameters of the 'deadweight' and 'displacement' factors. 'Deadweight' refers to those people who would have started self-employment anyway without the EAS, and 'displacement' occurs where new EAS-supported businesses displace other existing jobs and businesses. By combining estimates of deadweight and displacement, the Department of Employment has estimated that for every 100 people joining the scheme unemployment fell by 35 during the period of the allowance (Department of Employment, 1986). The NAO (1988) estimated the net cost to the Exchequer in 1987-8, taking account of income support saved and tax revenue gains, as £2,300 per person no longer unemployed.

The NAO also suggested that the Training Commission should consider greater checks on the viability of businesses established under the EAS. Gray and Stanworth (1986) identified two broad groupings within EAS participants - the 'serious' and the 'non-serious'. These categorisations roughly coincided with the different motivations detected for embarking on self-employment, so that those who had positively chosen to start a business were more likely to adapt to the demands of running it than those whose main motivation was simply to escape unemployment. This did not mean that some of the latter could not be successful, but most of those identified as 'non-serious' were clearly not suited to running their own businesses. Gray and Stanworth also identified a number of local and regional variations in the form and quality of support and decision making by Manpower Services Commission (MSC) staff which seemed to stem from a policy confusion over strategy for the scheme. This confusion centred on which of the two strategies should take precedence - direct unemployment reduction or longer term economic development.

The previous chapter explained how the availability of the Enterprise Allowance Scheme had influenced some people's decisions about becoming self-employed. Our study was not designed to evaluate this scheme, but it is useful to include here people's general observations.

People who had joined the scheme some years ago, such as one of the new entrants to farming, now had little to say about it. Those who had joined more recently, including all those currently still receiving payments, considered that it had generally been helpful. One aspect particularly mentioned was the availability in a local centre of advice and information that was freely offered without compulsion. People completely new to business had appreciated being helped with cash flows and profit forecasts at an early stage in the development of their ideas. Meeting other people with similar experiences of redundancy or unemployment, with similar hopes and facing the same anxieties, had been useful in early stages.

The main criticisms were that the capital requirement was easy to manipulate, and that there were a number of constraints of timing, for example not being allowed to advertise until the official start date. In addition, one person who had used the enterprise scheme in a business venture which failed, blamed pressure from the DSS in hurrying him into business before he felt ready to start. Once he mentioned that he might be interested in self-employment, he felt he had been swept along too quickly, before he had properly prepared the business premises. He and his former business partner still owed £6,000 from that venture.

In establishing the new enterprise scheme the Government appeared to be placing more emphasis on longer term development than on reducing unemployment. The planning framework for TECs, issued in January 1991 (Department of Employment, 1991b) encouraged them to adopt longer term strategies and gave them greater powers to restrict entry criteria on the basis of business viability or local industrial and labour market conditions. The unemployment qualifying period was reduced from eight to six weeks, and even further for people with disabilities, victims of large-scale redundancies and 'returners' who had been out of the labour market for at least two years.

There are not enough data yet available to indicate effects of these changes. It is not clear, for example, how people with businesses generating low profit margins will manage on enterprise allowance payments below the previous £40 level. Many of those on family credit will already be receiving maximum payments and will not qualify for increased awards. Similarly, self-employed families who receive the higher enterprise allowance over a shorter period may find that they lose much of the extra money by reductions in family credit and housing and community charge benefits. A follow-up telephone survey (Tremlett, 1993) of all new starters on the scheme in May 1991 was conducted in November 1992, 18 months after joining. However, most of the schemes from which participants received their payments were still operating the EAS system of £40 per week when they joined. There was some indication that there has been change in the types of businesses starting up using the scheme. Three industrial sectors covered two-thirds of all businesses started: distribution/catering and repairs (24 per cent), other services (22 per cent) and finance/business services (20 per cent). In terms of 'survival rates', 73 per cent of the scheme participants were self-employed in the same business, 18 months after starting on the scheme. The reason most frequently given by those who left their business was 'not making enough money' to survive.

The Business Start-Up Scheme ceased to recruit in March 1995. Resources previously attached to the scheme are now within the Single Regeneration

Budget (SRB). The SRB will fund locally-designed, economic regeneration projects which will include start-up support where this is seen as a local priority. The nature and extent of start-up support will therefore now vary considerably from locality to locality.

Finally, in this section on business start-up schemes, it is appropriate to mention the Prince's Youth Business Trust (PYBT). The Trust was founded in 1983, and provides business start-up grants and loans, and general advice and support, for disadvantaged young people, focusing help on unemployed young people from inner cities, areas of rural deprivation, the minority communities, people with disabilities and ex-offenders. Finance from the Employment Department boosts money raised in the private sector, and there is a regional network of administration and support.

A recent evaluation of PYBT (Dalgleish, 1993) showed that the average age of recipients was 22 years, and 82 per cent were also on the enterprise allowance scheme, for which unemployment was a condition. Two-thirds of the businesses survived three years. Businesses providing recreational or personal services had, initially, higher survival rates. The majority of businesses were in the services sector, but survival rates in the hotels/catering/repairs businesses were lower. The above report does not mention social security arrangements among the main findings of the evaluation, although some of the reported circumstances of recipients, such as disability, suggest that social security arrangements could well be significant aspects of the young people's lives.

This concludes our chapter on the use of social security benefits by self-employed people. Our study focused on means-tested benefits, primarily family credit. However, in order to understand the importance of means-tested benefits to some self-employed people, it was necessary to explain the general position of self-employed people in the overall British social security system. Setting this context has pointed to many gaps that exist in knowledge about the use of social security by the self-employed, and problems that remain to be resolved in the collection of data and estimates of take-up.

Our interviews showed, however, that self-employed people readily discuss their attitudes and views about financial support. They provide information about their experience of claiming benefits that throws considerable light on their opportunities and problems in the social security system. The people we interviewed were also prepared to discuss in detail how they managed on their low incomes, and the following chapter presents what they told us about their financial circumstances and overall living standards.

7 The living standards of self-employed people

The evidence presented so far in this book suggests that there is a substantial group of self-employed people, working in a variety of occupations from traditional small businesses to forms of marginal sub-contracting, with genuinely low and insecure levels of earnings. We have looked in detail at the work carried out by 73 families who had applied for family credit on the basis of self-employed earnings. Some of these people were higher earners in the past, either as employees or in more successful periods of self-employment, and they came from a variety of backgrounds, both professional and manual.

We have also seen that with the expansion of self-employment in the 1980s in the lower income sector, people working for themselves have had to engage more frequently with the social security system. There is a case for the self-employed having greater access to social insurance schemes, but certainly the means-tested benefits have been of key importance to many self-employed families. Our main focus has been on family credit and we have seen how this plays a number of important roles in helping people enter or survive in forms of self-employed work. In some cases it seems clear that without family credit people could not realistically have continued in their work. It has provided help to families in a position of severe income decline, as well as a step up for some who may go on to achieve lasting independence through their own efforts. The cushion of extra benefit income has also allowed people to pursue interests and enthusiasms which stand little chance of market success.

A period of family credit receipt may therefore represent different stages in the working careers of different families. It was argued earlier that the national income data from sources such as the Households Below Average Income (HBAI) series cannot conclusively show whether very low recorded incomes are a realistical reflection of the whole range of resources available to self-employed people. In the same way, information on earnings assessed for benefit purposes, which relates to a particular accounting period, may in itself tell us little about the living standards currently enjoyed by the family concerned. We now pursue this question further through qualitative interviews and observations which look for the links between declared incomes and current standards of living. The issues discussed include the composition of incomes and savings; other forms of financial or non-cash help; housing circumstances; patterns of financial management and budgeting; the acquisition and possession of household durables and other consumption items; family health and illness; and people's own perceptions of continuity or change in standards of living and quality of life.

The introductory chapter explained why we felt that these topics could fruitfully be explored through qualitative methods. Where appropriate, this chapter also includes some quantitative measures in order to locate the families interviewed within the broader patterns established through other large-scale studies. The detailed exploration of living standards was carried out with a sub-set of the whole study group, whose occupations and working lives have already been discussed in previous chapters. They included a group of people with businesses which showed relatively high turnovers in the period covered by their benefit applications. Since there was some concern that living standards among these families might be inconsistent with the aims of family credit as offering work incentives to low earners, it was important to include examples within the study.

Also, since self-employed family credit recipients apparently have much lower incomes than their employee counterparts, it seemed helpful to introduce some comparison in this component of the research. We therefore extended the work to include some interviews with a small group of families with an employed main earner. As with the self-employed families, they were chosen to include a range of family types, occupations, length of time in receipt of benefit and levels of benefit awards. In total, there were 40 self-employed families in the interview group chosen for the study of living standards, along with 10 employee families. Details of the methods by which the groups were selected can be found in Appendix B. Table 7.1 below shows their occupations.

Table 7.1
Occupations of main earner in families in the living standards study

Self-employed	*Employees*
Farmers (3)	Joiner
Fishermen (2)	Driver
Builders (2)	Garage manager
Child minders (3)	Factory worker
Professional consultants (2)	Maintenance worker
Salesmen (2)	Gardener
Shopkeepers (2)	Clerical workers (2)
Fish processor	Caretaker
Food retailer	Care assistant
Food wholesalers (2)	
Baker	
Taxi driver	
Cleaning contractor	
Motor mechanic	
Plumber	
Gardener	
Transport operative	
Scrap dealer	
Carpet dealer	
Craft retailer	
Giftshop owner	
Hairdresser	
Agents and distributors (2)	
Artist	
Musician	
Potter	
Therapist	
Minister	
Educational business director	

Our first focus of interest was on how much families were actually earning and what other resources they drew on.

Earnings and other financial resources

We saw earlier that there were a number of different routes into self-employment. Patterns of work and previous earnings influenced families' ability to manage on their present low incomes and were likely to affect their current living standards. Current incomes, however, may still be the main determinant of living standards for many families, particularly if earnings have remained around the same level for some time. We look here at business turnover, assets and net earnings; at other sources of regular or occasional income, including maintenance and informal work; at contributions from children; and at the role of non-monetary forms of help such as goods in kind and mutual exchange. We also consider savings and other capital accrued by the families, to see how much living standards during periods of low income were supported or protected by resources accumulated in earlier years.

Business turnover

Business turnover represents the total takings of an enterprise before any allowance is made for the cost of stock or other purchases, labour costs and other business expenses (Boden, 1993). If there are families with large amounts of cash coming in from their enterprises, why is it that they are apparently so poor? The family credit database does not record the level of business turnover, so the proportions of recipients with turnovers at different levels are unknown. Some indications come from a special exercise carried out by the Family Credit Unit, which examined a sample of new or renewed awards in a two-week period in 1993. Twenty-eight per cent of families reported turnovers in the previous six-month assessment period of more than £10,000. Nearly four-fifths were retailers, who made up 31 per cent of the whole sample. Most of the others with half-year turnovers above £10,000 were farmers and market traders (seven per cent each). Twenty-seven cases (eight per cent) had six-month turnovers greater than £40,000. Again, these were mainly retailers. The largest groups in the 'other' category were taxi drivers, child minders and window cleaners.

The exercise also recorded the percentage profits reported by the self-employed recipients relative to their gross receipts. More than a third had 'gross profit ratios'[1] of 20 per cent or less, of whom retailers, market traders and farmers made up the vast majority. This is not surprising, since as Boden (1993) pointed out, many retail businesses have relatively low mark-ups on goods traded.

If the results of this exercise are extrapolated to the whole self-employed recipient population, there may have been just over 11,000 families in 1993 whose businesses took more than £40,000 in gross receipts over the previous year, including some 4,000 with annual turnovers greater than £100,000. Turnovers at this level are not especially high in business terms, particularly for retailers who may have to meet high stock costs.

Apart from the small group specially selected because of their high turnovers, gross receipts for most of the businesses in the whole year preceding the last benefit claim were generally less than £20,000. Particularly low turnovers of under £5,000 were reported by around a fifth of the families.

The higher turnover cases were selected so as to include a range of gross receipts above a threshold of £25,000 for the relevant 26-week period. On the basis of the exercise reported, this threshold would have captured around one in seven of all self-employed recipients. Where businesses had received VAT refunds these were included in the receipts, along with any enterprise allowance paid and the value of any goods or produce taken from the business. It should be also noted that gross receipts would include any capital introduced into a business in the form of loans, according to regulations in force when the families' claims were last assessed. This has been a controversial rule, leading to a number of representations to the DSS by accountants representing self-employed claimants. A decision of the Appeal Court has since stated that certain forms of capital receipt should not be counted as income for family credit (Kostanzuk/Chief Adjudication Officer, by consent, 28 August 1992). One family, for example, had taken out a loan to buy a new car for use in the man's consultancy work, which had the effect of doubling their gross receipts for the year. Several others also had overdrafts included as part of their gross receipts. There was very little understanding of this rule, which appeared to contribute to some people' confusion about DSS assessments of their benefit claims.

Half-year turnovers in these families ranged from around £24,000 to just over £180,000, while gross profit ratios varied from zero, in the case of one loss-making venture, to over 80 per cent in the case of one of the men offering professional consultancy services. The gross profit ratio (GPR) formula can give some idea of whether a business is producing the level of profit to turnover which might be expected in comparable types of enterprise. However, it is generally only applicable to businesses buying and selling goods or adding value to raw materials. In other kinds of self-employed work, especially that involving professional services, GPRs are a less useful indicator, since it is not always obvious what should be included as 'purchases', as distinct from other kinds of business expenses.

For the farmers, purchases included sums spent on livestock, feed, fertiliser and other materials, as well as, in one case, a sum for the lease of milk quotas. Since these costs were substantial their gross profit ratios were relatively low.

The consultant's profit ratio, on the other hand, appears high in comparison with other businesses, partly because one of the major items of expenditure (for the production of advertising brochures) would not be counted as a purchase but as an advertising cost - and would thus come into the net rather than gross profit calculation.

Apart from purchases of stock, the other element commonly included in the gross profit equation for accountancy purposes is labour costs. We have seen that several businesses employed people other than the owner's spouse. This is a feature of small enterprise which might be seen as anomalous to the function and purpose of family credit. How can people who can afford to pay wages to others have net incomes low enough to qualify for supplementation? From the respondents' perspective, however, there was no anomaly. None was in the process of building up their businesses by taking on staff and any expansions which had taken place predated their claims for family credit. A shopkeeper, for example, had borrowed money to buy a second shop shortly before the recession began. This shop currently ran at a loss but he had been unable to sell it. Only by keeping both shops open for 14 hours a day, seven days a week could he generate enough sales to meet the interest payments on his loans. These opening hours required the employment of two young people to work part-time shifts. Interestingly, the owner had not claimed his staff wages as an expense. It is not clear whether this is because he misunderstood the application form or because he was employing them cash-in-hand and was reluctant to declare it. The effect, potentially, was to reduce his benefit entitlement, though in practice it made no difference, since he was judged to be making an overall loss.

Other businesses with some wage costs included the farms, who took on additional labour only as and when necessary for specific, labour-intensive, seasonal tasks. The amounts claimed as expenses for this purpose were small as a proportion of turnover.

One way in which profits may be kept low while the value of a business is increasing, is if the level and value of stock or other assets are allowed to build up. However, Boden (1993) pointed out that inflating the paper value of stock can also be a means of making a business appear more valuable than it is, for the purpose of obtaining loans or credit. Building up stock and assets is a legitimate, indeed laudable, aim in business terms, but it could be seen as problematic for family credit entitlement if profit margins are artificially depressed in the process. The study of the income assessment system (Boden and Corden, 1994) pointed to anomalies in the way the family credit regulations approach this issue in the accruals-based assessment procedures, such that no account can be taken of any net changes in stock levels.

There was no apparent evidence from the interviews or from examination of case papers that people were manipulating the rules to build up stock or assets to levels higher than could reasonably be required for the efficient performance of their business. Nor were the figures for goods purchased, such as perishable food, in excess of what would be seen as a normal level. The one business where the cost of the stock purchased seemed high in relation to sales was the food franchise. Franchises of this kind are financially very complicated, however, and it was clear that the terms of business were largely set by the franchise firm.

Overall, examination of the relationships between gross receipts and gross profits in these businesses suggested few unexpected patterns. The large gaps seen in higher turnover businesses between gross and net profits were attributable to business expenses and costs other than those of goods purchased or wages. Most of the types and amounts of business expenses claimed by applicants against their business takings were unsurprising, given the nature of the particular activities involved. Expenses included fuel and transport, interest on loans for equipment such as tractors, repairs to vehicles, commission paid on sales of livestock, and insurance for stock or machinery. None of these seemed unusual or excessive and all appeared to be legitimate.

The kinds of expenses claimed by people providing professional services may be more unusual so it may be helpful to look, as an example, at one of the consultants - one of the highest net earners in the study. He had supplied information for family credit through a full-year profit and loss account. He had substantial advertising and promotional expenses and although these were eventually recouped from fees, they had to be met from a business overdraft and accrued interest payments. Apart from a secretarial wage, the other main costs were for rent and rates for a workspace and car park, spaces in which he sub-let to cover most of the rent. A further expense was a substantial sum written off for bad debts. This expense was initially disallowed but after queries and protracted correspondence the decision was eventually revised in his favour.

Although most of the business expenses claimed seemed unexceptional, there were three areas where either the costs themselves or the treatment of them in the assessment process require some comment. These were interest payments on large business loans, rents for combined business and domestic property, and franchise costs. Boden (1993) drew attention to businesses that were highly 'geared' - that is, a high proportion of business assets were funded by loans. There was evidence of high gearing in several of the businesses in this study, including those of two farmers and the shopkeeper, such that interest payments consumed substantial proportions of the gross profit. Family credit regulations permit interest payments on loans taken out for legitimate business purposes to be counted as expenses against any business profits, and there was nothing in these cases to suggest that the loans involved were not legitimate under the regulations. Nevertheless, the presence of large business debts of this kind helps to explain how some high turnover businesses show little profit, at least during the period of loan repayment.

There were also two examples where rent for premises use for both domestic and business purposes had not been correctly identified in the family credit assessment. Only that part used for the business should have been included but total rent had been allowed as an expense.

The point has already been made that franchises are a special kind of self-employment, where certain costs are imposed on the franchise holder by the franchising firm. These can, at least in the early years, reduce substantially any gross profits made from the sale of goods. In this case goods were sold to the franchisee at an initial 25 per cent discount, but the business was then subject to a range of fixed or turnover-related costs, including:

- franchise fee of six per cent (of turnover)
- fixed fee for van leasing (£470 per month)
- fixed fee for road tax, insurance and operator's license (£118 annually)
- fixed fee for van maintenance (£150 per month)
- initial stock loan repayment (0.4 per cent of turnover per month)
- canvassing fee (one per cent of turnover per month)
- subsistence loan repayment (one per cent of turnover per month)
- fee for 'buying customers' - amounting to around six per cent of turnover
- telephone customer booking service (one per cent of turnover per month up to ceiling of £11,000)
- parking and recharging of refrigeration for the van - approximately £1,500 annually.

The franchisee also had to meet other work expenses, including fuel. Over time some of these costs would fall, bonuses could build up, and after a specified period sales rounds could be sold to other franchisees, thus reducing the debt to the company. Nevertheless, it is easy to see how the relatively large receipts from such an enterprise can be consumed by business expenses. The business transactions of such an enterprise are also particularly difficult for the applicant to explain on a cash-flow statement and for assessment staff to interpret from accruals-based accounts.

The study was not designed to be able to verify all the business expenses which respondents claimed on their applications. People talked about the different ways they recorded their expenses and often showed the researchers account books and other details. A common theme was how difficult it was to remember to keep all the necessary receipts and how some items went unclaimed because of the evidence being missing. People who had received family credit before had some understanding of the kinds of expenses which were allowable and those which were not. Use of the home as a business expense was one item which was rarely claimed where respondents did not have the advice of accountants. In general, examination of family credit application forms and discussion with the self-employed applicants indicated that business expenses claimed were those which would be expected in the occupations involved. What the research demonstrates is that higher turnovers should not necessarily be expected to produce correspondingly high net profits in small businesses of this kind. Nor, in fact, do low gross receipts always produce the lowest net earnings, as we now show.

The net earnings of the main worker

The difficulty of measuring self-employed earnings is one of main themes of this book. The problems related to survey data were reviewed in Chapter Two and the specific, technical questions involved in assessing earnings for benefit purposes have been discussed extensively (Boden and Corden, 1994). The researchers were not in a position to pass definitive judgement on the accuracy of either the information presented to the Family Credit Unit or the adjudication officers' assessments. We were often offered accounts and other documentation to inspect, and we also saw premises where work was carried out and observed equipment, tools and merchandise. Looking at the scale and nature of the work carried out, there seemed little reason to believe that earnings were different from those reported. Some undeclared work was carried out and this is discussed later. Several people also drew attention to apparent discrepancies between their standard of living and their current low earnings. Past earnings were referred to in a number of cases, but it was more common to emphasise the exercise of tight management on household budgets. These budgeting strategies are explored later in the chapter.

Table 7.2 shows the range of estimated net main earnings of families in receipt of family credit at the time of the interview, based on their most recent benefit applications. The figures include enterprise allowance where it was received and are net of allowable expenses, deductible tax and national insurance, and half of pension contributions if paid. The table includes the previous earnings of those who had stopped being self-employed and were now claiming out-of-work benefits.

Table 7.2
Net earnings of main employed and self-employed persons

£ per week	*Self-employed*	*Employed*
0 - 49	12	-
50 - 74	8	2
75 - 99	9	1
100 - 150	10	7
Total	39*	10

* Excludes a family whose claim had been disallowed because of excess earnings

Overall, the main weekly earnings of the self-employed families were clustered more in the lower range than those of the employees and the higher turnover families mostly had lower net earnings than the other self-employed recipients. Nearly three-quarters had net earnings below £100 per week. The highest earnings were those of the cleaning contractor, at approximately £140 per week, while the lowest net earner was one of the food retailers. She declared taking £30 - £40 per week from the business in food and other goods, but was still assessed as having net earnings of less than £5 per week. In spite of having a relatively high turnover, most was absorbed by the wholesale cost of food and the remaining profit margin was consumed by the costs of transport, refrigeration and rent for the retail unit. All the employees' earnings, by contrast, were between £50 and £150, with most over £75. The smallest amount was earned by a female factory worker, who averaged just over £50 per week for around 25 hours work during the assessment period. Her firm had lost work in the recession and her hours had been gradually cut back. The highest earner was a public sector caretaker, with just over £150 per week. Allowing for possible increases in earnings and the way in which the interview groups were selected, the distributions of earnings in the two study groups was not dissimilar to that found in the wider family credit population.

Very low self-employed earners are of special interest, but it turns out that they are not easy to categorise. Those earning below £50 per week included child minders - a group known to be low paid. As we saw earlier, two of the child minders were in dual-earner families, who might not be expected to remain claimants in the longer term. This group also included loss-making ventures which were among those with higher turnovers. There were both recent and long-term recipients, as well as members of all three career groups identified in Chapter Five. Some, as we will see later, were facing serious financial problems, while for others minimal earnings were manageable partly because of having no housing costs and because of a commitment to the lifestyle that went with the work.

Very low earnings were sometimes associated with limits to earnings which were largely beyond the control of the person involved. Subcontracted earnings, for example, depended on the amount of work made available by the employer, as in the case of woman working as a debt collector for a finance company. Hours of work could also be limited by the need to be available for family members needing care because of ill health or disability.

Also, earnings cannot necessarily be increased by extra work effort. A musician, for example, spent most of his non-performing time pursuing work and promoting his music. Higher earnings here would depend on an upturn in the market for his particular product.

It is worth noting that self-employed respondents often found it hard to estimate their earnings. Few drew a 'wage' as such: for most it was a matter of struggling from month to month to keep enough money coming in to meet bills and payments. As we saw in the last chapter, family credit and child benefit often constituted the main or only cash available for regular family expenditure. Thus the concept of net weekly or monthly earnings was often meaningful only in terms of figures produced for specific purposes, such as the family credit claim or tax returns. Respondents often answered questions about their earnings by reference to family credit assessments in terms like 'this is what they said I earned'. They were interested in these assessments, sometimes expressing surprise, either because they felt their earnings had been overestimated or, not uncommonly, because they were shocked to find how little they had apparently earned over a particular period. By contrast, most of the employees were able to state fairly precisely what their earnings were at the time and what they had been when they last applied for family credit.

Self-employed people may often be uncertain about what their net profits are, but one way in which these may be represented is as 'drawings'. We saw earlier that it has been the practice in some surveys, where self-employed people are unable to give an estimate of profit, to ask instead about money drawn from the business to meet living expenditure. The question of 'drawings' in self-employed enterprises is complex. What people take out of a business may be all they have to spend on a week-to-week basis, apart from benefits, but it is not necessarily the same as their 'earnings'. When businesses are starting up or struggling to keep going, the priority may be to leave as much of the takings as possible in the business, either as stock, or as contingencies to meet bills. Most respondents explained that they did not take a 'wage' as such, but just drew out the minimum needed to meet payments such as mortgages or fuel bills.

Where drawings were made, the amounts were influenced by three main factors. First, people drew no more than the minimum needed to cover essential household expenses. Secondly, amounts drawn would be based on some appreciation of the likely level of current profit, according to the most recent set of accountancy figures or people's own 'feel' for how they were doing. Thirdly, there were limits set by the level of bank overdrafts, since these were often the only regular source of drawings. These influences are illustrated in the following comment by the wife of one of the self-employed men:

> ... his drawings vary so much depending on what he can afford to draw at the time. Now we've just had the leanest six months ever so we've drawn just as little as we possibly can, you know, so that we're still drawing something from the business, but it's - we're not dipping into it too much because we're constantly at the end of the overdraft. It's constantly being, you know, topped up and dipped back into and that's it.

Her husband also talked about pressure from their accountant to draw out more money from the business than they thought they could afford in order to avoid suspicion of carrying out undeclared work.

Earnings were seen as constituting a 'wage' mainly in families where the main earner was a subcontractor or worked in a primarily male manual occupation, such as the building trade. It was very rare for estimated drawings clearly to exceed actual net earnings. In one shop the owners had been taking out around twice as much as their estimated net earnings. These drawings were necessary mainly to keep up the mortgage payments, which were already substantially in arrears as a result of a previous business collapse. Taking this much from the business was possible because they were having to make small payments only towards the cost of their start-up stock. However, the new business had not being going long enough for the owners to know whether it could sustain the level of drawings they found necessary.

If, as is suggested, the net main earnings in the self-employed families were a realistic reflection of the scale and type of the work concerned, it is still possible that some businesses could be amassing substantial assets rather than net profits. There was, however, little evidence that this was the case among these particular families. Some of the farms constituted substantial building and land holdings, most of which had been in the family for many years, but apart from these, there were no businesses which were capitalised in any major way. Assets were limited mainly to stock, vehicles, machinery and other small pieces of equipment or tools of the trade. The only business asset the potter owned, for example, was her kickwheel. Kilns and other equipment belonged to the people who had originally put capital into the business partnership, of whom she was not one.

Partners' earnings

An earlier chapter discussed the labour market participation of spouses and other partners in the two-parent recipient families. We saw that work outside the home was rare for women with self-employed partners. The more common pattern in these families was for the wife to help with the husband's business, but even where women were formally described as employees this was for tax purposes only and no actual money changed hands. The female-earner families were normally dual earners and participation in work by the women preceded their becoming the main family breadwinner. Most of the lone mothers had also been working before their marriages or relationships ended, which may have been a factor in helping them to continue to combine lone parenthood and work. This section looks at the sums of money earned by the partner of the main earner in two-parent families and the contribution they made to the household income.

Among the self-employed, male-earner families, in the few cases where women had paid work outside their partner's business at the time of the interview, the work took up only a few hours each week and was organised to fit in with family or child-care responsibilities. Two women each earned around £15 per week - teaching a dance class and running a playgroup. The latter was conducted on a job-share basis and the woman enjoyed it as much for the social life as for the income it brought it. Both women saw their wage as an important contribution to family income and wanted in the longer run to expand their work, but neither felt this was possible until their children were older.

One higher-earning spouse had taken a part-time job in a shop job five years before, specifically to pay for her children to go to a private school. She took home between £230 and £300 per month, which now made up most of their household earnings since the business was barely making a profit.

Earnings from the spouses of self-employed men, therefore, although present in only a few of the families, could be important in the overall household income. It was a somewhat different picture, however, with the female-earner families. While two of the men were becoming involved in their partner's business, the other three saw their main priority as getting back into the workforce themselves, and two had already done so by the time of the interview. Both families intended applying for family credit again, but suspected their present earnings might disqualify them.

There were some similar patterns of work among partners of the employed recipients. The lone parents had been working before their marriages ended and the female-earner families had previously been dual earners, just as in the self-employed families. One of the husbands of the women employees had found work since their last benefit claim, though only of a temporary nature. Unlike the women in the self-employed, male-earner families, most of the employed men's partners had recently been in work, but only one had a job at the time of the interview. She brought home just under £60 per week from part-time work in a shop - roughly half the earnings of her husband. The other women had stopped work for reasons which included the birth of children and the reduction in the availability of work that fitted in with child care. All hoped to return to work once children were at school or when suitable work became available, because the loss of their earnings was seen as making a serious impact on household finances. In these patterns of work and future expectations we can see example of the 'parachute' families identified by Marsh and McKay (1993).

Other income

In addition to money derived from the business or main job and any earnings by partners, some families had other sources of income, apart from benefits, including maintenance, and casual work. In general these other amounts of money were small, but in some cases they could make a considerable difference to cash available for weekly expenditure. This section considers these other sources of income, starting with child maintenance.

Maintenance

The receipt of maintenance was unusual among the lone parents in the study for a number of reasons. One woman, for example, had joint custody of her children, who spent equal time with their father. Another was a widow, while the former husband of a third now lived abroad. Losing maintenance as children leave full-time education can present difficulties for some lone parents, because it may be combined with loss of benefits at around the same time. The one self-employed lone parent who was currently receiving maintenance had just lost payments for her older son who was about to go to college. She anticipated maintenance soon finishing for her 17 year old as well. She was worried about how she would cope because she expected to lose over £80 per week in family credit, child benefit and maintenance - more than half her total disposable income - while her children were likely to remain partly dependent on her. Of the two employed lone parents, one was waiting for a court maintenance order, while the other was receiving the relatively high figure of £29 per week for each of her two children.

Maintenance receipt was more common among the employee couples because they included several reconstituted families, with three women receiving amounts varying from £10 to £20 per week for each child. In the couples, maintenance was regarded along with child benefit as the woman's income, though women said it was generally spent on items for the children. It was seen as an important, but not necessarily reliable source of income: the uncertainty of not knowing whether the money would arrive could add to financial problems.

With the advent of the Child Support Agency, it might be expected that maintenance payments to lone parents in particular would increase, but it would be wrong to see cash maintenance as the only way in which the expenses of children are shared with non-custodial fathers. Paying for holidays and outings, clothing, school equipment and special presents were all mentioned as important ways in which fathers helped with meeting the costs of children in both self-employed and employed families. Contributions of this kind could be crucial, since they helped with items which parents often described as the most difficult to afford. Time spent looking after children can also be important if it allows a lone parent to work. It could be easier to work in the school holidays if the other parent took the children away. The gardener, for example, had spent several weeks during the summer working long hours on subcontracted harvesting in addition to his regular work because his children were staying with their mother. This was likely to boost his income for that period substantially, but he said it could not have been undertaken with his children at home. Such non-cash contributions for children raise some questions about the likely impact of child support arrangements. Parents who are expected to pay new or increased sums of maintenance may be reluctant to continue other more informal and occasional, but still often valuable, contributions.

The extra work taken on by the gardener was declared and recorded for tax and family credit purposes. However, self-employed work is commonly associated with 'cash in hand', undeclared work and the informal economy, although as we argued earlier there is little conclusive evidence of the extent of such work. People engaged in undeclared work would be unlikely to admit to it in research interviews unless confidence in the researchers is built up over time. Our study was not designed to discover whether work was being carried out which respondents would not talk about. Some were, however, prepared to discuss it.

It has been observed in other research that in discussing whether they are involved in undeclared work while claiming benefits, people often explain their activities in ways that attempt to preserve their identities as rational and moral beings (Howe, 1990; Jordan et al., 1992). Such views are often as interesting and revealing as whether or not they are 'telling the truth'. Rationalisation of this kind was present in this study too, with explanations for both involvement and non-involvement being put forward. It was noticeable that there was rather less sign of any casual or undeclared work being carried out in the higher turnover families. This was partly perhaps because their businesses were even more time consuming and absorbent of family energies, though it is also improbable that any system, short of regular economic policing, would pick up all the forms of casual labour and mutual exchange which goes on in a farming community.

People in self-employed families described a number of sources of occasional extra income, which were mostly included on their family credit application forms. One lone parent, for example, was paid around £38 once a month to provide a weekend's respite care for a disabled child. She was thinking of trying to take on more work of this kind to make up for the imminent loss of her family credit. The wife of the employed caretaker received approximately £15 per week in expenses as a county councillor, which she also declared. Another man played occasionally with a band in addition to his main work and talked as though his fees were declared, though this was not clear from their family credit application.

Cash income which was clearly not declared appeared to be available mainly in building work, decorating and car repairs, though most participants stressed that the opportunities were infrequent and the amounts of money small - one man referred to it 'a little bit of pocket money now and then'. Only one man said that undeclared work could be substantial and justified it as the only way they could make a living:

> Oh yes, well we've got to do it. If we showed everything - well we never have done and we never will ... Some weeks it can be a wage, a cash in hand job can be a wage for the week. A Saturday morning can make your wage, quite a few times, for the week.

This was unusual, however. The more common view was that little work was available and that the returns were not worth the danger of being caught. The wife of a builder whose business had failed talked about working and claiming income support:

> I don't think we'd dare. I honestly don't because we've heard that much. Because you are - it's fraud isn't it? You're claiming off the State and then you're working, which is not, you're not supposed to do. So you get a heavy fine to pay and all your money that you've claimed you've got it all to pay back. In my eyes it's big debt, so I mean it's not worth the risk.

The vast majority of the self-employed respondents were adamant that everything they received went through their books or was declared for family credit. People were nervous about being caught out and having to pay money back. Several were also critical of other people they thought were 'on the fiddle' - a practice most commonly associated with working while claiming unemployment benefit or income support. Amidst widespread assumptions about the dishonesty of self-employed people, it may be salutary to note examples of scrupulous behaviour. One man, in the course of demonstrating his meticulous records, showed the interviewer that he had returned part of his enterprise allowance because he had found a new job shortly before the allowance period had expired.

One interesting situation was that of the church family. Mutual aid among the congregation was emphasised as important. The minister described a number of times when gifts of money came from their parishioners at opportune moments of need. Gifts of this kind were not the results of undeclared work, but in paying for items of clothing, car repairs and other such needs they were as substantial as many of the occasional cash jobs discussed above.

Studies such as those by Pahl and Wallace (1985) and others on the informal economy have suggested that it may be most prevalent among those in employment, but none of the employees in our group talked about any work which was not declared.

Goods and services in kind

Apart from cash earnings, some self-employed families had access to discounted goods or services in the building trade, or were able to offer other skills or goods in return for building work. There were also a number of other ways in which non-cash transactions or goods in kind were important. Most of these were occasional and did not represent a significant regular addition to family resources: where they did they were generally included in the family credit application. They are nevertheless important in understanding the economy of low-income self-employment and the ways in which the families managed to preserve their living standards.

The example of the food retailer who regularly took goods in kind from the business has already been mentioned. This was the extent of their drawings and was included in their assessment. In addition various forms of 'bartering' were mentioned which they carried out with other traders: they exchanged food for services such as word processing of their price lists. These exchanges, the women said, were all 'above board' and went through their accounts. Transactions of this kind seemed not unusual among the self-employed families. Food was also the subject of a number of other exchanges or ways of receiving minor goods in kind. The wives of the share fishermen both regularly exchanged fish from their catch with friends or relatives for other food. Similarly, other people talked of exchanging products or services for vegetables or other produce grown by neighbours and friends.

One of the farming families declared some consumption of their own produce, mainly milk. The tenant farmers did not produce milk of their own but they were able to take some from another farm run by the man's mother in exchange for help with her animals. Both a shopkeeper, whose goods included food, and the franchisee also said that consumption of their own goods was minimal. For the former the type of food he sold did not make up much of the family's preferred diet, while the franchisees felt they could rarely afford their goods, which were specialist and expensive:

> If we do we have to pay for it, there's no discount - we're just reducing our own profits.

Goods received directly in connection with work were less common. A lone parent who worked a few hours in a pub in addition to her self-employed work was able to eat meals there, and the leaflet distributor was also kept well stocked with free samples of the products which her leaflets were advertising.

Other forms of non-cash help came mainly from relatives, and these could be significant in some cases. A therapist, for example, worked from the front room in his parents' house. He contributed towards heating costs, but otherwise this facility was provided rent free. Another family's parents had housed them rent-free for nearly a year while they were establishing their business. In a later section on housing we talk about some of the other financial help provided by parents in the form of loans, gifts and help with deposits. In a number of cases parents also contributed physical help with work. One man's father, for example, had delivered leaflets as part of an advertising campaign, as well as lending money for new equipment. Another woman's parents both helped on her market stall from time to time. Overall, it is clear that forms of help or goods outside the immediate cash nexus were important for some of the self-employed families, even if they did not substitute significantly for earnings. They were part of the network of support and working relationships which seemed intrinsic to the kinds of work or the lifestyles that some of the families had chosen. As such, they contributed to living standards in two ways: first they allowed people to concentrate limited cash incomes on priority expenditures; secondly, they contributed directly to the quality of life the families enjoyed. There was less evidence of help of this kind among the employed families, although help from relatives was sometimes important for them too. Some talked about financial help, usually in the form of short-term loans to tide them over difficult periods.

Contributions from children

Having older children in the households who are no longer classified as 'dependent' for benefit purposes can have a marked impact on living standards. It was described earlier how children and young people in some families became involved in their parents' work and made important contributions. Young people may also contribute towards household expenses from earnings, benefits or training incomes received in their own right. On the other hand, 'non-dependent' young people may not be receiving incomes sufficient for them to live on without parental help.

The self-employed families contained a number of older children, both dependent and non-dependent. Their contribution to their parents' work was usually as a source of pocket money or as a way of saving up for an expensive purchase. One father, for example, had employed his son during the school holidays in return for a football season ticket. Even if the amounts of work carried out by children were not substantial, having a self-employed family business could be an important way of introducing young people to the world of work and of passing on skills.

Some young people had earnings of their own and these were generally seen as contributions towards the cost of their upkeep, but parents still had to meet the major expenses. One teenage child had recently finished college and found a job in a nearby town, contributing £10 per week towards her keep. A younger teenager was on a Youth Training placement on a farm and contributed £5 per week. These contributions in no way met the full costs of the officially non-dependent children's keep, although having their own incomes meant that they were able to buy some things for themselves for which their parents might otherwise have to pay.

Incomes might also have to stretch to help keep other relatives. The father of one of the farm owners lived with them and continued to work on the farm. He had his own state retirement pension, but was supported largely by the farm. The household of one of the consultants included a number of relatives. Their parents and parent-in-law had some pension income of their own, but much of their support still had to come from the couple's earnings. A younger relative who was unable to work was also living with them.

It is clear from looking at the range and sources of income and other forms of non-cash resources available that the complexity of individual circumstances cannot easily be represented by simple profit and loss figures or even by traditional measures of total cash income. Nevertheless, for all the heterogeneity of the self-employed families, there was little evidence to suggest serious discrepancies between these measures and the resources available to the families. One factor which is likely to have a marked impact on living standards, however, is the extent of individual or family savings. Even where families have no savings currently, capital held in the past may have been significant in buttressing families against the effect of declining incomes.

Savings and capital

Apart from people's homes (which are dealt with later) few of either the self-employed or employed families reported having any significant savings or investments at the time of the interview. The expressions 'not a bean' and 'not a penny' were each used on several occasions and people often pointed out that they had debts rather than savings. The only recipient in either group recorded as having tariff income was a retailer, who had declared a savings account of just over £6,000 on her application form.

Where there were savings at all (in about a third of the self-employed and two of the employed families), mostly they were only a few hundred pounds. Families sometimes referred to these as 'holiday money', or as money put aside against a possible future tax bill. Uncertainty about both amounts and timing of tax demands was common and people often worried about not having something put aside to meet them.

Those few self-employed families who had savings of £2-3,000 had money left from redundancy payments, previous periods of higher earnings or small inheritances. People who previously had savings or redundancy money described a number of ways in which these had been run down or used up entirely. The investment of redundancy money in setting up self-employed businesses has already been mentioned and other studies have also remarked on it (Lee, 1985; Leece, 1990). Savings had also been used to carry out necessary work on houses, for buying large items of household equipment, in paying mortgages during periods of unemployment and in keeping going during lean periods. Capital could very easily disappear in this way, though it had helped some families avoid starting with large business overdrafts. One man had previously owned a second home, bought before he was married. The family had recently had to sell this house in order to reduce their overdraft. Initially the Family Credit Unit had queried the use of the proceeds of the sale, considering that it might be seen as capital introduced into the business, but they later agreed that it should not be counted as such.

Similarly, before her business started a woman involved in a shop had some capital from an inheritance, but this was used for a number of purposes, including building an extension to their house and buying a car and some household goods. What was left had to be used to pay off an outstanding VAT bill from her partner's failed business in order to avoid his being declared bankrupt. She now had only a few hundred pounds left, saved mainly from her child benefit to spend on her child as future needs arose.

Relatively few of the employed families had previously had savings to spend, but those who had, gave similar accounts of how they had been run down. One family, for example, spent all their savings renovating the house which they were currently having to sell at well below its previous value. The only other person who talked about having access to any other forms of investment was a lone parent. Her husband had shares in the privatised utilities, which were the subject of negotiations in their divorce settlement.

Overall, while national data suggests that self-employed people are likely to have somewhat higher levels of savings than other households, there was little evidence among this group that their living standards were currently buttressed by large amounts of capital. One of the most common and important forms of investment, however, is housing and we now turn to examine the respondents' housing circumstances.

Housing circumstances

Tenure is often regarded as a key indicator of household living standards, so the observation that self-employed people have high rates of home-ownership tends to suggest that their living standards in general are likely to be relatively high. However, an important aspect of house purchase is the 'front-loading' of costs, which has meant that first-time buyers have needed to be relatively affluent unless they have had assistance from parents or other relatives. The financial strains of entry into the market felt by those less well off have been eased in periods of inflation and income growth by the gradual reduction of mortgage payments in real terms. Rising house prices have also led to the accumulation of substantial housing equity, which has served a number of important economic functions. First it has fuelled growth in household consumption through equity withdrawal (Holmans, 1991; Lowe, 1992). Secondly it has provided security for credit and loans used for consumption or business investment. Passed on to children or other relatives, it has also contributed to a spread of inherited wealth.

Critics of housing policies directed mainly at expanding owner-occupation have pointed to other less positive consequences, particularly in the 'residualisation' of local authority rented housing (Forrest and Murie, 1987). Being a local authority tenant has come to be associated with relative disadvantage, poorer housing conditions and restricted choices. A growing proportion of tenants in what remains the principal alternative tenure to home-ownership are unemployed or rely on some means-tested state benefits (Malpass, 1990). This is perhaps an oversimplified picture, since local authority housing policies in some areas have been key instruments in alleviating the effects of poverty among tenants (Bradshaw and Holmes, 1989), while the owner-occupied sector continues to hold pockets of severe disadvantage (Forrest et al., 1990). Nevertheless, it is widely accepted that developments in housing policy, production and consumption have created forms of social advantage and disadvantage which tend to be structured along tenure lines. In their study of low-income families Marsh and McKay (1993) also identified tenure as one of the 'fault lines', dividing those facing particular disadvantage from the rest.

Two developments in the owner-occupied housing market during the 1980s have simultaneously contributed to this tenure polarisation and made it less clear cut. The first was the 'right-to-buy' introduced by the 1980 Housing Act, which has seen well over a million properties sold to former tenants at substantial discounts. The second was the boom and subsequent slump in house prices which took place after the mid-1980s. The boom saw many people making large capital gains from sales of their properties or moving upmarket. More recently the combination of falling house prices and high interest rates left thousands of owners with mortgages they cannot afford to maintain and an estimated 1.5 million households in 1991 with negative equity (Dorling et al., 1992).

Newspaper reports have suggested that self-employed and small business people have been particularly badly affected by the twin problems of economic recession and high housing costs. Whether this is true for individual families may depend on when they bought their houses or last moved, because inflation has substantially reduced the real costs of mortgage payments taken out before the mid-1980s. In spite of the high level of interest rates payable up until 1992, housing costs for people who bought before the boom may not be problematic unless they took out large mortgages.

Nationally, more than four-fifths of households headed by a self-employed person own or are buying their own homes - a proportion higher than both the overall national average and that of households headed by employees (Central Statistical Office, 1991). The group of self-employed families whose living standards we looked at included 26 owner-occupiers and 14 tenants - a balance which is likely to reflect the low-income status of family credit recipients and the small scale of the businesses involved, as well as the life stage of some of the families. The employee group was divided equally between owners and tenants.

This section examines the families' housing circumstances, looking at their housing histories, the conditions and quality of their housing, costs, equity accumulated and withdrawn, problems with payments and arrears, and the use of housing as security for business loans. We consider whether there is evidence of identifiable divisions among these families on either employment or tenure grounds.

The first clear pattern to emerge from the accounts of the self-employed owner-occupiers is that most were established owners who had bought their properties some years before, or had owned other houses previously. The farmers, for example, had inherited their farms from their parents and had lived all their lives in the same house. Others had lived in the same property for ten years or more, and had often bought their homes when they married, with help from parents. Having financial help from relatives to start on the housing ladder was clearly important for several families. If housing costs were reduced or eliminated, it was possible to manage more easily on low earnings.

One family in the relatively unusual position among lower income self-employed people of having no mortgage were from a minority ethnic community. They had bought their present house 16 years before, a few years after the man arrived in Britain, on a short mortgage, which had been paid off some years earlier when he was employed in a factory. The man explained that this was a not uncommon pattern among people from the Asian sub-continent who were not born in Britain. People tried to acquire outright ownership of a home as soon as possible, to free them from one major worry among the many involved in settling in the UK. If this is a common situation, some low-income Asian home-owners may not face the constraints involved in the loss of mortgage interest support in moving from out-of-work benefits.

More recent first-time buyers had mainly come from renting, mostly from the local authority. Those who had bought their present houses with substantial discounts under the right-to-buy scheme included another Asian family. A relative had helped them to pay off the outstanding mortgage - a form of assistance they said was not unusual among Asian families.

Another group of families who had moved more recently had owned at least one house before and often several. The minister's family, for example, had moved gradually northwards over the years in the service of their church, which had left them with no housing costs because of the differences prevailing in the late 1980s between house prices in the south and the north of England. For most of the families, housing costs were manageable partly because they were over the first difficult years of mortgage payments or had enough equity from previous houses to keep newer mortgages at an affordable level. This is not to say that housing costs were unproblematic: several families had experienced difficulties with keeping up payments or were currently in arrears.

Most of the self-employed lone parents had also been home-owners in the past with their former partners, but whether they stayed in owner-occupation depended largely on the value of the marital home and the financial settlement. Those who had moved into council housing had used up much of their settlements in setting up home again, though they planned to buy again if earnings became more secure.

Half of the employee families in the study were also home-owners, compared to only 36 per cent in the PSI survey (Marsh and McKay, 1993). Owner-occupation among this group of families was associated with two main factors. They had either bought their houses when they had two earners or they had bought council houses with substantial discounts - a factor described earlier as helping to spreading home-ownership down the income scale. Although the use of local authority discounts and dual earnings were both present among the self-employed families, there was only one example of both in operation simultaneously.

Unlike some of the self-employed owners, none of the employees talked of having received financial help towards buying houses from parents or relatives. This is not surprising since their parents were largely manual workers and often council tenants themselves. They would have been less likely than some of the parents of the self-employed families to be able to offer financial help.

It is worth noting here that nearly all the female-earner families were home-owners. This seemed to be partly because most were normally dual earners and previously had higher incomes, as we saw in the last chapter. One who had not bought as a dual-earner family had taken advantage of a local authority discount.

Most of the tenants among the self-employed families lived in local authority housing. In many ways the self-employed council tenants were the most homogeneous group of families in the study, and they shared a number of characteristics with their wage-earning counterparts. Most had been local authority tenants for much of their adult lives and had male earners who had carried on the same manual trade or occupation since leaving school. The employed council tenants had also been in local authority accommodation most of the time since they had started having children. They too were families with male breadwinners in manual jobs, though they were mainly younger than the self-employed families, with only intermittent periods of work since leaving school.

We can see here how the link between housing and work status can affect families in different ways. The instability of some work, whether employed or self-employed, means that people are regularly moving between the two and it may be unhelpful to draw too clear a distinction between them. These accounts of the housing histories of the self-employed and employed families suggest that help from relatives made it easier for some of the self-employed to buy houses, and that most bought their first homes well before the late 1980s boom in house prices. However, a substantial minority were long-term council tenants: their employment background and the types of work they carried out were not dissimilar to those of the employee recipients. With some exceptions the self-employed displayed somewhat more settled patterns of residence, which reflected both their age and their work histories. This could be disturbed by relationship breakdown, however, which would not always allow the lone custodial parent to resume home-ownership in the short term.

Housing conditions and quality

The interview groups were chosen from families living in two large regions. The families lived in a wide range of different locations, from inner cities to sea-side villages. Most families, both self-employed and employees, lived in housing of a good standard with which there was a high level of satisfaction. The quality of housing was nevertheless variable, both within and between tenures, and people identified a number of problems, mainly connected with the amount of space they had for the sizes of their families.

Most of the self-employed families lived in houses or bungalows and the predominant housing type was the three-bedroom terrace, but two families occupied flats over shops. Most houses had some form of garden, though these varied considerably in size, and the majority had also garages, some of which were rented separately and used in connection with the business. None of the houses lacked the basic amenities, though about a quarter were without full central heating. Nearly half of these were local authority tenancies, but one of the owner-occupier couples had chosen not to install central heating and two of the farms were heated with solid fuel stoves and open fires.

Although terraces were the predominant housing type, these varied considerably from attractive Victorian artisans' cottages to council houses on run-down 1950s estates. It is also important to note that some of the poorer housing was in relatively wealthy rural areas. The gardener, for example, lived in a small, unmodernised council house on the edge of an attractive village, the residents of which made up many of his customers. It is one of the features of low-paid self-employment that it is likely to be geographically scattered and frequently found alongside affluence.

The size and number of rooms in houses varied with the number of children, as would be expected. Since some families were relatively large, sharing of rooms by children was common and was experienced as a severe problem in some cases. Over half the families had children sharing, mostly two or three to a room and there was some anxiety about how they would manage as younger children grew older, particularly with children of different sexes.

The most severe space problems were those experienced by a lone parent who was trying to sell her house. She had large mortgage arrears and had moved, with her mother and her two children into the flat above her shop, which had only one bedroom and a small living room. She herself was sleeping in a converted store room at the back of the shop. Another family with a particular need for extra space had a severely disabled son who was unlikely to be able to live fully independently as he grew up.

As we saw in the previous chapter, space problems can also be expected to arise where people are running businesses from home. There may be a need for office space or for storage for goods and equipment, and health and safety may also be an issue where people are actually carrying out their work at home. There is an obvious difference between people working *from* their homes, where the home may be the business address, and those actually working *at* home. In this study there were few of the latter apart from the child minders and, in a different way, the farmers. Most either had separate fixed premises, such as shops and stalls, workshops and offices, or worked mainly away from home in other ways, including at sea, driving a taxi or working in other people's homes and premises.

Most properties were in a reasonably good state of repair, though several families saw redecoration as one of their current priorities once they could afford it. Larger houses were particularly expensive to keep in good repair. Both farmhouses needed major refurbishment: one needed a new roof and the work required on the other, including roofing, had been estimated as costing over £40,000. The family were currently applying for a means-tested improvement grant.

Beyond a certain point the condition of housing is largely a subjective question, but in the opinion of the researchers only a small number of houses could be described as 'shabby'. More than half of the owner-occupiers and a few of the local authority tenants had carried out extensive work on their homes since they had moved in, including installation of central heating or new gas fires, rewiring, damp courses, new kitchens and bathrooms, loft conversions, opening up downstairs living rooms and general redecoration. Mostly these works had been carried out by the longer term owners and completed some years before. Only two families were currently engaged in major repairs or improvements, though two others were considering borrowing money to build extensions.

The poorest quality housing was found in a flat rented above business premises; it was small and in a poor state of repair, with no central heating. The tenants were responsible for internal and external repairs and though they had painted the outside, they had been unable so far to redecorate inside. There were only two bedrooms, so the three children all shared one room.

At the upper end of the housing range was the home of one family who had bought and sold several houses in the past. This had allowed them to purchase a large detached house in a relatively expensive area, with five bedrooms and three other living rooms. Over the years they had gutted and reconstructed the house and garden. The property was now fairly valuable, but was currently for sale as the owners felt obliged to reduce their way of life to that which could be sustained from their present earnings.

We speculated earlier that some self-employed people might have access to trade discounts or forms of mutual exchange, so it is of interest to see how much transactions of this kind had contributed to their housing repairs and improvements. Respondents identified a variety of ways in which they had received help, including loans or gifts of money from relatives, access to cheap materials, mutual exchange of labour or goods, capital from sales of other houses, loans secured on the house, and grants. There was a strong emphasis, however, on DIY: families carried out as much work as they could themselves.

Access to discounted goods or labour was clearly not a general feature of self-employment. Several respondents pointed out this was restricted mainly to the building trades. One of the builders had renovated his house by carrying out the work himself, using mainly materials which were 'surplus' on contracts he was carrying out: 'I don't pay for a lot of the things I get. It's like perks really'. Both the other builder and the plumber had installed or augmented central heating in their council houses, having received substantial trade discounts on the materials. One of the share fishermen also had a room of their council house knocked through and a fireplace built with 'recycled' material by his brother and brother-in-law, who were both builders.

Other examples of mutual exchange included central heating installation in return for repairs to a car, while tiling and plumbing work had been exchanged for supplies of fish. One man involved in such exchanges commented that he did not see this as anything intrinsically linked to self-employment: 'It's just a working and living and growing relationship with people around'.

Overall there was somewhat less variation in housing quality and conditions among the employed families than among the self-employed. All but one lived in towns or suburban areas: the exception was a garage manager who rented a house next to his garage, outside a small coastal town. Most families also lived in houses, while one occupied had a first floor council flat. All the houses had gardens and four had garages. None was lacking any basic amenity and all had central heating, though only partial in two cases. All the properties had two or three bedrooms. The smaller sizes of the employee families meant that only two had children sharing rooms.

Some employee families had also carried out major works on their homes in recent years, apart from decoration. One involved a loan of around £2,000 from a finance company which the man said was for home improvements, and repayments were currently causing problems.

We have seen that there was considerable variation in the type and quality of housing occupied by the families receiving family credit, and that some of both the better and the poorer housing was among the self-employed families. A key factor, however, in household finances and living standards is the cost of housing.

Housing costs

Looking first at home-owners, we can see that the level of mortgage payments to be met by a particular family obviously depends on the price of their housing, when it was purchased and what percentage of the cost is being met by the loan. House prices are further dependent on location, type, size and quality. One would therefore expect a wide range of mortgage costs among the owner-occupier families, which would reflect their different family sizes, ages, previous employment histories, residential areas and preferences.

The mortgage payments made by the owner-occupier families in the study groups varied, but overall they were not as high as might be expected, in spite of interest rates still being relatively high during the period when the interviews were carried out. As was mentioned earlier, several families referred to their low housing costs as making it possible for them to work for low returns.

Table 7.3 shows the range of mortgage payments families were making when they were interviewed during the summer and autumn of 1992. Payments include endowment insurance where this was payable and extra payments being made towards arrears, but not extra sums for additional non-housing loans.

Table 7.3
Range of mortgage payments made by self-employed and employed owner-occupiers (£ per week)

	Self-employed	*Employed*
£0	6	-
£1 - 20	2	1
£21 - 40	5	3
£41 - 50	6	-
£51 - 100	3	1
£100 - 150	4	-
Total	26	5

Those with no direct housing costs owned their houses outright. In all nearly three-quarters were paying the equivalent of less than £50 per week. At the other end of the scale, however, there were four families, including three of those with higher turnovers, with payments of more than £100 per week. All were in arrears with their mortgages and those whose arrears had passed £2,500 were facing possible repossession. One family was in 'desperate straits', finding it hard to keep up their £550 per month repayments, as well as a further £74 per month for a loan secured on the house. Their arrears amounted to some £6,000. It was evident that where there were substantial outstanding mortgages, these self-employed home-owners found it difficult to meet repayments and sustain the kind of housing that some had been used to having in earlier periods of higher earnings.

None of the employed families had either zero or specially high mortgage costs. The highest was £63 per week, but this was being met by the husband of one of the lone parents, until a financial settlement had been reached. Otherwise all the payments were under £30 per week.

House values and equity

Respondents were also asked to estimate the current value of their homes. This is clearly not a scientific exercise, but most people were fairly definite about what they saw as a realistic value in the context of the current housing market: several had recently had valuations carried out or were aware of the selling prices of similar houses nearby. The cheapest houses were estimated at under £30,000 - one a terraced house in an economically depressed area of the North-East and the other an ex-council house on an estate in a new town north of London. Over half were estimated as worth under £60,000, including four of those owned by employed families. Not surprisingly, the most valuable properties were found among the higher turnover families, in particular the farms, one of which was estimated as worth around £450,000 - although this was regarded as 'a paper value'. The other farm owner regarded the market value as irrelevant since he had inherited it and intended to pass it in to his children. Nevertheless, since neither of these farms had mortgages attached, they clearly represented substantial equity, in spite of the business loans for which the farms acted as security.

Estimating equity, like value, is an imprecise exercise, and the results from our group of families is not statistically generalisable to the wider family credit population. Nevertheless, by comparing the estimated current values of their homes with the amount of outstanding mortgages it is possible to get an indication of the capital different families had stored in their houses. This gives some idea of the level of security underpinning people's employment decisions. Table 7.4 shows the estimated ranges of equity accruing to the two groups of owner-occupiers.

Table 7.4
Estimated housing equity of self-employed and employed owner-occupiers

	Self-employed	*Employed*
Negative equity	4	-
£0 - 20,000	6	1
£21,000 - 30,000	2	1
£31,000 - 40,000	5	2
£41,000 - 100,000	6	1
Over £200,000	3	-

The table shows that in spite of the drop in house prices which took place after the boom of the late 1980s some of the owner-occupiers had substantial levels of equity stored in their houses. More than half of both self-employed and employed families had estimated equity of over £30,000. Equity, of course, does not equal liquid capital or a form of usable income. It is only translatable into cash if an owner moves to a cheaper house, or if it is used as security for other loans. Few of the owners had withdrawn equity from their homes for any purposes. This was partly because not many had moved in recent years and those who had, moved either within the same locality to more expensive houses or between areas of comparable expense. The one family who had traded down by moving from the South to the North had been able to pay off their mortgage and have some capital left to spend on renovating and redecorating their house.

It is noticeable that in most cases where people received some capital from a house which had to be sold because of problems in meeting payments, or because of a relationship breakdown, there was not sufficient left to buy again immediately. This money tended to be absorbed by the costs of setting up and equipping new rented accommodation or by living expenses in periods of poor takings from the business. Occasionally some was spent on lump-sum business purchases such as vehicles, or on items of domestic expenditure which would not otherwise have been affordable.

Negative equity was associated with both falling house prices and accumulated mortgage arrears. One of the most expensive houses in the study was estimated by its owners to be subject to an equity gap of over £20,000. One of the least valuable houses in the study had been bought on a 100 per cent mortgage, which was increased by a further £3,500 for building work. When business began to decline, the bank called in the loans and the owner was left owing some £38,000 on a house estimated as worth around £28,000.

Rents

Like mortgages, rents vary with the size of the properties and the area, but they are still likely to be more uniform than mortgage payments, in spite of pressure from Government on local authorities to raise council rents nearer to prevailing market levels. The full rents of the properties occupied by the families renting from local authorities ranged from £25 to £40 per week, with most under £30. The highest rent was that of a family with six children and a four-bedroomed house.

The private sector rents were higher, but fairly similar to each other, mainly ranging from just over £60 per week to around £90 per week for the educational business. The rent paid for tied accommodation was only £11.50 per week, but this employee said his pay was correspondingly low to take into account the subsidised housing.

A more valid measure of the housing costs of tenants relative to owner-occupiers is to compare mortgage payments with net rents after housing benefit is paid, since no comparable allowance is available to mortgagees. There were some difficulties with arriving at realistic figures for rebated rents since several respondents explained that their housing benefits varied at different intervals, according to changes in their earnings and the level of family credit received. This was seen as one of the main difficulties with the interaction of in-work benefits. Although some tenant families were not receiving housing benefit at the time of the interview, most had applied at some point and there did not appear to be a major problem of take-up among the family credit recipients. Overall, the range of net payments varied among both the self-employed and employed families and there were no clear patterns of differentiation between them.

A comparison with the mortgage payments of the owner-occupiers shows that net housing costs were generally higher among the home-owners, but there were still tenants with net housing costs greater than some of the owner-occupiers. Likewise, there were no clear patterns of difference between the self-employed and employed families because of the variations in tenure, mortgage costs and levels of housing benefit received.

Our study found a somewhat higher incidence of arrears among the small group of employees than in the PSI survey of low-income families (Marsh and

McKay), but for the self-employed the proportions were similar, suggesting that our families were not untypical. Not surprisingly, mortgage arrears were more serious than rent arrears, both in the amounts owed and in the possible consequences. The former tended to be directly caused by major events such as redundancy, business failure or relationship breakdown. Rent arrears were more commonly the result of temporary fluctuations in earnings, or because some other urgent expenditure need had arisen which had taken precedent over the rent in the juggling of household budgets. Alternatively they arose from revisions of housing benefit following family credit awards.

One reason why more of the owner-occupiers did not have mortgage arrears in spite of many having low or fluctuating incomes was the high priority placed on keeping up payments. Respondents were well aware of the potential consequences of not doing so and anxious about any threat to their homes. Several talked in terms like 'paying the mortgage, then seeing what's left' or 'giving the building society the first bite'. To some extent mortgage payments were also protected by the run-down of savings.

It is important not to under-estimate the traumatic effects of losing one's home in these circumstances. The self-employed families who had lost their houses or seemed likely to do so all expressed resignation and it seemed to be too sensitive an issue for open discussion with an interviewer. One woman, however, talked about the work her husband had carried out on their house and said:

> He's done all that, and it would ... it would break my heart to lose this house because of all the work that he's done.

Uses of the home as security for loans

It was suggested earlier that one of the links between self-employment and owner-occupation may be the opportunities this tenure affords for running businesses, including the possibility of loans on the property. There was little evidence of this among the study group at families' present level of business operation, except among the farmers. Other families had taken out secured loans for consumption items such as new cars, or for home improvements, but only one non-farmer specifically said that she had borrowed money against the house to develop her business.

One reason for infrequent use of loans against housing equity may be that most of the kinds of work in which the families were engaged were not capital-intensive and had relatively low entry costs. It also appeared to reflect a widespread caution about using credit and a fear of borrowing beyond well-defined limits. Several respondents talked of banks trying to lend them more money than they felt comfortable owing. The carpet seller, on the other hand, mentioned having had difficulties persuading banks to lend him money, in spite of having considerable equity in a house. He saw this as an aspect of the difficulties many business people from minority ethnic communities have with the banking establishment.

Apart from using the home as security for loans, there is a more general question of how much people felt being an owner-occupier helped in being able to be self-employed. In fact few families made any direct connections, except, again, the farmers. Even the retailer who had borrowed money against the house felt home-ownership had not been an issue up to then in the establishment of her work, since she had started running the stall when occupying the same house as a council tenant. The motor mechanic talked about how useful it was having a garage with the house, but he too had previously rented the house as a tenant and buying the house came after setting up the business. Similarly the baker had started her business on a small scale from her council house and only when the work outgrew her home kitchen did she move to a retail 'start-up unit' leased from the local authority. Home-ownership in these cases was associated with expansion or consolidation of business rather than start-up.

In other cases the linkage appeared to work in the opposite direction. One of the builders, for example, had been able to afford to buy a cheap house and renovate it only because he had the skills to do it himself, and because of the availability of free, surplus materials from other jobs. A further dimension to the link between owner-occupation and self-employment is illustrated by the situation of a couple who, having lost their house, saw *renting* rather than buying as a way of allowing them to set up a business. Thus they felt they could keep running at a low profit level until such time as economic conditions improved, because a high proportion of their rent was met by housing benefit. Overall, it appeared that the link between self-employment and owner-occupation was less causal than reflective of dual aspirations. Home-ownership and self-employment were both seen as ways of achieving independence, self-reliance and choice.

To summarise the findings on respondents' housing circumstances, it appeared that the home-owners were broadly divided between those who had inherited their homes, like the farmers, or paid off an earlier mortgage, and those who had been caught in the house price boom and decline since the late 1980s. The size, quality and conditions of accommodation varied considerably, with people's housing generally reflecting their previous incomes, social status, or inheritance rather than necessarily their current earnings. Several households also included extra adults for whom the claimants had at least partial financial responsibility. In spite of a generally good standard of housing, some of the self-employed tenants had accommodation no better than, or even inferior to, some of the employees in the main study, and both of the owner-occupied farmhouses, while valuable, needed repairs or improvements which the owners had not been able to afford.

People with outstanding mortgages who had bought fairly recently had difficulty with repayments and in some cases faced possible repossession and negative equity. Nevertheless, the value of housing was relatively high among this group and there were several families with substantial equity.

Irrespective of the level of housing costs, one feature of all the families' experience was that of having to manage carefully their finances and household budgeting. We now move on to look at how they managed and at the choices and constraints they faced over expenditure.

Managing and budgeting on low incomes

'Managing' here is used in two ways: first it used in an administrative sense, referring to how families organised their business and household finances; secondly, there is the more colloquial sense of the word, referring to how families 'made ends meet'. These two meanings may be linked, in that how families organise their money may affect their capacity to balance expenditure and income. The links between these two processes are therefore explored, looking at patterns of management and decisions about expenditure, the constraints people felt and the needs they prioritised, and the various strategies they had adopted for budgeting with limited incomes.

Patterns of financial management and control

To a large extent the way finances were organised reflected the scale and the nature of the different businesses or types of work. Only just over half of the self-employed families kept bank or building society accounts for their work which were clearly separated from household or personal accounts. These were mainly people with genuine trading or service businesses, which were more likely to require such arrangements in order to function effectively. Earnings from subcontracted or quasi self-employed work were more likely to pass through the same bank accounts, either individual or joint, as household expenditure.

Families with separate business accounts often stressed the importance of keeping business and household finances distinct. Some had experienced difficulties with keeping their records in order before they set up separate arrangements. Failure to keep business and household finances distinct had sometimes compounded other problems in the business itself.

Where drawings were taken from business accounts for household expenditure the general pattern was to transfer these sums to personal or household accounts, from which people paid bills or standing orders for mortgages and insurance. Such transactions were less clear cut in businesses where parts of the takings were in cash. A common arrangement was to pay cash into a personal account for household bills, whereas cheques went into a business account to service an overdraft. Another arrangement was for small amounts of cash takings to be kept at hand for shopping and other regular spending. Although there was the potential for some confusion here, it was often stressed that the cash was still formally recorded as income: it was only separated so that there was a source of ready money not absorbed by overdrafts.

The picture was rather more blurred in the families where earnings, expenses and other household monies all passed through one account or were handled entirely in cash. The latter was unusual - only the former partner of the scrap dealer said that all their financial transactions were in this form. The taxi driver's takings were mainly in cash, but this and the expenses were still dealt with through a separate work account. Where both business and household money went through the same accounts, people talked of money being 'all in one pot', within which they had to juggle their incomes and expenditures, or of 'not drawing a line down the middle'. These families did not generally operate with substantial business overdrafts and the emphasis was on trying to keep earnings and expenditures in some kind of balance, or 'keeping above water'. This was not always easy. People without good banking records or with irregular takings often had the most difficulties because banks were less likely to allow them to overdraw. This was one of the reasons why the failed builder, for example, had to give up. Having no overdraft facility, any running deficit on the business had to be covered out of general household income, a situation which his wife found increasingly intolerable.

The last chapter discussed in some detail the ways in which family credit was used, but we can also see that the way that finances as a whole were organised in different families could affect both the viability of businesses themselves and the amount of money available for household spending.

Budgeting and control over resources in two-parent families

A growing body of research has shown that managing and budgeting in families need to be separated analytically from control over resources (see, for example, Brannen and Wilson, 1987; Pahl, 1980, 1989). This is an important issue for a study of living standards because, as the research has shown, family incomes may not be allocated fairly. Where limited resources are diverted away from basic household needs or where disagreement exists about priorities for spending, effective management may be difficult. What is particularly interesting in this study is to see how far the financial structures of small-scale self-employment may affect the control or allocation of resources in families.

In two-parent families the most common view, expressed by both partners, was that financial decision making was a joint process, while women tended to deal with most of the household budgeting and expenditure. Men sometimes took responsibility for handling larger bills, like mortgage payments. This was true in both male-earner and female-earner families and among both the employed and self-employed. It is a pattern which has often been observed in lower income families, but it does not always mean that women have equal control over the allocation of resources. As Pahl (1989) found in her study of money and marriage, it is common to talk of joint decision making, but the actual way in which resources are allocated may not conform to this image. The rhetoric of egalitarianism in marriage is often in advance of actual change.

'We just sit down and talk about it' was the kind of expression commonly used by people in this study and it seemed in many cases that such discussion did take place over items of major household expenditure (though not always where business expenditure was involved). However, patterns of allocation for day-to-day expenditure varied considerably and there were examples of all the allocative systems identified in Pahl's (1980) well-known typology.

In the employed families, patterns of allocation tended to conform most closely to those defined as 'whole wage' or 'wife management' systems and 'allowance' systems. In the first, wages are handed over the wife, or into her general control if paid into a bank account, for her to deal with bills, shopping, children's needs and all the various expenditures required. The second system involved a housekeeping allowance being paid to the wife out of the husband's wages. Both these systems place the main responsibility for managing money on women, without necessarily allowing them equal power over deciding priorities in expenditure or permitting them to have money for themselves. Men, however, commonly expect to be given or to hold back sums for personal spending.

This was the case in several employee families in the study. Money from benefits like family credit and child benefit were most likely to be seen as 'her' money, but in practice this was almost invariably spent on items for the children or general household costs. The following comment was typical:

> The cash I get we sort of call it mine, but it's not really mine that I get from the family credit and the child benefit. That's mine to spend as I see fit if the

children need something that week. He lets me decide whether they need nappies or whether they need this or that because obviously I know better than he does what we've got in the house and whether they need shoes and socks ... I don't think I've ever bought anything out of that money for myself. Sometimes I try to, but I always end up buying something for them. He used to allow himself £20 a week spending money - I don't know why. I don't know what he spent it on, so that was just his, but he's cut down now.

Other women in the employee families also talked about having to ask their husbands for money if they needed it. While both partners tended to say that there was little money ever left over after necessities for personal expenditure, some men still talked about keeping small amounts of spending money for themselves. Although some women clearly were involved in deciding how the overall resources of the family should be spent, the existence of the male wage as the main source of income still appeared to support a fairly traditional system of allocation.

In the self-employed families allocation systems were much more varied. Where the men worked in traditional manual trades, particularly subcontracted work where earnings were received in a form close to wages, couples tended to use modified versions of the 'whole wage' system. This was commonly explained by both partners in terms of men's inability to manage money. Two men in particular talked about themselves as 'terrible with money', or 'spendthrift', as opposed to their wives who were 'shrewd' and knew 'exactly how to stretch our means'. Another woman described herself as having 'an older head on younger shoulders' than her husband when it came to managing money. There was an expectation here too among some of the men that they would normally be able to hold back spending money for themselves, for drinks or other purposes, though several men remarked that this was harder than in the past because of tighter budgets.

There was a rather different picture in some of the more established businesses, where women were more directly involved. The long hours worked by some of the men and the effort needed for the work itself often meant that book-keeping and other financial aspects of the business were carried out by the women. Even if this sometimes made it hard for them to think about taking other jobs of their own, having this kind of detailed knowledge of the business finances put them in a stronger position to exercise decision-making power as well as responsibility for household budgeting. As was observed earlier, this also put some women in a relatively strong position for applying for family credit if their husbands were reluctant.

Allocation in these households operated more like 'pooled' systems, where both parties had access to money. Often there was still a division of responsibility: men tended to deal with paying larger bills like the mortgage or other regular outgoings which required funds being transferred from business accounts, while women dealt with shopping, food and things for the children. Yet there was a sense in some of these families that women had as least as much say as men about how money was allocated. Several men talked of having no real idea about the finances. It was all up to their wives and they had to ask them if they needed something for themselves.

There were exceptions to this pattern, of course. Where women were less directly involved in businesses, the divisions of responsibility tended to be more traditional. Yet even here, because in the self-employed families family credit tended to make up a relatively high proportion of family income, women still often had more household cash in their hands than in most of the employee families. There seems little doubt that the success that some of these families had in managing on low incomes was directly due to the executive power exercised by the women - a factor widely acknowledged by the men.

One area where there could be potential conflicts over spending was on business expenses. One of the musicians, for example, had recently spent a substantial sum on a new instrument. He saw this as a lasting investment and better value than the cheaper but less durable instruments he had previously used. It was counted by family credit as an allowable business expense, which had reduced the net earnings figure. His wife, however, saw the purchase as reducing the immediate amount of money available for household spending.

Overall, although there was great variation among the families, it was clear that whatever level of power or control over financial decision making was held by women, they had the major responsibility for budgeting and managing. This may often have helped the families keep going, but the responsibility could be burdensome. In several cases there was a striking difference in the interviews between the optimistic tone taken by men in describing their hopes and plans for their work, and the anxiety and doubt expressed by women about the risks being taken and the difficulties of making ends meet. It is mainly in the women's accounts that we find the details of how families prioritised expenditure and the constraints they experienced.

'Levels of managing'

In a study of living standards in unemployment, Ritchie (1990) grouped families into four 'levels of managing', depending on whether they said they regularly balanced income and expenditure ('made ends meet'), and whether they had acquired debts or arrears during their periods of unemployment. On this basis families were categorised as:

- *managers* - people whose expenditure did not normally exceed their income or resources and were not in debt or arrears

- *marginal managers* - people who usually made their expenditure just match their income or resources, but who were in or moving into debt or arrears

- *marginal non-managers* - people whose expenditure was just exceeding their income and who were in or moving into debt or arrears, or

- *non-managers* - people whose expenditure consistently exceeded their incomes and were fairly deeply in debt or arrears.

Although the situations of people working and receiving family credit may be rather different from those of families experiencing prolonged spells of unemployment, a typology of this kind is helpful for summarising the financial position of the families in the study. For the self-employed, however, classification is made more complex by problems in defining current earnings and by the common use of overdraft financing - a particular issue for some of the families with higher turnovers. Also, some arrears had not been acquired recently and were not currently accumulating, even if repaying them sometimes proved difficult. A further complication is that community charge or 'poll tax' arrears were widespread, not least among some of the families with no other substantial debts or arrears. These were often treated as a low priority, for reasons which are discussed later. In determining whether families were 'making ends meet', therefore, we base our assessment on respondents' own perceptions of how well their incomes matched their expenditures. Where poll tax arrears were small and not considered a serious problem, they are disregarded as a sign of 'non-management'. Similarly, arrears are not taken to include the normal use of a business overdraft, unless respondents indicated that they were regularly exceeding limits or facing problems with creditors.

On this basis, three-fifths (24) of the self-employed families could be seen as *managers*, while five were clearly *non-managers*. The remaining 11 families were primarily *marginal managers* in that they all had arrears or debts, but usually made ends meet on a month-to-month basis. However, fluctuations in earnings and cash-flow problems meant that some families were always hovering on the margins of management and non-management. The builder who had gone out of business is a good example. While he was still trying to maintain his work they were increasingly failing to manage and falling into debt. It was only through stopping being self-employed and claiming income support that they were able to stabilise their finances. They were currently managing, though at a level which meant their spending was severely constrained.

Among the employed families, only two were clearly *managers*, without debts or arrears and balancing income and expenditure. The other eight were mainly *marginal managers*, with varying degrees of debt and some hovering again on the margins of managing.

The self-employed *non-managers* all had large mortgage arrears arising from redundancy or business decline. Their inability to match incomes with outgoings was directly related to accumulation of unmanageable debts. All were at or near a crisis point and were attempting in various ways to stave off repossession, juggle creditors' demands, or cut their losses by selling their homes. Despite cutting back on all kinds of expenditure, they were unable to prevent the debts mounting. For a child minder the crisis stemmed from the severe drop in household income brought on by her husband's redundancy. Lone mothers who were inexperienced in running businesses also admitted to being poor managers of household finances. One in particular had a history of other arrears and non-take-up of means-tested benefits. It is inevitable that financial pressures of this kind bring psychological strain and all expressed feelings of stress and depression.

Most of the self-employed higher earners were, as we might expect, in the majority group who generally made ends meet. Higher earnings were clearly not the only issue, however. The *managers* also included several of the lowest earners and families with all the different career profiles identified in earlier chapters, as well as most of the longer term family credit recipients. In this group have to be included some who were actually making losses, of which the farm owners are a prime example. Because they owned valuable property and generated steady flows of cash from their activities it was possible for them to maintain their loans, which would expand and contract as business ebbed and flowed. Banks in these areas are accustomed to such business - indeed their lending practices are shaped by it - and they are able to take a long view, absorbing losses in some years up to a certain point. This is not to say that even these families did not experience financial difficulty. But through careful control of expenditure they were currently managing to meet their outgoings and avoid increasing indebtedness to the point where lenders would begin to baulk at further support. Where this level of support from banks or other lenders was not available, managing was considerably more difficult, particularly if families were still carrying commitments or expectations from earlier, more affluent times.

There were several different factors at play here in families ability to manage. First, having had higher earnings in the past meant that some families were well stocked with household goods. Secondly, expectations often seemed as important as earnings. Some families who had persistent low earnings had adapted to the restrictions on expenditure this imposed. Others, as we have seen, prioritised the freedom and satisfaction their choice of work brought them and found ways to make their lives more pleasant and comfortable which involved minimal expenditure. It is also clear that some families were able to adapt better than others to restricted incomes, and often it made a difference how much they had access to family support and the other non-cash resources identified earlier in the last chapter.

Having said that, few of even the higher earners found managing easy. Indeed it was some of those previously on higher earnings who found adapting to new patterns of expenditure particularly difficult and were disappointed at not having been able to improve their situation. Tight management and careful budgeting were the explanations offered by several respondents in these families for such success as they had in maintaining their standard. Even for families like these, managing was not easy. 'Scraping by', or 'just keeping our heads above water', were expressions commonly used, although some people also pointed out that they were doing better than others in the current recession.

Nevertheless, virtually all the families in the study reported some kinds of restrictions on spending or having had to cut back in some way. Even where basic needs were adequately met, it was almost universal that some form of personal expenditures, social activities or 'little extras' had been curtailed. This was not always seen as a problem: as has been pointed out before, some families accepted these limitations voluntarily as part of their chosen lifestyle or as a sacrifice they were prepared to make in the short term, in the hope of future business success.

The strategies adopted for economising on expenditure were familiar from other studies of survival on low or insecure incomes (Ritchie, 1990; Huby and Dix, 1992), and in this respect there was little difference between the families with self-employed and employed earners, or between the families with higher business turnovers and the others. However, these non-essential 'extras' which were cut out sometimes included items like house insurance, or private pensions, which could have longer term consequences for standards of living and future security.

Constraints and priorities in expenditure

We continue here by examining briefly some of the areas of spending which are known from other studies to be problematic for families with low incomes. We look at how families prioritised particular needs or calls on expenditure, at the constraints they felt, and the areas where spending had been restricted or cut down. Constraint is of course to some extent a subjective feeling. Most people, at whatever income level, experience feelings of being unable to afford things they would like. There is a difference, however, in having to refrain from luxuries and in feeling unable to afford basic items commonly enjoyed by the mass of the population.

Food is a basic necessity and eating patterns are often taken as key indicators for measuring living standards. The PSI survey of low-income families found a core of around 10-15 per cent of family credit recipients registering some form of deprivation on indicators of food consumption which families ascribed to affordability rather than choice (Marsh and McKay, 1993). However, there was little difference between those families with an employed earner and those supported by self-employment.

In this study food was frequently mentioned as a priority, particularly, as we would expect, for children. It was one of the first demands to be met from weekly budgets and no families felt they ever actually went short. One strand of experience was that little had changed in family eating habits for many years. People said they 'ate well enough', but that this reflected a restraint that was longstanding: 'We've never gone for luxuries'. There were also questions of taste. Several families were mainly vegetarian and felt they had both a cheaper and more healthy diets than other families. As we have seen earlier, food was often one of the forms of mutual exchange which some families were involved in and several others had access to fresh produce from their own gardens. The other common view was that food was an area where people had been forced to cut their expenditure. This was usually by cutting out 'luxuries', buying cheaper cuts of meat, having less variety, or shopping around for bargains. One lone parent explained how checking prices and looking for cheaper items was a constant way of life:

> I have to think about what I'm going to buy all the time. All the time I have to. When I buy my meat I have to work out 'right, you know, I can't pay that much a pound'.

The most drastic changes in the buying of food took place in families who had seen severe drops in income - one woman talked ironically about being sent 'food parcels by pensioners' - her parents.

Heating and other fuels were another priority for most families and few had any arrears at the time of the interview. One reason was, as one woman put it, 'if you don't pay it you get cut off'. There was still often a need to economise. One lone parent had started using 'keys' for both gas and electricity because of being in arrears in the past: 'They said it's very expensive but I'd rather do that than get into more debt'. She said that in winter it was costing her up to £25 per week so she had stopped using it unless it was bitterly cold. This was not unusual: several other people said they only used their central heating in particularly cold weather.

Clothing was one of the items of expenditure which families most frequently felt they had to do without and very few parents said they had bought any new clothing for themselves in the recent past recently. Often this had changed since they started being self-employed or moved from a previous job. One change came in buying clothing for children as Christmas and birthday presents and in asking for clothes themselves for presents. There was also use of second-hand and charity shops, while shoes were often cited as an expense needing to be spread over time and were often ordered through clubs and catalogues.

The question of clothing came up most often in the interviews in the context of children. Parents expressed a number of conflicting feelings here. 'If they need things they need them' was a common feeling and sometimes if this meant going into debt or not paying the rent for a week or two then this had to be done. On the other hand they were reluctant to meet the costs of fashionable clothes which children sometimes demanded. This was an issue raised frequently in the self-employed families, who generally had older children. One way this problem could be eased was where children earned some money for themselves. They were then expected to meet at least part of the cost of inessential clothes or other goods. Buying school uniforms or other items for school was another problem mentioned by some families, and a few had applied for school clothing grants from their local authority.

Other costs which are known to be difficult for lower income families include school trips or holidays and Christmas and birthday presents. Most said that they tried to find the money for school outings even if this was difficult, and some of the lone mothers said that the children's fathers occasionally helped out with costs of this kind. Family credit also came in useful here. Longer school trips sometimes attracted forms of subsidy so that children of less well-off parents did not have to meet the full costs. Several people said they had taken advantage of these arrangements, though they were not always happy about doing so.

Buying presents for children was often done with help from other relatives. People talked about having 'a whip round' of relatives, for presents like bicycles and making up the difference themselves. Even so, events like Christmas generally required saving up in advance and clubs and catalogues were also used to spread costs. For some families who had been used to a higher standard of living in the past, explaining to their children that they could no longer afford to spend as much as before could be a problem. Having been a relatively low-earning family for a long time seemed to make it easier in this respect for some parents. They felt their children had been brought up not to expect too much.

Although sharing costs became easier for some families as children got older and found part-time work, there were still often great difficulties where sons and daughters were notionally no longer dependent on their parents and benefits for them had stopped. The benefit or training income the young people received in their own right only met part of their costs, and they often remained largely dependent on their parents financially.

Holiday and leisure activity among a group as diverse and heterogeneous as these self-employed families were influenced more than almost anything else by choice, lifestyle and priorities as much as by whether families could afford them. Clearly cost was a major factor in whether families had been able to take holidays. Many had not taken what they considered a proper family holiday for several years, and had made do with visits to relatives. A few had managed to have foreign holidays in the previous two years, but always only with help from relatives or friends or by dint of special saving. In some cases people had managed to send their children away for organised trips or holidays, but these were often subsidised in some way, either by a relative or the holiday organisation.

Making economies on a low income often means cutting out regular bills or payments which may seem 'non-urgent', or appear to bring no immediate benefit. For some of the families in this study such payments included private pensions and some forms of insurance.

Pensions and insurance

Commitment to paying National Insurance Contributions among self-employed family credit recipients was variable not just among the sub-set interviewed about living standards, but across the whole study group. Several people appeared not be paying contributions when they should have been, and at least two were in substantial arrears. How much of a problem this may be for future pension entitlements depends on people's previous contribution records and how long they stay in self-employment. As Meager et al.'s (1994) analysis of the incomes of formerly self-employed people in retirement shows, low incomes while in work can persist into later years.

One way in which people can compensate for any gaps in their contribution record is by taking out private pensions, for which half the premiums are deducted from income in the family credit assessment. Most self-employed families were aware of the need for some form of pension protection if they stayed long in self-employment and they had often made enquiries about different schemes. Many judged the premiums unaffordable from their present earnings, but wanted to take out pensions when circumstances allowed. Others were prepared to wait - some of the younger people in particular felt there was 'plenty of time yet'.

The analysis of administrative statistics found that only 17 per cent of self-employed recipients were recorded as contributing to private pension schemes. Among all the self-employed families interviewed less than half were currently making payments, crossing all family types and occupations. Payments were generally small, mostly between £20 and £30 per month, though for one farmer the premium was only around £50 per half year and seemed unlikely to offer much of a return. It also appeared that pensions are a 'soft' area of expenditure which families would be likely to cut out or suspend if circumstances became difficult. In addition to the current subscribers, there were other self-employed families and a few employees who had previously been contributing to private pensions but had stopped paying, leaving their existing contributions frozen. None had any clear idea of the likely value of their discontinued payments.

Other families had not yet been able to afford to start pension plans, though they were all aware of the difficulties they might face in retirement if they did not start contributing soon. In talking about planning for retirement one expressed an anxiety common to many of the respondents:

> I try not to [think about it], because it worries me when I do and I've got other things to worry about which are much more immediate. But I will have to do something about that fairly soon.

Some self-employed people are likely to have previously been in occupational schemes from earlier periods of employment. Where they were higher earners, these contributions might be expected to increase their chances of having some pension protection in later life. There were examples of people in this situation among the families interviewed, some of whom had either had their contributions transferred to their private schemes or left their contributions in the previous funds. Mainly, however, they had cashed in their payments and used them either during a period of unemployment or to help start the self-employed business. None of the employees had been in occupational schemes in previous jobs, which perhaps reflected the temporary and insecure nature of much of their work experience, though one was a member at the time of the interview.

In general it appeared that families were more likely to have and maintain small life insurance policies than pension plans. This may be because the premiums are smaller and because they tend to have shorter terms, with more prospect of a return from the investment. Building insurance was compulsory for owner-occupiers, and most of those needing personal liability insurance in connection with work made a priority of keeping up these payments (though there were exceptions). House contents insurance was different, however: nearly a quarter of the self-employed families and several employees currently had no insurance or had recently given up paying. Invariably people said they had stopped paying for insurance because they felt they could not afford the rising cost of premiums. Expressions like 'we've got nothing worth robbing' were also common. Some had experienced burglaries and were not happy having no insurance but felt there was no option: 'something has to go'.

While pressures on expenditure were common to most families, some were clearly able to manage more easily on their incomes than others. Sudden drops in income or large demands on expenditure were the hardest to handle, sometimes leading to debts or arrears which could compound their difficulties. Responses to these financial pressure differed little between the employed and self-employed families, though more of the latter had some protective cushion of savings, previous earnings, or family support. Where such cushions did not exist, managing could involve the use of credit or going into debt.

Credit and debt

The use of credit as a means of managing on low incomes has been referred to at various points earlier in the book. It is also discussed later where we look at how families acquired various consumer goods. This section draws together the various strands of discussion on this subject and looks at the extent to which the families in the study had accumulated forms of non-housing debt. The national literature on debt tends not to disaggregate information by employment status, so little is known about levels of indebtedness among the self-employed specifically (Berthoud, 1989; Parker, 1990; National Consumer Council, 1990). This is perhaps because many self-employed people are so habituated to living with large loans and overdrafts that until a crisis is reached they do not regard these 'debts' as a problem. Nevertheless it is clear that the recession of the early 1990s caused considerable financial problems for large numbers of small business owners, some evidence of which emerged from cases taken to Citizens Advice Bureaux (Brown, 1992).

The difference between credit and debt is not clear cut. One person's credit is another person's debt and the difference is sometimes a matter of degree or attitude. The distinction is even more uncertain when applied to business, since the use of overdrafts or deficit funding is a conventional business practice. Often it excites little concern unless loan repayments become unmanageable or there is a change of policy or attitude on the part of lenders. The distinction was not always clear in the minds of respondents in this study and people took differing views of their situations. It was not unusual, for example, for someone to say that they had no debts, but that they ran a £1,500 overdraft and were paying hire purchase payments for a car, whereas others would refer to small sums outstanding on a catalogue purchase or a credit card as a debt. This section talks first about the use of credit and then outlines some of the debts people saw themselves as having. It follows broadly the kind of analytical distinction most commonly expressed by the families interviewed, but it is recognised that for some people the division is artificial.

In general, people were highly reluctant to use credit unless they had no alternative. To some extent this was based on previous experiences. Several families recounted stories of difficulties in the past resulting from the use of credit cards or from buying too many items on hire purchase. Some of the self-employed people explained that they used credit cards for small work-related expenses like petrol, but emphasised that they always tried to pay off the balance each month. The only person who reported heavy use of credit cards used them to pay for overseas buying trips and did not regard the repayments as a problem. Others had cut up credit cards or returned them to the banks. One woman referred to them as 'fool's gold'. Overall there was a strong ethos among both employed and self-employed people on saving up and keeping within current means. As one man put it:

> We try and keep to what we can afford and if we can't afford something then we go without.

There was nevertheless fairly extensive use of certain types of credit. This mainly fell into four categories. First, the self-employed people in the building trade usually ran monthly accounts with suppliers. Secondly, some people used hire purchase or other similar arrangements for large items which they felt were essential but could not save for. Thirdly, there was widespread use of catalogues and clubs, mainly for smaller items of expenditure like children's clothing.

The fourth important form of credit was the business overdraft. The use of authorised overdrafts has been referred to earlier and was clearly essential for many of the self-employed businesses. Those reported mainly ranged between

£900 and £2,000, though some of the farming overdrafts were higher. The users were mainly in the larger trading businesses and the families involved were generally those with higher overall living standards. As we have seen, overdrafts were often the source of such drawings as were taken from the businesses and they were constantly being repaid and 'topped up' again. Respondents emphasised that they were often crucial in allowing them to keep on meeting household bills and urgent payments, while using family credit for shopping and other day-to-day expenditures.

We have seen that most families had used up any savings they previously had, either in setting up self-employed enterprises or seeing them through lean times. Many had only managed to maintain their present living standards by taking on debts in addition to mortgages and overdrafts. The 'non-managing' families among the self-employed were, as has been mentioned, facing severe debts on top of mortgage arrears.

Only a minority of both self-employed and employee families were without some non-housing debts, leaving aside catalogue and hire purchase payments or small credit card bills which were seen as manageable. Community charge arrears were common, ranging from a few weeks' payments to almost two years. Other debts of between £1,000 and £2,000 included loans from family or friends. There were also substantial arrears of tax and national insurance and the previous chapter has already discussed the problems which can arise from not keeping up these payments.

Among the employees, poll tax arrears were again common and few were up to date with their payments. Several families had bank loans or overdrafts of up to £600 and others had borrowed sums of up to £200 from relatives, or in one case from an employer. One employed family with major debts had lost their house because of the failure of a previous business. As well as mortgage arrears they owed a total of over £2,000 to companies and relatives.

Not all of the debts described were seen by the families as serious problems. The family loans in particular were very flexible and repayments were only made when the money was available. Nevertheless they still placed constraints on family expenditure and were often experienced as a constant worry. Although families were generally managing on their present incomes of earnings plus benefits, doing so required careful household budgeting. Most had cut down on some areas of spending and there was rarely much money left for anything other than necessities. For a few families, business collapse or redundancy had left them owing large sums of money, and others had only avoided major debt by drawing on savings. Sharp drops in income were difficult to deal with, but families who previously had higher incomes tended to find managing easier because they were already well equipped with household goods and consumer durables.

Household possessions and consumer durables

The way that consumer durables and other household possessions are used as indicators of living standards was discussed in Chapter One. It was suggested that access to goods may be an important aspect of the quality of life people expect to enjoy, but that quantitative data alone is limited in what it tells us about the relationship between ownership of the various items and income. Factors such as the source, condition and purpose of goods are also important. This may be particularly true for groups like the self-employed families in the study, whose earnings have often changed or fluctuated substantially over time.

The varying patterns of previous earnings identified suggest a number of likely outcomes for the different groups of families in the study. Some families may be managing to preserve living standards based on earlier periods of greater prosperity, though they could be facing future problems of repair and replacement of goods. Others may have existed for long periods with second-hand or poor-quality goods: lacking the surplus income which allows them to save, some may have been obliged to take on credit payments for expensive new items. Higher earnings, inheritance and other factors such as taste can also mean that some families may have expensive and long-lasting goods, whereas others may have settled for cheaper and less durable purchases. Finally, questions of choice and preference may be relevant. As we have seen, some respondents expressed a lack of interest in acquiring possessions. For these people, being without certain goods does not necessarily indicate deprivation, although some may have learned to live with lowered expectations. In a survey measuring ownership of goods, all these different groups of families might exhibit characteristics which give no real indication of the quality of their lives.

Useful information about household possessions is hard to get at and difficult to interpret, but it is important in families where the relationship between earnings and living standards is not clearly understood. Here qualitative methods can help to put flesh on the bones of quantitative data by looking at the ways in which goods were acquired, their value and condition, and any problems people face with repairing or replacing them.

Table 7.5 below compares data on the percentages of households with a range of standard consumer durables from the 1991 General Household Survey and the Policy Studies Institute survey of low-income families (Marsh and McKay, 1993). The GHS data is for all households in Great Britain, not just families with children, whereas the PSI data is based on families in receipt of family credit at the time of their survey in 1991. The PSI survey found families in both employment groups with higher levels of ownership than the national average for a number of items, such as videos, fridge-freezers and washing machines. This is not surprising among a sample of families with children. The most striking differences between the two groups in the survey were whether they had telephones and motor vehicles, but one might expect more families with a self-employed main earner to have both of these in connection with their work.

The table also includes the distribution of household durables amongst the families we interviewed. As we have emphasised before, comparisons between small qualitative study groups and national representative samples are not meant to suggest that data from the former are statistically generalisable in the same way. The purpose is merely to see where the particular families who were selected for in-depth interviewing were located within the broader picture derived from the national surveys. This provides a background for further qualitative exploration. Not all the same questions were asked in the two surveys and the current study. We, for example, asked about personal computers, answer-phones and fax machines because we were interested in their use by people operating small self-employed enterprises.

The self-employed families in our study appeared to be marginally better endowed with most consumer durables than the equivalent families in the PSI survey, as were the small group of employees. As we saw earlier, the distribution of earnings among these families was also slightly higher than the national average within the family credit population. The differences between the two self-employed groups were slight, however. Fridge-freezers and washing machines were omnipresent in both groups and ownership of vehicles and telephones was higher among the employed families than both the PSI sample and the national average. Colour television sets were also virtually universal. Dishwashers were still a minority possession, present in only seven self-employed and two employed homes. While we might expect some self-employed people to have computers for business use, it is interesting to see that four of the employed families also had some kind of personal computer in addition to any games consoles they may have acquired for their children.

Table 7.5
Consumer durables: comparison of data from the study groups with those from national surveys

Percentage of households with:	*GHS 1991*	*PSI survey* Employed	*PSI survey* Self-employed	*Qualitative interview groups* Employed	*Qualitative interview groups* Self-employed
Colour television	98	94	93	100	95
Video	68	78	82	90	84
Home computer	21	-	-	40	27
Children's games computer	-	-	-	50	51
Microwave oven	55	59	67	60	60
Fridge-freezer	83	96	99	100	100
Washing machine	87	93	94	100	100
Dishwasher	14	4	7	20	16
Telephone	88	75	88	90	92
Answer-phone	-	-	-	10	51
Facsimile machine	-	-	-	0	5
Car or van	67	45	83	80	89
Base	9,995	760	103	10	37*

Sources of national data: OPCS (1992), Marsh and McKay (1993)

* Excludes three families not in receipt of family credit at the time of the interview

Household goods: acquisition, use, value and condition

The interviews provided rich detail on the source and condition of household goods, although the amount of information people were able to offer varied. In general, few of either the self-employed or employee families had made major purchases of consumer goods in recent years, with the exception of motor vehicles. Even the apparently better-off families had acquired most of their more expensive possessions in previous years when their earnings were higher. Often they still had the major items like cookers, washing machines, beds and suites of furniture which they had bought or been given when they first married. Items like microwaves, videos and computers which were acquired more recently were often second-hand, sometimes passed on by family and friends who had bought new items for themselves. Second-hand items were generally quite acceptable and there was a widespread emphasis on 'making do' and repairing goods to keep them going for as long as possible.

When families had to buy new items, the preference was for saving up and there was a widespread reluctance to use credit facilities. There were two main groups among those families who had recently bought expensive new items. First, there were lone parents who had left many of their shared goods behind in their marital home: lump-sum divorce settlements had been used to equip new homes. The second group comprised couples who had bought large items like washing machines to replace broken ones. These were usually families without a large existing stock of household goods from earlier, more prosperous periods. Several explained how they had reluctantly used credit because their earnings were insufficient to allow them to save the sums required.

The families who had dishwashers were mostly, as one might expect, those with previous higher earnings and all had been purchased some years before. One family's needs had changed and they had chosen to buy a dishwasher by selling an expensive pram and other baby equipment, while another had acquired a second-hand model cheaply when her husband was in the removals business.

Most families felt that were reasonably well equipped with the main consumer goods which were important to them, and only a few listed urgent necessities which they felt they lacked. Others talked of things they would like to buy when they could afford it, including new furniture or kitchen equipment, but they did not usually describe these as either necessities or priorities. There were, nevertheless, frequent anxieties expressed about the replacement of worn-out equipment. People who had machinery like washing machines, cookers and refrigerators which were old and malfunctioning spoke of the problems they would face if they broke down beyond repair. Central heating was another large expense mentioned by families whose systems had been in place for many years, and they worried that the boilers might need replacing. Other items most commonly mentioned as needing replacement when funds allowed included beds, carpets and new suites. People pointed to worn patches of carpet or uncarpeted stairs, and commented on the age or discomfort of their furniture. Finally, it was common for people in both self-employed and employee families to say that they were short of bedding: several talked in terms of having 'one set on and one in the wash'.

Items like computers tended to have been bought partly for business use and partly for educational or entertainment purposes where families had older children. Several of these were again second-hand or had been gifts, though in two cases they were included in family credit applications as business expenses. One of the fax machines belonged to a retailer who had to communicate with overseas dealers.

In general there were few signs of luxury items in any of the homes. Some of the households had music systems, but only one included a modern CD player. They were mostly old, cheap systems, in several cases given to children as Christmas presents or bought by them from pocket money and after-school jobs. Children on farms sometimes had access to ponies, but these were thought to 'cost less for a country child than a new bicycle'.

Within this overall picture there was still considerable variation. In order to give a flavour of the complexity and the contrasts which lie behind the simple statistics, we look first across the two study groups at three key consumer items - motor vehicles, washing machines, and televisions. Then we look in more detail at a wider range of household goods in four different families, who illustrate the range of variation found within one small group of the self-employed.

Motor vehicles

There were cars or vans in the households of most the families in the study who had an adult in self-employed work at the time of the interview. About a third had more than one vehicle - usually a van used in connection with the self-employed work or a farm vehicle, though in several cases one or other of the vehicles was either defunct or 'on its last legs'.

If we look at the range of occupations involved, including farming, taxi driving, sales and delivery work, the building trades and various kinds of retail, it is apparent that vehicles were important or essential for many families. In a few cases purchases had been offset against tax liabilities and, where loans were involved, included in family credit assessments. Vehicles were also important in that around a third of the self-employed families lived in rural areas where public transport was limited or non-existent. People with disabled children or other relatives also needed a second car when one partner used a vehicle for work. The need for vehicles had to be balanced against the cost, however, and few had been bought new or nearly new in recent years. Virtually all the respondents said they had bought or acquired their car or van second-hand and none of them were in any sense 'luxury' vehicles. Even the highest earners in the study made do with old vehicles - both were second-hand and one was described as being worth 'only scrap value'. Vehicles were often acquired with help from parents or relatives - either by them buying second-hand cars or handing on used vehicles. The only recent purchase of a new car had been financed with a loan on a three-year finance agreement. The car was needed in connection with a sales occupation and the loan had been included in the family credit as income, offset by the interest payments.

Although people were generally reluctant to use loan finance, there were some occupations where investment in a presentable vehicle could help secure work:

> Everyone told me just get a battered old van to start with - something I didn't want to do. I wanted to project an image and that was important to me. I'd rather not have done it all if I couldn't project the image of being a professional.

However, keeping payments for the purchase of vehicles could be a heavy drain on the business. One person had seen both a car and a van repossessed, leaving her still owing some £7,000 in repayments.

It was mentioned in the last chapter that the cost of keeping cars on the road was among the expenditures some families found it hard to meet, and families who did not currently own vehicles had sold them for this reason. Another alternative was to leave cars untaxed. There was also great emphasis on repairs and keeping old cars on the road as long as possible. One lone mother and several of the men had car maintenance skills and one car was referred to as being 'saved from the scrapyard' two years before, though it was not expected to last much longer.

Family use of vehicles was important for some respondents and was seen as better value financially than some other forms of transport. One woman pointed out the economies involved in running a van, particularly with a large family:

> See people say 'how can you afford to run a van?' But when you think about it, if you've got seven of you going out for the day, imagine going on a bus or train. You're cheaper to go by car.

The high level of car ownership was an indication of the importance families placed on mobility and the necessity in many cases for self-employed people to have access to transport. Some self-employed families had bought their cars when they were previously employed with higher earnings, and others had been able to take advantage of the legitimate arrangements within tax and family credit to count the purchase of a vehicle partly or wholly as a business expense. However, the kind of vehicles the families possessed and the ways in which they were acquired did not suggest the presence of large amounts of available income, nor did they in general indicate an especially high standard of living or a level of consumption inconsistent with receiving support through family credit.

Washing machines

A high proportion of all households and over 90 per cent of low-income families in the PSI survey had washing machines. This suggests that they have come to be seen as important or even necessary as a household good, particularly in families with children. They are also expensive items which other research shows families on very low incomes find it hard to afford. The official evaluation of the social fund by Huby and Dix (1992), for example, found that washing machines were among the top needs causing concern to people applying to the fund in 1990.

We have already seen that both of the groups in this study contained families with a slightly higher average level of earnings than we would expect to find in the family credit population as a whole. Some had higher earnings in the past and there were also several families with large numbers of children, as well as other adults or disabled children in the household. It is not surprising, therefore, to find that all the families had washing machines, which in itself does not indicate unusually high living standards. Washing machines were the item most frequently mentioned as a necessity, particularly though not only by women, and they were also one of the causes of the greatest anxiety if they went wrong. They were often too expensive for families to save for, so if people wanted new machines buying them was the most common use of hire purchase or other credit. Nevertheless, very few self-employed families said they had acquired new machines within the two years before the interview. Hire purchase, credit from electricity boards, or catalogues were the most common sources of finance, as well as money from divorce settlements and inheritances. A couple with six children expected to wash three loads most days. This heavy use had worn out their previous machine and buying a new one had been essential. For this family, hire purchase was the only way of meeting such a large cost, a situation seen as general among families with one low earner:

> Like most people we have to either get it on credit or get a loan from the bank for bigger items. Unless there's two of you working and in pretty good jobs, I think generally speaking most people are like that, you know.

The majority of the families who had originally bought new machines had owned them for between three and seven years, often bought when they were in previous jobs, or brought by women from previous marital homes. Most had been repaired several times and some were hardly functioning. One machine brought from a previous marriage had been repaired 'umpteen times' and another woman felt she had 'half a machine': it did not spin and often leaked. She spun her clothes in an 'ancient' spin dryer handed on by a friend.

Many other washers had been acquired second-hand and some families were emphatic that this provided better value:

> I won't buy a new one - they don't last. I'll buy a second-hand one for say £20-25, get a couple of years use out of it.

There were few appreciable differences between the employed and self-employed families in the ownership of washing machines. Because some of the employee families were younger and more recently established they had bought machines more recently, but there were also several families with machines more than ten years old which were regularly breaking down. The lone parents still used the machines they had when they were married. The only new washer acquired in the previous two years had cost £500 and had been bought through a catalogue. As the husband explained, this was one of their uses of family credit:

> Family credit helps there, because that's what we pay it with. Well that's what we have been paying it with in so many words ... We drew the money out of the bank and just gave it to my mum who gave it to the club.

Television sets

Television sets hold an ambiguous position in the consensual view of household necessities. Almost all households have one, as did more than 90 per cent of low-income families in the PSI survey. On the other hand, only 58 per cent of people surveyed for the Breadline Britain 1990s study (Frayman, 1991) thought they were necessities. This apparent contradiction may not be difficult to explain, however. Most people appear to make distinctions between goods like refrigerators, cookers, washing machines or beds, which are seen as basic to the production of everyday health, nutrition and cleanliness, and television sets or videos, which are seen as primarily for entertainment.

Such distinctions were commonly expressed by people in this study when asked to say what they saw as necessities. This did not mean that television sets were not important to them. As in many other studies of people on lower incomes, watching television or videos was a prime leisure activity and it was frequently mentioned in words like 'our only form of entertainment'. Compared to going out to pubs or other kinds of evening entertainment - which most people said they could only rarely afford - television represented good value for money. Without it, many people would clearly feel deprived of an important aspect of their individual and social lives.

As with the other goods discussed, there were wide variations in the age and value of television sets and the ways in which they were acquired. The exact ages of television sets was not always clear, but few self-employed families said they had bought new colour sets within the previous three years. Lone parents had sometimes bought new sets along with the other equipment they acquired from the proceeds of their divorce settlements. Indeed for one woman this felt like 'the first chance I ever had to buy anything new'.

Renting television sets was one option. Among those who paid by slot meter was a lone parent could not afford to save up or buy a set on credit and had previously had difficulties keeping up a monthly rental payment. Other family television sets were mainly four to ten years old - some expensive sets acquired during more prosperous times and others bought second-hand for as little as £10, or handed on from parents. Just over a third of the self-employed families had more than one set - a feature which appeared to be associated mainly with having several children, who were the primary users of these other sets. The extra sets had often been given by relatives, friends, or in one case the non-custodial father of a child.

Ownership and access to all these three key household goods appeared overall to bear some relation to patterns of past and present earnings, but they also were crucially influenced by networks of family support and the various strategies of household financial management discussed earlier in the report. The variation between families which lies behind the statistics of ownership of consumer goods shows that is difficult to draw clear inferences about living standards from quantitative data alone. One way of looking at the question in more detail is to choose a few families and take a case study approach. This helps us to see how past and present earnings, family support, and choice all combine in different ways for different families. In order to illustrate the diverse circumstances of families in the self-employed group, we therefore look at a range of household items belonging to three couples. They are chosen to represent the three main groups of self-employed families identified as having differing work histories and patterns of earnings - the 'male manual workers', the 'career changers' and the 'developers'. They also include the two families with the highest and lowest net earnings, as assessed for family credit, in order to show how current earnings are not necessarily the dominant factor.

Three self-employed families

1. Mr and Mrs A (both in their 30s) had five children of school age. Mr A had worked for 20 years on and off in a manual industry, both as an employee and as a self-employed subcontractor. His earnings were variable but generally in the mid-range of incomes for family credit. Although their income had been more stable and secure at some times in the past, it had never been much higher than it was currently and Mr A had experienced several periods of unemployment. They had been receiving family credit continuously for nearly 18 months, though they had also claimed both family credit and FIS at other times in the past. They lived in a small, owner-occupied, terraced house without central heating in a rundown area of a small town. The house was well decorated because this was Mrs A's hobby, and it was adequately, but inexpensively, furnished and carpeted. Their television set and video were both rented and they had no stereo or music system except for a small radio cassette player - 'nothing flash' - bought as a present several years before. They had a second-hand, twin-tub washing machine and no tumble dryer or dishwasher. Their vacuum cleaner had just broken and Mrs A was currently borrowing a neighbour's. She was planning to use her next family credit payment to buy a new one. They had an eight year old microwave oven, but the turntable was broken. Children's presents were a priority for them and they had bought a second-hand games computer for their sons the previous year. Mr and Mrs A were resistant to buying anything on hire purchase, having got into serious debt after their marriage, and they had saved up to buy an old van which they use for family outings. Mrs A did not drive and rode a second-hand bike. Mr A's earnings had always been too low for them to accumulate savings except for specific purposes like the van or the occasional holiday. The only other money they had put away was a few hundred pounds for a future income tax bill. Mrs A felt they had just enough bedding for the children:

   'They've got like the sheet and their quilt covers, so it's a case of washing it, ironing it and put it back on. They haven't got loads and loads of changes or anything like that.

They were 'happy with what we've got', but one item they would like was a new bed, not having had a new one since they got married. Their current priority was the mortgage as they were about to move to a more expensive house.

2. Mr and Mrs B (both in their 40s) had three children under 14. They represented the 'career changers'. Mr B's main work experience was as a manual worker employed by various different companies. He had been made redundant twice in the past. Seven years ago they set up an agency business with some financial help from his father. Until she had children Mrs B had also worked, in a clerical job. They currently had the highest net earnings among the families, though this was still less than he had earned in his previous work. They were coming to the end of their second year on family credit. The B's lived in a detached, modern house with central heating, in the suburbs of a small town. The house was bought with help from their parents. They had a business van, bought with a family loan, and a car - jointly valued at around £8,000. The house was well decorated and comfortably furnished, though some of the household equipment dated back to their marriage 17 years before. This included a gas cooker, a fridge-freezer and the vacuum cleaner. They had a dishwasher, bought some eight years before by selling baby equipment:

> I had a very nice pram and all the other equipment and sold that, and I virtually had enough money out of all the things I sold to buy the dishwasher.

Mr B's parents had given them a washing machine, again several years before. They had decided to buy a microwave oven with cash given to them as 'a very generous present' by a close friend. They had three colour television sets - the main one was bought more than seven years ago, along with a video, before they started their business, and the others, used by the children, were gifts. They also had a modern stereo system and an answering machine bought for the business. Mrs B explained that they had bought very few things for the house since her husband became self-employed. Most of the goods and furniture had been bought in the past with two sets of redundancy money and with maternity pay and benefits she had received from her previous jobs. They had also been left some money in the past and had rarely had to use hire purchase or credit, but they had no savings as: 'when we've ever come into an amount of money, we've generally put it in the house'. She would like to buy a computer for the business and for the children, but this would have to wait until they could afford it. They felt they were basically well set up for household goods, including bedding, but worried about having to replace large items like the washing machine and the central heating boiler.

3. Ms C and Mr D (both in their early 30s) were a cohabiting couple with one child pre-school age child. They represent the 'developers'. Ms C had given up her previous professional job as it was difficult to fit in with having a young baby. Two years before she started on a small scale selling food and other dietary products. A year later Mr D gave up his job to join her. They currently had the lowest net earnings of any family in the study and received maximum family credit payments, of which they were on their second award. The couple lived in a small Victorian terraced house, bought ten years before with parental help. There was no central heating, but open fires, and the house was simply painted and furnished, with a few antiques. Ms C had the highest level of cash savings reported among families. They had a small van previously belonging to Mr D before they met. This was used to transport goods for her business, but was in need of replacement. They also had an old car given to Ms C by a parent. Their washing machine, fridge-freezer and cooker were all bought new three years before, when Mr D was in full-time work. They also had an old hi-fi system and a black and white television set, but no microwave, dishwasher, tumble dryer or video, and said that they did not particularly want any of these. No major household items had been bought since Ms C started her business. Ms C said she would quite like a computer, a food processor and a new wardrobe for their clothing, but she was:

> ... not really bothered. I mean you know, it's like the more you have the more you want. The less you have the less you seem to need in a way.

Measured by possession of standard domestic goods, the differences between these families are not extreme. All owned many of the major consumer goods generally used as indicators of living standards, apart from central heating and dishwashers in two cases. For Ms C, not having central heating was not a sign of deprivation. The As managed with the goods they had because they did not have high expectations, whereas the Bs had benefited from substantial help from family and friends. We can see from these case studies that the influences of previous earnings and work patterns, parental support and choice combined to produce quite different standards of living for three families whose equivalised net incomes after taking benefit into account would be fairly similar.

Up to this point we have looked mainly at material aspects of living standards, including housing, incomes and consumer goods. We have seen that even the better-off, self-employed families found aspects of their lives constrained by having to manage on restricted incomes, although some were sustained by a strong commitment to their way of life and the work that supported it. We now conclude the empirical findings from the study by discussing people's own views of their living standards and how these have changed, their perceptions of their health, and their hopes and aspirations for the future.

Respondents' own views of their standards of living

It was stated in the introductory chapter that the idea of 'living standards' is complex and contested. While this is true, the term is still widely understood as having common sense meanings, and people in this study talked about it in similar ways. There were three basic layers of discourse used by respondents:

- *material* - people referred first of all to material factors, like disposable incomes, their homes, their spending power and possessions

- *comparative* - people compared themselves to other people or, more often, described changes in their own standards of living

- *subjective* - people talked about their states of mind, the position they saw themselves as occupying in the world and the processes of relating to it. Terms used included 'struggle', 'security', 'contentment', 'bettering ourselves', or 'falling behind'. States of mind were often further explained by reference to factors such as 'choice', 'expectations', or 'ambition'.

These layers of discourse were clearly not discrete. Indeed, they were closely linked, so that, for example, people's states of mind often depended on how they compared themselves in material terms with previous circumstances. So far we have concentrated on the material aspects of living standards, but the other two facets were as important for the people concerned, and some discussion of these is necessary to provide a fuller picture of how people saw their lives as low-income families. The comparative discourse dominated the structure of people's comments, but they employed the descriptive or explanatory terminology of the subjective discourse and this structure is followed in the discussion.

Comparisons with other people took two main forms. First, people compared their situations favourably with those of others, reflecting a common recognition that while they might be struggling they were still objectively better off than most people without work at all. This position was held more widely among the self-employed families, but it was present among the employees too. It was expressed most forcefully by two people who had direct involvement through their work or voluntary activities with the lives of unemployed and poorer people in their neighbourhoods.

The second form of comparison with other people was generally used in reference to wider economic problems and was expressed as 'it's the same for everyone' and 'we're all in the same boat'. It was interesting to find that comparison with other people who were better off was rare, although respondents occasionally referred to other families getting as much income from the dole as they themselves did by working.

The more common comparison was with the families' own circumstances in the past. Mostly people's views of changes in their living standards reflected to some extent the patterns of past earnings analysed in earlier chapters. This relationship was perhaps most transparent among the two-parent employed families, where half directly attributed decline in living standards to recent redundancy, loss of a business, and interruptions in periods of temporary work. In the self-employed group the link was also clear for people like a fisherman whose earnings had fallen and whose wife was on sick leave from her work. He described their living standards as having fallen 'dramatically'. Similarly, the wife of the builder who had stopped trading compared their current circumstances with how life had been when he started: 'It was very good and now compared to that it's very poor'.

Among those in the group of families with higher turnover businesses who felt a distinct drop in standards was one of the farm owners, who spoke of having to 'tighten their belts' and referred to a time in the 1970s before he was married and before his father became ill:

> The money was there then, new clothes and everything, but now the money isn't there. I just can't do it, it's gone.

Similarly, a shopkeeper felt that their living standards had declined in the last few years, though he hoped they might improve once one of their loans was paid off in just under two years time.

However, there are two aspects of change in living standards which need to be disentangled. First, people's comparisons depended on their reference periods and how long they had been in their present work. For some this meant looking back to previous earnings in employment - the time when they felt their living standards had been at their highest. For others the start of self-employment was the reference point, from which they could trace gradual improvement. In one family these two viewpoints were both demonstrated simultaneously. The husband saw the trajectory of their living standards as a gradual upward path from the point when he was made redundant, whereas his wife emphasised the 'struggle' to manage on a much reduced self-employed income. Both these perspectives were equally valid ways of looking at the same situation, but the difference illustrates the way that people's perceptions of change depend on their points of reference.

A second aspect of change in living standards is that fluctuations in income by themselves are not the only cause. Often relationship breakdown, the birth of new children or other alterations in family composition are just as important. For a builder's wife, loss of earnings was clearly significant, but crucial too was having two more children during the period since her husband became self-employed.

The views of some of the lone parents offered a further perspective on this question. For the two self-employed lone fathers, setting up home on their own with their children meant 'starting from nothing'. Although both still earned less than in their previous jobs, the gradual acquisition of household goods and the building up of a new life represented a clear improvement. As one put it: 'Starting life again, like, with me and the lad, everything's a bonus'. For lone mothers a common experience is that living standards seem higher when they are on their own, even if their new income is less than the family income when they were married (Bradshaw and Millar, 1991). Greater control over money, as well as over their lives generally, can bring a sense of greater well-being, even if managing is still a struggle. Life can be seen as better even though it is financially more circumscribed:

> Oh, it's changed a lot, because now I can do what I want. I've nobody to answer to.

Life stage, as well as relationship breakdown, can influence people's perspectives on changes in their living standards. In spite of long periods of insecure and fluctuating earnings, several families saw their living standards as on an upward path, linked partly to their children growing up and moving towards independence.

People's perceptions of changes in their living standards, therefore, were influenced by factors over and above their current incomes. Having said that, most families, both self-employed and employed, felt that their circumstances had not changed appreciably for some time. 'Just plodding along', 'treading water', 'hanging on', 'ticking over' and 'hopeful survival' were all expressions used to describe a state of insecure balance, which was undoubtedly the most common single view among all the families. The families reporting no recent change included half of the employees and many of the lower earning self-employed families who were not facing crises, as well as most of the longer term family credit recipients. But they also included the highest self-employed earners, who, while managing, were pessimistic about improving their situation:

> I really can't see it going a lot further than we are at the moment ... It's a small business and I really think it's going to stay a small business.

No change was not necessarily a negative position, among the self-employed at least. A few families eschewed great ambitions, as was described earlier, and saw their quality of life as located in things other than material success. A child minder whose husband was unemployed said:

> In my life I wouldn't change anything at all. I am very, very happy with my life, very happy.

Even for this family, however, maintaining the equilibrium which they enjoyed depended on family credit. Without this, she said, they would be 'struggling'. An earlier chapter discussed the range of functions performed by family credit and it was clear that many of the families depended heavily on the benefit for the maintenance of their living standards. In this respect there was no difference between the employed and self-employed families, in spite of the different levels of award.

For some families the strain they had experienced as a result of trying to survive in self-employment had taken a toll on their health, while there were others who had chosen self-employment as a way of being able to keep on working even though their work was circumscribed by their own ill health or that of a family member.

Health and illness

There are a number of ways in which questions of ill-health and disability may be of special importance to self-employed people. Chapter Two discussed evidence that some people choose self-employment because of a limiting illness or disability, or as a way of combining work with the responsibility of caring for an ill or disabled person. Self-employed work itself can also involve risks to health and safety and it has been argued that self-employed people are poorly protected against such risks in social security and under legislation on occupational injury (Brown, 1992). Recent work by Ford et al. (1994) on the circumstances of lone parents has also suggested that increasing numbers are reporting health problems which reduce their labour market activity, or have a household member whose poor health requires their time and attention.

Our study found a number of ways in which health problems or disability had affected people's self-employed work and had contributed to financial constraints. There were also examples of problems facing self-employed people if they find they are not entitled to sickness benefits. This could happen in two ways. First, ill health or injury on the part of the self-employed people themselves could limit the amount of work they could carry out, and thus potentially reduce their earnings. Financial problems might be non-entitlement to sickness benefits or difficulty in obtaining income support. Secondly, work could be interrupted or limited by the illness of another family member.

In all, around half the self-employed workers and a small minority of the employees said they currently had health problems or had suffered illnesses or injuries in the past which still affected them. Thus, although ill health was not restricted to the self-employed, it was more prevalent among these families at least than among the employees.

Some of the accidents or illnesses which had limited work in some way during the previous two years were longstanding injuries which continued to cause problems, but most were recent occurrences. The conditions described included back strains and injuries, sciatica, stomach and throat problems, and stress or stress-related conditions. As we saw in Chapter Six, part of the nature of self-employment is that work has to carry on for the business to survive, and most of those affected said they took little time off even when they felt very ill. Some of these illnesses were a potential threat to people's long-term livelihoods. The musician's throat problems, for example were currently under control but he was anxious about future re-occurrences.

Even if there were no immediate crises, trying to run a small business in times of recession was often stressful. Several people talked of being under psychological strain which they felt had brought on various physical conditions. A man with stomach problems which doctors had ascribed to worry and stress said he hardly ever slept: 'the business is always on my mind'. Stress of this kind was intensified where families were facing imminent loss of homes or businesses. A woman breadwinner's thyroid complaint was felt to be exacerbated by tension and anxiety, and a shop owner currently required medication to control his blood pressure.

Although there was evidence of considerable ill health, those people who talked positively about their well-being were also mainly from the self-employed families. They often ascribed their good health to their way of life and the integration they had achieved between work and family life through self-employment. It appeared that self-employment could have both positive and negative health associations, depending on the circumstances.

The employees, as we have said, mainly reported being in good health. The slight disability of one of the clerical workers had not so far caused any serious problems with her work: until the recent birth of a child she was the main earner in a couple. Another woman who did clerical work was also managing to keep going to her job, although this could be difficult at times. Since her divorce she had been severely depressed and had developed associated physical symptoms.

Loss of earnings through ill-health can be a problem for both self-employed people and those who work for employers. As we saw in the previous chapter, however, the self-employed people tended not to think that they could rely on social security to provide a minimum income through periods of illness.

Illnesses were not restricted to the main self-employed earners themselves, but in only a few cases were other adults' conditions described as related to or affecting the family's present work or financial circumstances. Partners of the main earners reported various ailments, including a heart defect, asthma, backstrain, migraines, pneumonia and gynaecological problems, and at the time of the interview one woman was waiting for an operation.

If partners were ill, the self-employed work effort could be disrupted or constrained: for example, a woman with cancer often needed her husband to be at home. Loss of a second earner's wages could also be a problem if the partner had to take time off work through illness. One woman was currently on long-term sick leave from work with repetitive strain injury - a situation which had influenced her partner's decision to leave his area of self-employed work and look for other means of employment.

Illness among children can also potentially disrupt work in any family. Most children in the families whose living standards we examined closely were reported as normally being in good health, apart from occurrences of the usual childhood illnesses. Where there were instances of longer term conditions, the most common of which was asthma, parents in the two-parent families generally said that they had not caused major problems with work. This was mainly because in most families one of the parents was not working outside the home. On the other hand, children's long-term conditions limited some women's opportunities to look for work of their own.

More difficulties were experienced by some of the lone parents. A lone father whose son had required several operations and other visits to hospital had needed to take considerable time off work, causing loss of earnings and extra expense. He had also only recently discovered that he could apply for help with fares to the hospital. Children's ill health was a further source of stress to other lone parents with health problems of their own.

Overall, in this group of 40 self-employed families whose living standards and quality of life we explored, the proportion who reported some kind of ill health was rather higher in the PSI survey (Marsh and McKay, 1993). Illness or disability among the partners or children of self-employed people also seemed rather common. This may just be the effect of differences between a small qualitative sample and a larger representative survey, which are to be expected. However, in-depth interview techniques are also likely to encourage people to reflect more deeply on their circumstances than they do in responding to a survey. Even so, it is hard not to see in this high incidence of ill health some more general reflection of the lives of low-income families.

Looking to the future

The future plans or intentions of some families have been mentioned in earlier chapters. It is useful here to conclude the substantive findings by bringing together the various aspirations of the families as a whole. This is relevant to a discussion of living standards, because it indicates how families were reflecting on their circumstances and responding to changes or events in their lives.

We have already seen that the unemployed men in some of the female-earner couples had found jobs or were hoping to do so soon. They were expecting to be earning enough in the near future so that they would not need to claim family credit, although they were likely to re-apply for the time being. There was also quite a strong move out of self-employment into what people hoped would be more secure waged work. One formerly self-employed woman had just found herself a job as an employee. She needed to sell her house to pay her debts and was doubtful about trying self-employment again. She thought her new wage might take her out of family credit, but she planned to apply again anyway.

The fishermen too were looking for ways out of the industry and were trying for more secure waged employment. Several other families also expressed interest in possible moves out of the current area of work, including the taxi driver, though his plans were less developed. One man was considering retraining for the prison service where his brother worked: 'More for the security and pension side of things, I think, for later on in life'. One of the consultants was also looking at other alternatives:

> There's a strong possibility that I could get out of [this work] and actually sell the business. We're looking at that because I can't see it getting any better. I can only see it getting worse, so we're looking at different avenues.

By contrast, two quasi self-employed people had aspirations to become more genuinely self-employed. The fish processor was hoping to start a fish round and was trying to save money for equipment. A child minder and her husband were thinking about trying to run a shop or off-licence. This was a long-term plan and depended on money she was expecting to be left by a relative.

Not surprisingly, the farmers were the most settled in their way of life and they derived great satisfaction from it, even though there were financial worries. The two farm owners hoped that their sons would follow them in their occupation and expected to hand on the farm to them. Similarly the tenant farmer hoped to pass the tenancy on to his son if he was allowed to take over his mother's farm. Most of the other families saw themselves as continuing in their present work, hoping, in the case of the trading businesses, to survive the recession and gradually build up their work. The Asian carpet dealer felt he was constrained by racism from banks, suppliers and market authorities, but expected gradually to do better.

Some families, as we have seen, were motivated by satisfaction with their work and their ways of life. They did not expect their living standards to improve in the near future, but saw no reason to change their work, at least in the short term. Some people expected to increase family income in the future when children were older, either because partners in two-parent families would find work, or because lone parents would be able to expand their own working hours.

All the families currently receiving family credit planned to apply again, except for the man with the smallest award of all the families. His earnings had increased further and his partner had found a part-time job, so they did not expect to need family credit unless circumstances changed again. Several hoped they would not need to apply in the future. The following comment was typical:

> Yes I think so, you know. While they say it's ok for me to. But I mean as soon as I earn enough to keep myself the happier I will be.

For the employees the main hope was to hang on to jobs or to find work which was not temporary. One couple was particularly worried about the future if the husband could not find work, as the woman's hours were being slowly cut back and there was a danger the factory might close altogether. Another young couple was thinking of moving to another part of the country where there were more job opportunities. The only person who could see immediate prospects was the care assistant who was studying for her qualifications. She thought there might be openings arising from the new community care arrangements.

As we saw earlier, most of the women in the two-parent families wanted to find jobs when their children's ages allowed, though they were not optimistic. Only one family seemed likely to try self-employment in the near future: the man had previously been self-employed and his wife thought he might try again at some point, since there was 'no bright future' in his present work. All the families expected to continue claiming family credit.

Summary

It has been emphasised at various points that neither the way living standards are conceptualised nor how they are measured are subject to universal agreement. We have taken a qualitative approach to the question, because so much is unknown about low-income self-employment and needs explanation as well as measurement. We have looked at material questions such as the value and cost of housing, the level of earnings and other income, and the ownership and value of consumer goods, and then sought explanations from families for how and why their present material circumstances came about. We also sought respondents' views on the importance of different aspects of their living standards and quality of life, and how they perceived them changing or developing. In doing so we tried to trace the way that current living standards are often linked to patterns of expenditure determined by previous different circumstances.

For the self-employed, the relationship between current earnings and living standards often depends on how far previous earnings and expenditure still cushion them from more recent falls in family income. Thus, in general, the longer they have been at their current levels of earnings, the more direct the relationship becomes, as household goods deteriorate and savings dwindle. However, the relationship is mediated by other factors, so that in some cases expenditure may exceed net incomes over specific periods. Help from families, the use of credit or the accumulation of debt all act in different ways to make the link more tenuous. Low housing costs also can also help families to meet essential bills from the minimal drawings their overdrafts permit them to take out of their businesses.

Maintaining living standards with incomes at this level requires careful management and women clearly play an important role, particularly where their involvement in the business gives them greater direct influence on household expenditure. Nevertheless, surviving in low-income self-employment can be a continuing struggle - and one which can take a toll on people's health.

Note

1. This is an accountancy term referring to the percentage of turnover remaining after purchases of stock and labour costs are deducted.

8 Self-employment and the role of social security

When the authors planned their research on low-income self-employment and means-tested benefits they were entering an area in which little previous work had been attempted. The recent growth in self-employment was well-charted, and there was a substantial sociological literature on the culture of business and the attitudes and motivations of the 'entrepreneur'. However, almost nothing was known about the lives of families working on their own account, or in newer marginal forms of self-employment, who were bringing up children on earnings low enough to qualify for support through means-tested benefits.

Despite this relative paucity of real understanding, or perhaps because of it, there was no shortage of scepticism in the views expressed to the authors as they began their work. In a number of arenas the authors were offered familiar anecdotal references to the situations of people who continued in apparently non-profitable self-employment while occupying comfortable, well-furnished houses and driving around in big cars. From an early stage in our work, a key concern was for the research to test whether this widespread prejudice had any real foundation.

Since we started our work, other researchers have entered the field and reported on aspects of low income self-employment. Brown's policy analysis of social security provision for self-employed people (1992) has provided essential background material for understanding the financial circumstances and opportunities of self-employed people. The large-scale work recently reported by Meager *et al.* (1994) has also furnished a broad picture of the financial circumstances of the self-employed and supported quantitatively some of the patterns detected in our own research. This work confirms the existence of a substantial low-income group, some of whom may face problems in retirement. Other research on low-income families by Marsh and McKay (1993) has included self-employed people and acknowledged the importance of disaggregating findings by employment status when investigating working patterns and use of benefits. Most recently, early evaluation of the disability working allowance (Rowlingson and Berthoud, 1994), has highlighted the special significance of this benefit for self-employed people and when full findings become available yet another piece of the jigsaw will have been completed. Overall, we have begun to build up a substantial body of systematic information about the real circumstances of low-income self-employed people.

There remains room for considerable further work. We have yet to make sensible attempts at including self-employed people in measures of take-up of benefits, despite the importance of this topic and all the policy and research attention it has attracted during the past 30 years. Some of the administrative problems in dealing with claims from self-employed people for means-tested benefits remain to be understood properly and resolved. Nevertheless, compared with the sketchy outline of low-income self-employment that was available at the beginning of this decade, the current picture now has some details and colour.

This concluding chapter brings together some of the main findings from our programme of research. Our exploration of the lives of self-employed families has included their day-to-day experiences of combining work with bringing up children, financial management and living standards, and hopes and plans for the future. We have found richness, satisfaction and fulfilment in the lives of some families, as well as clear evidence of financial problems and anxieties for many, with risks and insecurities for their current and future lives. These findings have encouraged us to make some observations on the role of social security support in the wider economics of self-employment.

Heterogeneity

One of the most striking findings from the research was the extreme heterogeneity among the low-income self-employed families, as in the self-employed population generally. The range of occupations and organisation of work extends in all directions, bringing in activities indistinguishable from low-waged work for an employer as well as autonomous trading businesses at all stages of development. It extends across the traditional productive communities of farming and fishing and into the newer service industries characterised by franchise or free-lance organisation. It includes people in small craft industries or with individual and sometimes unusual skills developed to a high level of expertise, as well as others carrying out repetitive and unskilled work that is more traditionally associated with the low-waged sector.

People come into self-employment at different stages of their lives and through different routes. Some come through redundancy, or in a determined attempt to break out of unemployment. Others are simply continuing a way of life established by their parents and grandparents. Some dislike the routines and impositions of waged work, or have had a longstanding desire to work independently. Still others are almost surprised to discover that their small-scale leisure activities or interests have developed to the extent that they are formally categorised as 'self-employed work'.

The range of business activity within individual families is also considerable. In some families, self-employment means that one breadwinner is engaged in remunerative work away from home. In others self-employment is a way of life for an extended family, drawing in both spouses, children and grandparents into a general family activity, much of it based around the home. Some of the work contributing to self-employed activity is invisible within the formal economy, such as work done by children and, to a much greater extent, work done by women.

Women in two-parent families frequently play a vital part in business activities but the extent of their contribution is often not acknowledged in formal measures of economic activity and earnings. Indeed the requirements of some self-employed work may have the effect of reinforcing gender divisions of labour, particularly where women's involvement in the enterprise reduces the opportunity for them to pursue their own, independent labour market participation. However, where women are closely involved in the financial or clerical side of businesses, they seem often to be in a stronger position to influence decision making about both business and household finances. This can be an important factor in helping families to maintain their living standards during periods of financial pressure.

Heterogeneity is not only a feature of employment circumstances, but is apparent in all family and personal characteristics. People we interviewed included families at all stages of formation, growth, and for some, dissolution. In each sphere of work can be found lone parents, traditional male breadwinner couples and other two-parent families where the woman has, temporarily at least, become the main earner. It is also a dynamic population, where self-employed people move back into employed work or unemployment, while redundant workers and people who believe they can develop a personal skill or interest try setting up on their own. Changes in living standards often lag behind such occupational shifts, or reflect different stages in life trajectories: the low-income sector includes both people who are contemplating retirement and younger parents who have just embarked on their working lives or on bringing up children.

Diversity of personal characteristics extends into aspects of family health. While some of the families interviewed enjoyed robust physical and mental health, others were coping with the effects of serious illness or disability, or had responsibility for other family members whose health was poor. A characteristic shared by all the families, however, was low income.

Family incomes

Although long working hours were common among the families we studied, and the commitment and energy of whole families went into some of the small enterprises, incomes were currently low enough to qualify for financial support through in-work benefits. There were many different reasons why incomes were so low. Some people were just starting out in business, others were facing business failure and likely to return to unemployment or seek work elsewhere. Some had little control over their earnings or the amount of work available, or had personal or family circumstances which limited their time or effort. There were different levels of skills, qualifications and business expertise. All had decided, however, that incomes were insufficient for family needs and had applied for the means-tested family credit.

Findings from the study underline again the crucial role played by family credit in the lives of many self-employed families. For many, it was essential for maintaining a reasonable standard of living, which was evident from the way they described it as a 'lifesaver' and a 'godsend'. The passport benefits to which family credit brought entitlement were highly valued. Although some people felt they would have found ways of continuing in their work if family credit had not been available, for all of them it would have been a struggle. Without it some would have been certain to return to unemployment. Family credit provided regularity and security of a proportion of family income - a particular advantage when earnings were unpredictable or uneven.

Although all the families had applied for family credit they were not heavy users of other social security benefits. Self-employed people are excluded from some of the contributory and contingency schemes to which employees have access, and so are not entitled to unemployment or industrial injuries benefits. They are entitled to sickness and invalidity benefit, but the families we spoke to rarely made use of them. Of course, if they had not been keeping up their national insurance contributions, or were working at earnings levels below the contribution threshold, they had no entitlement, anyway.

Those who appeared to be entitled, however, did not readily claim sickness benefit. Few tried to claim income support during periods of ill health. Expectations of problems in demonstrating entitlement, or preference to keep 'soldiering on' without recourse to sickness benefit or income support, suggests that there is likely to be considerable non-take-up of entitlement by self-employed people. Families had rarely made adequate private provision for illness or accident, or indeed, for their future retirement, and this also had repercussions for their current and future living standards.

Living standards of self-employed families

There are a number of ways of thinking about family living standards. The introductory chapter explained that neither the way living standards are conceptualised nor how they are measured are subject to universal agreement. The qualitative approach adopted here seemed appropriate, because so little was known about self-employment that the way it affected living standards required explanation as well as measurement. We have looked at material questions such as the value and cost of housing, the level of earnings and other income, the ownership and value of consumer goods, and then sought explanations from families for how and why their particular circumstances came about. Respondents' views on the importance of different aspects of their living standards and how they perceived change or development in this respect helped us to trace the way that current living standards are often linked to patterns of expenditure determined by previous different circumstances.

How people come to their work and when, the level and support from parents and relatives, and earnings from previous work, all contribute to the living standards they now have. Within this diversity, it is possible to discern some groups of families who shared common characteristics and similar living standards. Male manual workers and other subcontractors, or 'quasi self-employed' people were one such identifiable group. They basically had the standards of living to be expected from long-term employment in low-wage sectors of the economy. They were accustomed to living on relatively low earnings, even if these fluctuated. Their incomes were reflected in the housing they occupied and the quality and condition of their household possessions.

Another, smaller, group with some features in common were the families who developed some self-employed work out of a consuming personal interest, or chose a way of working which suited a particular lifestyle. Few of these had histories of high earnings, although some came from professional backgrounds. They were sustained by low expectations of material rewards and by support from families, or networks of mutual aid. To some extent, their living standards might be said to reflect personal choice or preference, but it would be wrong to exaggerate the differences between them and the more traditional 'entrepreneurial' self-employed. They may have adapted well to surviving on low incomes, but they shared many of the same motivations and commitments to the work ethic, supporting their families and 'struggling through' that were exhibited right across the self-employed spectrum.

The highest material living standards were found among some of the people with independent businesses. They had high expectations and had placed importance on the standard of their housing and household goods, which was mainly where money had been spent in the past. Some pointed out that their living standards might appear incongruous with eligibility for means-tested benefits, but it was only by careful budgeting, by using overdrafts and by exhausting previous savings that they were able to keep up these standards. However, also among this group of people were some whose current incomes were furthest from those earned in previous periods of relative business prosperity or high salaries. Their apparently high living standards in terms of housing, household goods and equipment, and general participation in social activities masked their mounting personal overdrafts and business debts, and high levels of anxiety and financial distress.

There was little evidence that families were living a high life at the expense of the tax payer. Rather, by keeping businesses afloat through the early stages or through lean times, means-tested benefits might be said to be giving some would-be entrepreneurs the possibility of eventually rising above the need for them. This was certainly the hope of many. Appreciative as they were of the financial support they were receiving from social security, most would prefer not to have to rely on it.

One important point when considering the extent to which financial support should be made available to self-employed families is whether people are accumulating assets in a business rather than taking profits. It is, after all, a sensible strategy in some circumstances, especially in the early stages of trying to get off the ground, to take as little as possible out of the business. Survival and success may depend on being prepared to 'plough everything back'. However, if this means that self-employed people are choosing to reduce current family incomes to levels so low that they are entitled to means-tested support, it could be argued that this is not a proper use of public funding. We looked particularly at the accumulation of assets in businesses generating high turnover relative to recorded net profits, and among families with valuable premises, stock or equipment, such as farmers, boat-owning fishermen and hoteliers. There was little sign that such accumulation of assets was taking place. While some of the traders did have valuable assets and stock, these had usually been built up in previous more profitable times and debts were more common than substantial assets. The businesses with the most valuable stock were those which, by their nature, were also more likely to generate higher turnovers: such businesses have higher costs and expenses as well.

In general, the highest levels of gross receipts were demonstrably based on the high cost of the traded goods and the expenses involved in their acquisition and sale. The reporting of finances and the measurement of self-employed income is, however, a complex and interesting area.

Measuring low incomes

There are a number of problems in measuring earnings from self-employment, in comparison with estimates of the incomes of employees or people outside the labour force. Uncertainties in the definition of self-employment, differential response rates, time-lags between survey dates and earnings periods, apparent under-reporting of income and conceptual aspects of measurement of earnings and profits have all contributed to the exclusion of self-employed people from income surveys in the past, and likewise from official estimates of take-up of benefits.

Such problems have to be tackled directly, however, in assessment of the entitlement of self-employed people for means-tested benefits. Considerable attention was paid in this study to the assessment of earnings from low-income self-employment. A conceptual and theoretical approach was followed by detailed study of some of the self-employed businesses by an accountant with Inland Revenue experience of assessing small businesses. She observed premises, equipment and working practices, and had access to financial data which formed the basis of business accounts and assessment by Inland Revenue, VAT inspectors, and the Department of Social Security. There seemed little reason to believe that earnings reported by the self-employed families were not an accurate reflection of their true incomes, even if they might occasionally be boosted in some trades by a little undeclared work.

From our study of the families there appeared to be little evidence of purposeful misreporting of financial data, or of any improper manipulation of the assessment system or deliberate false accounting. This does not, of course, rule out the possibility that there are individuals among self-employed people claiming in-work benefits who are manipulating the system. The complexity of accounts and financial data in some of the larger businesses did allow greater scope for both error and manipulation. However, there was little to suggest that there is anything intrinsically different about the validity of data about incomes supplied by self-employed people, compared with employees.

How the DSS deals with the different components of reported income from self-employed people, and which components provide the best basis for assessment of eligibility for means-tested benefit, to promote equitable treatment across employees and self-employed people are separate matters.

They have been discussed at length previously by Boden and Corden (1994). On balance, their conclusion was that cash-flow procedures were generally a more helpful and accurate way of assessing earnings for an income-related benefit. Closer study of the higher turnover businesses suggests, however, that the complexity of finances of the small proportion of self-employed businesses with high turnover may require some special attention by assessment staff.

Taken together, we have confidence in the validity of the details of business and household incomes described by the self-employed families in our study. Findings from a qualitative study focusing on family credit cannot be used to make generalised observations about self-employed people in other contexts, of course. Nevertheless, we feel that our findings do offer a challenge to the widespread belief that self-employed people purposefully under-report earnings in order to maximise their situations. It is our belief that the problems researchers meet in measuring self-employed incomes and in fitting the data available to the methodology of household surveys, statistical modelling or take-up estimates may have more to do with assumptions made by researchers and the under-development of research expertise in self-employment than the characteristics of the self-employed people they are researching.

The wider context

It has been Government policy for some time to encourage entrepreneurial activity, both as a dynamic force in the economy and as a way of reducing unemployment. Many of the self-employed families in the study had responded to this encouragement, some using the enterprise allowance and others putting in redundancy money, savings, or cash from the sale of their homes.

The interviews were carried out at the height of a long recession which was reflected in the economic position of the respondents. Most were struggling, managing to 'get by', like many other low-income families, but not without sacrifice and anxiety. Many felt insecure and vulnerable and, for some, trying to support families without the protection of a guaranteed weekly wage was putting strains on family relationships and had taken a toll on their health. Often the sacrifice was acceptable: some people were motivated by the possibility of future success as well as by the satisfaction which came from working for themselves. Yet it seemed that strategies for short-term survival might be undermining longer term security. Non-payment of national insurance or suspension of pension contributions meant that some were not building up a contributions record to protect them and their dependants in case of illness and disability, or as they reached retirement age. Nor had they, in compensation, made private provision. Others appeared to be conducting work under conditions that could well be jeopardising their current and future health and safety; not only of themselves and their families, but also members of a wider public.

On the other hand, many people told us about the emotional and psychological well-being that they associated with their current occupation and way of working, which is likely to have long-term effects on their health and security, and that of their families. They described a richness of life, a sense of purpose and achievement and a strong belief in the suitability of their family environment for bringing up children, which research has often found lacking amongst similar parents in low-waged work or unemployment.

A key policy question then is, what role should a means-tested benefit play in the economic support of self-employment? The issue has at least three aspects. First, is it the role of a social security benefit to encourage people to enter a world of insecure self-employment? It seems that there is a balance to be struck here, and it would be useful to know where the balance currently lies. On the one hand, positive outcomes are clear. Some families are helped to move into work and establish a form of employment that brings them satisfaction and well-being, provides goods or services that meet demand, and eventually generates sufficient profit to make the family financial independent. On the other hand failure may not only mean financial crisis for the family involved, but can also lead to wider repercussions in local economies.

The second aspect concerns the viability of businesses, and the role of a benefit such as family credit in supporting those which show little sign of producing anything other than minimal net profits, or indeed, trade at a loss. There is certainly room for debate about how far social security should directly subsidise a non-profitable market sector.

Thirdly, there are questions about how far family credit really is fulfilling its purpose as a bridge to financial independence in the case of some of the self-employed ventures. Some of the enterprises supported by family credit showed very low returns for long periods of time, with the families involved depending on relatively high levels of family credit and other benefits. Using the current terminology of policy making, is this encouraging enterprise or dependency?

One policy option, to address some of the above issues, might be for family credit to be more selectively targeted, perhaps, at those enterprises which *do* show some potential for economic viability. This is the direction in which policy making appears to be travelling in the field of business start-up schemes. However, social security has a range of policy aims much wider than encouraging business start-up.

Another option might be to restrict the availability of family credit to self-employed people with specially low earnings, or for a limited amount of time.

The problem with addressing policy measures towards people with particularly low earnings, however, is that there is no neat way of categorising them for administrative purposes. Long-term recipients of family credit, with earnings which had grown little since they first applied, often had little control over their earnings or the amount of work available, or had family circumstances which limited the time and effort they could put into their work. In so far as there may have been extra work capacity among a few families or the ability to earn more money if they chose, this was mainly not among the lowest earners but more among those with incomes in the middle range. To impose a requirement to earn to full capacity would be difficult since this would run against the trend of reducing the minimum working hours for family credit. It will be interesting to see the effects on self-employed claimants of the 1995 measure to pay an extra £10 in the family credit awards of people who work over 30 hours per week.

Categorising families by their level of living standards is also problematic, since the factors influencing these standards are so complex and vary a great deal among self-employed families.

There is little evidence at present on how long different kinds of business can be expected to continue at very low levels of profits. Some might, given time and a more favourable economic climate, gradually grow and prosper, whereas others are unlikely to produce substantially greater earnings. It could be argued that continued support for marginal enterprises is an inappropriate role for family credit, but for some self-employed people any alternative would probably result in a transfer from one kind of state support to another. In terms of the broader quality of their lives it might be a poor exchange.

Appendix A
The family credit database

How the sample is drawn

Tabulations of family credit statistics produced for publication in the Department's annual statistical returns are based on a five per cent sample of claims in payment on a particular day each month, extracted from the main claimant database held at North Fylde. The sample is drawn according to a particular sequence of final digits in individual national insurance numbers (NINOs). This produces a random sample of the required size and allows cases to be followed during their full period of claim. It also permits identification of cases where people have claimed again, having previously received the benefit. In order to protect confidentiality the national insurance numbers were removed before the data were transferred to SPRU. They were replaced by alternative, unique identifiers which allowed us to trace individual claims over time without compromising confidentiality.

The sample data, being collected for the purposes of basic administrative tabulations by the Department, do not include all the information on individual claims or awards which is held on the main database. For practical reasons it was not possible to use the latter for this exercise, though using only the administrative sample makes some forms of analysis impossible. For example, the sample does not cover claims where applicants have been judged ineligible for benefit. There is also no information on the treatment of gross profits, or on how the assessable earnings figures have been calculated.

It is also important to emphasise that the data themselves are collected primarily for the administration of benefit delivery rather than for research. Reports by the Chief Adjudication Officer and the National Audit Office have suggested that there has been a relatively high degree of error in family credit adjudication (DSS, 1990; NAO, 1991a). Such errors may be located both in decision making and in the keying in of information. Either way, errors are not always detectable in secondary analysis of data. The primary variables contained in the five per cent sample records are listed below.

Primary variables in the family credit sample dataset

NAME	(Removed)
AWARDS	Total number of claims
RTYPE	Record type
	1 new, renewal, repeat
	2 revision
RUNDATE	Run month and year
NINO	National insurance number - main (replaced with non-identifiable case number)
CLAIMNO	Claim number
OCLAIMNO	Old claim number
DOB	Date of birth
DOBINT	DOB - Number of days since a specified date
FAMTYPE	Family type
	1 couple - male main earner
	2 couple - female main earner
	3 single - male
	4 single - female
POSTCODE	
PCOUNT	Number of postcode changes
LOCATION	LO code + region code + country code
OFFICE	
REGION	2 Northern
	5 London North
	8 Wales and South West
	9 Midlands
	10 Northwestern
	11 Scotland
	15 London South
COUNTRY	1 England
	2 Scotland
	3 Wales
PNINO	National insurance number - partner (removed)
PDOB	Date of birth - partner
PDOBINT	DOB - partner: number of days since a specified date
CHILD1	Number of reckonable children aged 0-10
CHILD2	Number of reckonable children aged 11-15

CHILD3	Number of reckonable children aged 16-17
CHILD4	Number of reckonable children aged 18 & over
NRCRDS	Number of no credit children
CAGE1-16	Age of 1st -16th reckonable child
CHBEN	Amount of child benefit weekly
OCCUP	Occupation code

1 General Managerial
2 Professional & related supporting management & admin
3 Professional & related, in education, welfare & health
4 Literary, artistic, sports
5 Professional & related; science, engineering, technology
6 Managerial (excl general management)
7 Clerical and related
8 Selling
9 Security and protective services
10 Catering, cleaning, hairdressing and other personal services
11 Farming, fishing and related
12 Materials processing (excl metal)
13 Making and repairing (excl metal and electrical)
14 Processing, making, repairing etc - metal & electrical
15 Painting, repetitive assembly, product inspect, packaging
16 Construction, mining and related (not elsewhere classified)
17 Transport operating, materials moving and storing & related
18 Miscellaneous
19 Unclassified

ETYPE — Employment type

1 Self-employed
2 Employed, private sector
3 Employed, public sector - central government
4 Employed, public sector - local government
5 Employed, public sector - NHS
6 Employed, public sector - other
7 Employed, unclassified

WKHRSW — Weekly hours worked

EARNS	Weekly earnings - main
TAX	Income tax
NICONT	National insurance contributions
SACONT	Superannuation contribution
OBTYPE-OBTYP5	Other benefit types
	IS Income Support
	IV Invalidity Benefit
	MA Maternity Allowance
	MS MSC Training
	OT Others
	SB Sickness Benefit
	SM Statutory Maternity Pay
	SS Statutory Sick Pay
	UB Unemployment Benefit
OBREC1-OBREC5	Other benefit recipients
	1 Main
	2 Partner
OBAMT1-OBAMT5	Other benefit amounts
OITYP1-OITYP5	Other income types
	B Benefits in kind
	M Maintenance
	O Others
	R Rent
	T Tips
OIREC1-OIREC5	Other income recipients
	1 Main
	2 Partner
OIAMT1-OIAMT5	Other income amounts
PETYPE	Earned income type - partner
	1 Whole time
	2 Part time (less than 24 hours)
PEARNS	Earned income amount - partner (net)
DEARNS	Earned income amount - children
NTINC	Notional tariff income
SAVINGS	Amount of savings
TYPE	Type of award
	1 New
	2 Renewal
	3 Repeat
DOCLAIM	Date of claim
CLDAYS	Date of claim
WKCRED	Weekly rate of credit
DOSTART	Date award commenced

DOSTOP	Date award terminated
DAYSTA	Date award commenced
DAYSTO	Date award terminated
PREVIOUS	Previous award indicator 0 New, repeat renewal with previous 1 Renewal, no previous
CURSTART	Date current credit commenced
DAYSCUR	Number of days since current credit commences

Appendix B
The methodology of the qualitative studies

The selection of families for interviews

Interviews were conducted in three waves, involving three separate groups of people chosen according to different aspects of theoretical interest and administrative practicality. The figure below represents the three stages of the research programme.

Wave one

In the first wave of interviews the focus of interest was the nature of low income self-employment and the way in which social security supports this way of working. Information was also needed to inform a study of the basis of assessment of self-employed earnings for the purpose of determining entitlement to family credit. The key requirement in choosing people to interview was a group in which a range of occupation types was represented, at different stages of business development and both with and without enterprise allowance. The aim was to include some dual-earner households as well as sole-earner self-employed people, and some business partnerships (both spouse and non-spouse) as well as people working on their own. A range of family types and sizes was also required, as well as some people who had been refused family credit. In view of the importance of self-employment in some minority ethnic communities, it was decided to include families of minority ethnic origin in the proportions in which they appeared among the names passed to the researchers (in so far as they could be identified from surnames).

To generate such a study group, the Family Credit Unit drew quotas of cases fitting the occupational criteria as people entered new or renewed applications during the period from June to September 1991. Seventeen per cent of names drawn declined to participate when approached by letter from the DSS. The researchers then contacted 43 families and achieved 33 interviews, including four pilot interviews.

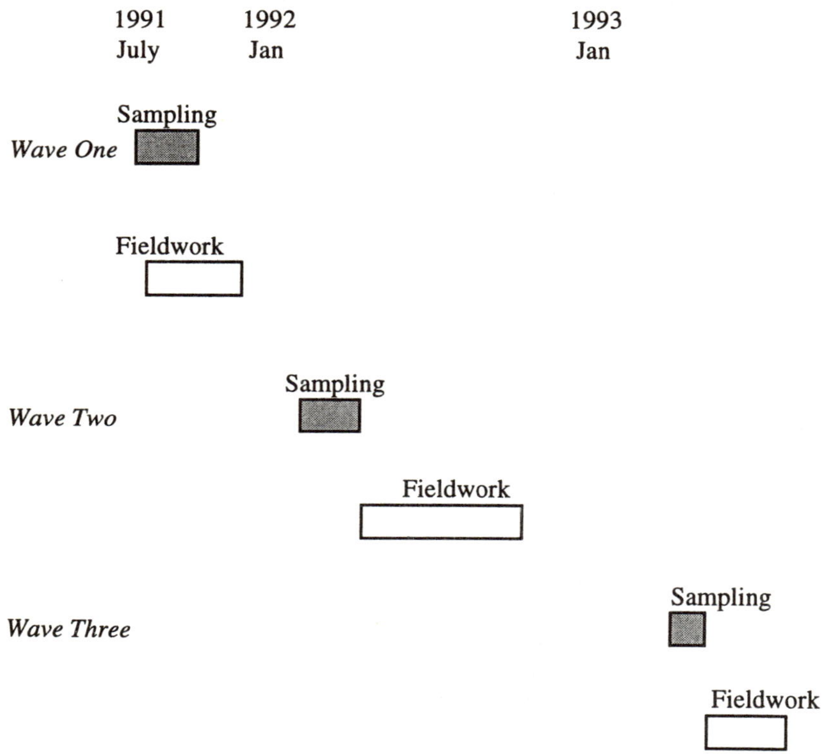

Respondents lived in the northern counties - Lancashire, Cheshire, Derbyshire, North Yorkshire, Cumbria, Northumberland - and North Wales. Fieldwork started in August and was completed in November 1991. In 21 of the 24 interviews with two-parent families both parents were present.

Wave two

For the study of families' living standards the primary requirement was representation of a range of incomes and levels of family credit awards spread among the three main family types (male-earner couples, female-earner couples and lone parents), whose different characteristics were identified in the analysis of administrative statistics. An initial interview 'pool' of families in two DSS Regions was randomly drawn by computer from the family credit database, stratified by family type and also programmed to include a small number of dual earners and unsuccessful applicants. Nineteen per cent of people whose names were drawn declined to participate when approached by letter. From the remaining pool the researcher constructed a smaller interview group using a simple matrix of family type and high, medium or low levels of award, based on the percentage of the maximum available. The selection also took into account the range of occupations and numbers of previous awards.

The researchers made contact with 39 self-employed families and achieved 30 interviews, including five pilot interviews. Respondents lived in the northern counties and North Wales, as in the first wave, and in North London, the northern home counties and East Anglia. Fieldwork started in July 1992 and finished in November 1992.

A similar process was undertaken for the selection of a smaller interview pool of employee recipients in September 1992. Forty recipient families were selected at random from the database, comprising 20 male-earner couples, ten female-earner couples and ten lone parents. Approximately half came from each Region and five of the couples had two earners. The researchers selected a smaller interview group to include a range of family types and levels of family credit. Contact was made with 16 families and 10 interviews were achieved.

In constructing the study groups one consideration was that of ethnic origin. The randomly selected interview pools for the living standards study produced a relatively high proportion of families with Asian surnames in the two regions chosen. Again the decision was taken to include some of these families in the study groups. However, the apparently substantial use of family credit by self-employed people of New Commonwealth origin may be a subject meriting further specific research.

Wave three

In the third wave of interviews the aim was to look at a small number of businesses apparently generating 'high turnovers'. High turnover businesses were defined as those with gross receipts in the 26-week assessment period of £25,000 or more (or £50,000 for those providing full-year accounts). The quickest and most effective way of drawing a sample was for Family Credit staff to search randomly among recently processed cases on two alphabetical sections until they had found 100 families in the defined higher turnover bracket who lived in the same two regions as used in the earlier study

(Northern and London North). In order to include some farmers a separate trawl was carried out in Wales.

There was a considerably higher level of opting out amongst this group than among people in the first two waves. Altogether 40 out of 103 cases drawn from the two regions declined to participate in response to a letter from the DSS, plus two farmers out of ten cases drawn from Wales. In addition a further eight families chose not to take part when they were contacted by the researchers, including two farmers. Proportionately there was a higher level of opting out amongst families with surnames indicating origins in South Asia. Apart from ethnicity there were no other obvious patterns among the opt-outs.

A higher opt-out rate among Asian families is not surprising, given the possible language problems and the anxieties inevitable among minority groups with experience of discrimination and racism. It is difficult to interpret the meaning of a higher level of opting out generally. Those who opted out on contact often expressed their reluctance to take part in terms of being too busy: it is possible that some of the people running larger scale businesses may well have found less time available to talk to a researcher than some of those in the main study carrying out more low key activities from home. One woman was worried about the confidentiality of the discussion, in spite of reassurances offered, and it was clear from the contact with some families that talking to strangers about details of family life and finances was an unusual and not altogether comfortable experience. It is also possible that people with somewhat higher levels of business activity and more complex finances may be more reluctant to talk about them to researchers acting on behalf of the DSS. This is not in itself evidence of a desire to conceal information or of false accounting, though these cannot be ruled out. Overall the higher level of opting out should be noted, but without a different kind of study explanations cannot be determined.

Interviews

A semi-structured topic guide was used for all interviews. This differed according to the particular focus of interest in each series of interviews. The topic guide used for the living standards study allowed for the collection of a core of structured data for use in comparing the self-employed with the employee families and with other quantitative data. Where separate interviews were held with both partners in two-parent families, the same topic guide was used for both interviews, and information and perceptions on all the issues were sought from each partner. Where it was clear that a division of responsibility or knowledge existed in the household, the researchers pursued particular areas of enquiry in greater depth with the relevant partner.

Most interviews took between one hour and an hour and a half, though a few lasted longer because respondents wished to talk at length about their work or their current situation. All of the main interviews took place in the respondents' homes. This was sometimes where the person worked and the researchers saw the work premises. In a few other cases where work was carried out at fixed premises separate from the homes, these were also visited. In most cases interviews were tape-recorded, but when this was not possible the researchers reconstructed the interviews immediately afterwards.

At the end of the interviews with self-employed recipients, the researchers asked written permission from the respondents to look at their last family credit application form. Throughout the complete series of interviews only four people refused permission: they felt their applications were a private matter. Signed letters of consent were passed to the Family Credit Unit, who made available copies of application forms and associated correspondence. Following the interviews, letters of thanks were sent to the respondents.

Analysis

The tape-recordings from the interviews were transcribed. In addition, researchers made notes of observations during fieldwork visits or of relevant comments made by respondents before or after the tape-recorders were turned on or off. Data from these sources and from the respondents' family credit application forms were extracted manually onto index cards. On each card there were further sub-divisions. Colour codes were used to distinguish contributions by gender, and other visual marking techniques used to indicate employment and family types, and, for couples, separate or joint interviews. Summaries of respondents' comments on each topic were extracted onto the cards or into separate files, sometimes using actual words indicated by quotation marks.

The material was analysed by a process of sorting the information held on the cards across topics and by categories such as family type, gender, age, employment type, length of time in business, previous occupation, tenure, and size of award. From this sorting process lists, charts and diagrams were drawn up and concepts developed based on patterns, linkages, explanations and exceptions.

Separate records were kept of the structured data collected from some respondents on questions such as earnings, housing type and costs, fuel costs, debts and benefits and possession of consumer goods. None of the three study groups was statistically representative, so these data cannot be extrapolated numerically to the wider population. Nevertheless, they help to locate the families interviewed within the national statistical framework and provide a descriptive context for the qualitative material.

References

Allen, D. and Hunn, A. (1985), 'An evaluation of the Enterprise Allowance Scheme', *Employment Gazette,* 93 (8) pp.313-317.

Allen, S. and Truman, C. (1992), 'Women, business and self-employment: a conceptual minefield', pp.162-174 in Arber, S. and Gilbert, N. (eds.), *Women and Working Lives: division and change*, Macmillan, London.

Arber, S. and Gilbert, N. (1992), (eds.), *Women and Working Lives: division and change*, Macmillan, London.

Ashworth, K. and Walker, R. (1992), *The Dynamics of Family Credit*, Working Paper No. 154, Centre for Research in Social Policy, Loughborough University of Technology.

Atkinson, A.B. and Micklewright, S. (1983), 'On the reliability of income data in the Family Expenditure Survey 1970-1977', *Journal of the Royal Statistical Society (A)*, 146 (1) pp.33-61.

Atkinson, J. (1985), 'Flexibility: Planning for an uncertain future', *Manpower Policy and Practice,* 1, Summer, pp.26-9.

Atkinson, A.B., Smith, J.M. and Sutherland, H. (1986) *'FES data on the self-employed',* Taxation, Incentives and the Distribution of Income, Research Note 11, London School of Economics, May.

Austrin, T. (1980), 'The lump in the UK construction industry', pp.302-315 in Nichols, T. (ed.), *Capital and Labour: Studies in the Capitalist Labour Process*, Athlone Press/Fontana, London.

Baker, P. (1993), 'Taxpayer compliance of the self-employed: estimates from household spending data', IFS Working Paper No. W93/14, Institute for Fiscal Stuies, London.

Baldwin, S. (1985), *The Costs of Caring: Families with Disabled Children*, Routledge and Kegan Paul, London.

Benefits Agency (1993), *Self-Employed and Business Cases Handbook*, HMSO, London.

Bercusson, B. (1991), 'New forms of employment and social protection: the emerging social law of the European community'. Paper given to the European Institute of Social Security International Colloquium on *Social Security and Technological Innovation*, Florence, October 1991.

Bercusson, B. (1993), 'Solidarity and Diversity: social protection for self-employed persons in the European Community', Paper for the European Commission conference *Social Protection for Self-Employed Persons*, Florence and Siena, 14-16 October 1993.

Bergman, J. (1991), '1992 and social security: critique and proposals', pp.91-102 in Room, G. (ed), *Towards a European Welfare State?*, School for Advanced Urban Studies, Bristol.

Berthoud, R. (1989), *Credit, Debt, and Poverty*, Social Security Advisory Committee Research Paper 1, HMSO, London.

Bevan, J., Clark, G., Banerji, N., and Hakim, C. (1989), *Barriers to Business Start-up: A Study of the Flow Into and Out Of Self-Employment*, Research Paper No. 71, Department of Employment, London.

Beveridge, Sir William (1942), *Social Insurance and Allied Services*, Cmd. 6404, HMSO, London.

Blackwell, J. (1994), 'Changing work patterns and their implications for social security', pp.79-99 in Baldwin, S. and Falkingham, J. (eds.), *Social Security and Social Change: new challenges to the Beveridge model*, Harvester Wheatsheaf, Hemel Hempstead.

Blanchflower, D. and Oswald, A. (1989), 'International Patterns of Work', pp.15-29 in Jowell, R., Witherspoon, S. and Brook, L. (eds), *British Social Attitudes: Special International Report*, Gower, London.

Blanchflower, D. and Oswald, A. (1990), 'Self-employment and Mrs Thatcher's enterprise culture', in *British Social Attitudes: the 1990 Report*, Aldershot: Gower.

Blundell, R. and Walker, I. (1982), 'Modelling the joint determination of household labour supplies and commodity demands', *Economic Journal*, 92, pp.351-364.

Board of Inland Revenue (1994), *Inland Revenue Statistics 1994*, HMSO, London.

Boden, R. (1993), *The Living Standards of Self-employed Recipients of Family Credit with Higher Turnover Businesses: Background paper on accountancy issues*, Working Paper DSS 1127, Social Policy Research Unit, University of York, York.

Boden, R. and Corden, A. (1994), *Measuring Low Incomes: Self-Employment and Family Credit,* SPRU Papers, HMSO, London.

Bogenhold, D. and Staber, U. (1991), 'The decline and rise of self-employment', *Work, Employment and Society,* 5 (2) pp.223-239.

Borooah, V., McGregor, P. and McKee, P. (1991), *Regional Income Inequalities of Poverty in the UK,* Dartmouth, Aldershot.

Borchardt, K-D. (1989), 'Improvement of national protection in the field of social security in the light of the co-ordination of Community law', *Social Europe,* 2/89, pp.59-61.

Bradbury, B., Encel, D., James, J. and Vipond, J. (1988), *Poverty and the Workforce,* Social Policy Research Centre Reports and Proceedings No. 72, SPRC, Sydney.

Bradshaw, J. and Ernst, J. (1990), *Establishing a Modest but Adequate Budget for a British Family,* Family Budget Unit Working Paper No. 2, University of York, York.

Bradshaw, J. and Holmes, H. (1989), *Living on the Edge: a study of the living standards of families on benefit in Tyne and Wear,* Child Poverty Action Group, London.

Bradshaw, J. and Morgan, J. (1987), 'Evaluating adequacy: the potential of budget standards', *Journal of Social Policy,* 16 (2) pp.165-181.

Bradshaw, J. and Millar, J. (1991), *Lone Parent Families in the UK,* Department of Social Security Research Report No. 6, HMSO, London.

Brannen, J. and Wilson, G. (1987), (eds.), *Give and Take in Families: Studies in Resource Distribution,* Allen and Unwin, London.

Bresnen, M.J., Wray, K., Bryman, A., Beardsworth, A.D., Ford, J.R., and Keil, E.T. (1985), 'The flexibility of recruitment in the construction industry: formalisation or re-casualisation?', *Sociology,* 91 (1) pp.108-124.

Brown, C. (1988), *Taxation and the Incentive to Work,* OUP, Oxford.

Brown, J. (1990), *Social Security for Retirement,* Joseph Rowntree Foundation, York.

Brown, J. (1992), *A Policy Vacuum: Social Security for the Self-employed,* Joseph Rowntree Foundation, York.

Brown, J. (1994a), *Escaping from Dependence: Part-time workers and the self-employed,* Institute for Public Policy Research, London.

Brown, J. (1994b), 'Social Protection for the Self-employed: a Background Paper', prepared for the European Commission conference *Social Protection for Self-Employed Persons,* Florence and Sienna, 14-16 October 1993 (revised January 1994).

Brown, P. and Scase, R. (eds), *Poor Work: Disadvantage and the Division of Labour,* Open University Press, Milton Keynes.

Brownlee, H. and McDonald, P. (1991), 'The Australian Living Standards Study: concepts and methodology', paper presented to the annual conference of the Social Policy Association, University of Nottingham, July.

Campbell, M. and Daly, M. (1992), 'Self-employment into the 1990s', *Employment Gazette*, June, pp.269-292.

Carter, S. and Cannon, T. (1988a), *Female Entrepreneurs: A Study of Female Business Owners; Their Motivations, Experiences, and Strategies for Success*, Research Paper No. 65, Department of Employment, London.

Carter, S. and Cannon, T. (1988b), 'Women in Business', *Employment Gazette*, 11, pp.565-571.

Casey, B. and Creigh, S. (1988), 'Self-employment in Britain: its definition in the Labour Force Survey, in tax and in social security law', *Work, Employment and Society*, 2 (3) pp.381-391.

Central Statistical Office (1991), *Family Expenditure Survey: Report for 1989*, HMSO, London.

Citro, C. and Michael, R. (1995), (eds.), *Measuring Poverty: A New Approach*, National Academy Press, Washington DC.

Commission of the European Communities (1988), 'Employment trends and prospects in Europe', *Social Europe*, 1/88, pp.9-12.

Commission of the European Communities (1990a), *Underground Economy and Irregular Forms of Employment: Final Synthesis Report*, Brussels.

Commission of the European Communities (1990b), *Social Europe: The Labour Market for Information Technology Professionals in Europe*, Supplement 1/90.

Corden, A. (1985), 'The process of claiming family income supplement: study 3 - increasing take-up in Cumbria', Working Paper DHSS 214, Social Policy Research Unit, University of York, York.

Corden, A. (1987), *Disappointed Applicants: A Study of Unsuccessful Claims for Family Income Supplement,* Avebury, Aldershot.

Corden, A. (1991), 'Women's business? claiming and using family credit', *Poverty*, 80, pp.9-11.

Corden, A. (1995), *Changing Perspectives on Benefit Take-Up*, SPRU Papers, HMSO, London.

Corden, A. and Craig, P. (1991), *Perceptions of Family Credit*, SPRU Papers, HMSO, London.

Corden, A., Eardley, T. and Boden, R. with Elliott, J. (1993), *Housing Benefit for Self-Employed People: report of a group discussion with local authority officers*, Working Paper DSS 1048, Social Policy Research Unit, University of York, York.

Cordova, C. (1986), 'From full-time wage employment to atypical employment: a major shift in the evolution of labour relations?', *International Labour Review,* 125 (6) pp.641-687.

Cragg, A. and Dawson, D. (1981), *Qualitative Research Among Homeworkers*, Research Paper No. 21, Department of Employment, London.

Creigh, S., Roberts, C., Gorman, A., and Sawyer, P. (1986), 'Self-employment in Britain: results from the Labour Force Surveys 1981-1984', *Employment Gazette*, 94 (5) June.

Curran, J. (1990), 'Rethinking economic structure: exploring the role of the small firm and self-employment in the British economy', *Work, Employment and Society*, special issue, May, pp.125-146.

Curran, J. and Burrows, R. (1989), 'National profiles of the self-employed', *Employment Gazette*, July, pp.376-385.

Curran, J. and Burrows, R. (1991), 'Not such a small business: reflections on the rhetoric, the reality and the future of the enterprise culture', pp.9-29 in Cross, M. and Payne, G. (eds.), *Work and the Enterprise Culture*, Falmer, London.

Curran, J., Burrows, R. and Evandrou, M. (1987), *Small Business Owners and the Self-Employed in Britain: an Analysis of General Household Survey Data*, Small Business Research Trust, London.

Dale, A. (1986), 'Social class and the self-employed', *Sociology*, 20 (3) pp. 430-434.

Dalgliesh, M. (1993), 'An evaluation of the Prince's Youth Business Trust', *Employment Gazette*, January, pp.661-666.

Dallago, B. (1991), *The Irregular Economy*, Dartmouth, Aldershot.

Daly, M. (1990), 'The 1980s - a decade of growth in enterprise: data on VAT registrations and deregistrations', *Employment Gazette*, November, pp.553-565.

Daly, M. (1991a), 'The 1980s - a decade of growth in enterprise: self-employment data from the Labour Force Survey', *Employment Gazette*, March, pp.109-134.

Daly, M. (1991b), 'Statistics on the self-employed', lecture given to the Royal Statistical Society, London, 16 October 1991.

Daly, M., Campbell, M., Robson, G. and Gallagher, C. (1991), 'Job creation 1987-89: the contributions of small and large firms', *Employment Gazette,* November.

Department of Employment (1983), 'Industry analysis of the self-employed', *Employment Gazette*, June, pp.257-259.

Department of Employment (1986), 'Two years after the Enterprise Allowance - special feature', *Employment Gazette*, 94 (9) pp.405-408.

Department of Employment (1990a), 'Women in the labour market: results from the 1989 Labour Force Survey', *Employment Gazette,* December, pp. 619-636.

Department of Employment (1990b), *Employment and Training for People with Disabilities: Consultative Document*, Department of Employment, London.

Department of Employment (1991a), 'Ethnic origins and the labour market', *Employment Gazette,* February, *pp.*59-72.

Department of Employment (1991c), *Training and Enterprise Council: Planning Framework 1991-92,* Department of Employment, London.

Department of Employment (1993), *Labour Force Survey Historical Supplement - April 1993,* Department of Employment, London.

Department of Employment (1994a), *Labour Force Survey Quarterly Bulletin*, No. 10, December.

Department of Employment (1994b), *Employment Gazette Historical Supplement*, No 4, October.

Department of Health and Social Security (1980a), *The Self-employed and National Insurance: a discussion document*, DHSS, London.

Department of Health and Social Security (1980b), *Industrial Injuries Compensation: A Discussion Paper*, DHSS, London.

Department of Health and Social Security (1989), *Family Credit Take-up Estimate 1988: Technical Note*, Statistical and Research Division, 3/89.

Department of Social Security (1990), *Annual Report of the Chief Adjudication Officer for 1989/90 on Adjudication Standards*, HMSO, London.

Department of Social Security (1991a), *Social Security Statistics 1990*, HMSO, London.

Department of Social Security (1991b), *Stocktaking*, Report of the Working Group on Households Below Average Income, November.

Department of Social Security (1991c), *The Industrial Injuries Scheme and the Self-Employed in Construction and Agriculture: A Consultation Paper*, Industrial Injuries Advisory Council, HMSO, London.

Department of Social Security (1992), *Households Below Average Earnings: A Statistical Analysis 1979-1988/89*, HMSO, London.

Department of Social Security (1993a), *Households Below Average Earnings: A Statistical Analysis 1979-1990/91*, HMSO, London.

Department of Social Security (1993b), *Social Security Statistics 1993*, HMSO, London.

Department of Social Security (1994), *Income Related Benefits: estimates of take-up in 1990 and 1991*, Analytical Services Division, DSS, London.

Department of Social Security (1995), *Income Related Benefits: estimates of take-up in 1992*, Analytical Services Division, DSS, London.

Dilnot, A. and Morris, C. (1981), 'What do we know about the black economy?', *Fiscal Studies*, 2 (1) pp.58-73.

Dilnot, A., Kay, J. and Morris, C. (1984), *The Reform of Social Security*, The Institute for Fiscal Studies, London.

Ditch, J. and Pickles, S. (1991), 'The social policy implications of the Single European Act', Working Paper WP 834 7/91, Social Policy Research Unit,University of York, York.

Donnison, D. (1988), 'Defining and measuring poverty: a reply to Stein Ringen', *Journal of Social Policy*, 17 (3) pp.367-374.

Dorling, D., Gentle, C. and Cornford, J. (1992), *Housing Crisis: Disaster or Opportunity*, Centre for Urban and Regional Development Studies Working Paper No. 96, University of Newcastle, Newcastle upon Tyne.

Dorsett, R. and Heady, C. (1991), 'The take-up of means tested benefits by working families with children', *Fiscal Studies*, 12 (4) pp.22-32.

Equal Opportunities Commission (1980), *The Experience of Caring for Elderly and Handicapped Dependants: Survey Report*, EOC, Manchester.

Felstead, A. (1991), 'Testing the self-employed label: the motif of the Eenterprise culture'', in Leighton, P. and Felstead, A. (eds.), *The New Entrepreneurs: Self-employment and Small Business in Europe*, Kogan Page, London.

Fevre, R. (1987), 'Subcontracting in steel', *Work, Employment and Society,* 1, (4) pp.509-527.

Fevre, R. (1991), 'Emerging 'alternatives' to full-time and permanent employment', pp. 56-70 in Brown, P. and Scase, R. (eds.), *Poor Work: Disadvantage and the Division of Labour*, Open University Press, Milton Keynes.

Ford, R., Marsh, A. and McKay, S. (1994), *Lone Parenthood in 1989, 1991 and 1993: Three cross-sectional survey reports*, Policy Studies Institute, London.

Forde, M. (1979), 'The self-employed and the EEC social security rules', *Industrial Law Journal*, 8 (1) pp. 1-18.

Forrest, R. and Murie, A. (1987), 'Marginalisation and subsidised individualism: the sale of council houses in the restructuring of the British welfare state', *International Journal of Urban and Regional Research'*, 10, pp. 44-66.

Forrest, R., Murie, A. and Williams, P. (1990), *Home Ownership: Differentiation and Fragmentation*, Unwin and Hyman, London.
Foster, K. and Lound, C. (1993), 'A comparison of questions for classifying income', *Survey Methodology Bulletin,* 32, 1/93.
Frayman, H. (1991), *Breadline Britain 1990s*, Domino Films/London Weekend Television, London.
Fry, V. and Stark, G. (1992), *The Take-up of Means-tested Benefits 1984 - 1989* (preliminary report).
Gaselee, J. (1983), 'Variations on the permanent health insurance theme', *Post Magazine and Insurance Monitor*, Vol.CXLIV, No. 7, 17 February, pp. 377-378.
Gilbert, B. (1966), *The Evolution of National Insurance in Great Britain*, Michael Joseph, London.
Glendinning, C. (1989), 'The financial needs and circumstances of informal carers: final report', Working Paper DHSS 529, Social Policy Research Unit, University of York, York.
Glover, J. (1995), 'Secondary analysis in cross-national research on women's employment: Three approaches', paper presented to the Cross-National Research Seminar on Methodological Approaches to International Comparisons, Loughborough University, 28 January 1995.
Goffee, R. and Scase, R. (1985), *Women in Charge: The Experiences of Female Entrepreneurs*, Allen and Unwin, London.
Goldthorpe, J. (1980), *Social Mobility and Class Structure in Britain*, Clarendon Press, Oxford.
Goodman, A. and Webb, S. (1994), 'For Richer, For Poorer: The Changing Income Distribution in the UK, 1961-91, *Fiscal Studies*, 15 (4) pp. 28-62.
Gray, C. and Stanworth, J. (1986), *Allowing for Enterprise: A Qualitative Assessment of the Enterprise Allowance Scheme*, Small Business Research Trust/ MSC, London.
Gray, A. (1987), *Trial by Restart: a study of the Restart Programme in London*, Unemployment Unit/Trojan Press, London.
The Guardian (1990), 'Self-employed failing to pay £250m a year', 5 March.
The Guardian (1992), 'Writer has last word over DSS', 9 June.
Hakim, C. (1985), *Employers' Use of Outwork,* Research Paper No. 44, Department of Employment, London.
Hakim, C. (1987a), *Home-Based Work in Britain: A Report on the 1981 National Homeworking Survey and the DE Research Programme on Homework*, Research Paper No. 60, Department of Employment, London.
Hakim, C. (1987b), 'Trends in the flexible workforce', *Employment Gazette*, 95 (11) pp. 549-561.

Hakim, C. (1988), 'Self-employment in Britain: recent trends and current issues', *Work, Employment and Society*, 2 (4) pp.421-450.

Hakim, C. (1989a), 'New recruits to self-employment in the 1980s', *Employment Gazette*, 97 (6) pp. 286-297.

Hakim, C. (1989b), 'Workforce restructuring, social insurance coverage and the black economy', *Journal of Social Policy,* 18 (4) pp. 471-503.

Hallam, C. (1994), 'Child Support Agency: Calculating the cost', *Accountancy*, April, p.87.

Hancock, R. (1988), *Income Variation and Family Credit: Evidence from the Family Finances and Family Resources Surveys*, STICERD Discussion Paper no. TIDI/109, February, London School of Economics, London.

Hansard (1991), House of Commons, col. 908, 26 January.

Hansard (1994), House of Commons, col. 506, 4 May.

Harris, J. (1972), *Unemployment and Politics, 1886-1914,* Oxford University Press, Oxford.

Haskey, J. (1990), 'The ethnic minority populations of Great Britain: estimates by ethnic group and country of birth', *Population Trends*, 60, pp. 35-38.

Heady, P. and Smyth, M. (1989), *Living Standards During Unemployment*, HMSO, London.

Hepple, B. (1986), 'Restructuring employment rights', *Industrial Law Journal*, 15 (2) pp. 69-83.

Hinrichs, K. (1989), 'Irregular employment patterns and the loose net of social security: some findings on the West German case'. Paper given to the International Social Security Association Seminar on the Sociology of Social Security, Edinburgh University, July 1989.

House of Commons Social Services Committee (1982), *Age of Retirement: Evidence*, HMSO, London.

Holmans, A. (1991), *Estimates of Housing Equity Withdrawal by Owner-Occupiers in the United Kingdom 1970-1990*, Economic Service Working Papers No. 116, Department of the Environment, London.

Howe, L. (1990), *Being Unemployed in Northern Ireland: An Ethnographic Study*, Cambridge University Press, Cambridge.

Huby, M. and Dix, G. (1992), *Evaluating the Social Fund*, Department of Social Security Research Report No. 9, HMSO, London.

Hutson, J. (1990), 'Family relationships and farm businesses in South West Wales', in Harris, C. (ed.), *Family, Economy, and Community*, University of Wales Press, Cardiff.

Institute for Employment Research (1987), *Review of the Economy and Employment*, University of Warwick, Coventry.

Jenkins, S. (1994), 'Winners and Losers: a Portrait of the UK Income Distribution During the 1980s', University College of Swansea Department of Economics, Discussion Paper No. 94/07.

Jenkins, S. (1995), 'Accounting for income inequality trends: decomposition analyses for the UK, 1971-1986', *Economica*, 62, pp. 29-63.

Johnson, P. and Rodger, J. (1983), 'From redundancy to self-employment', *Employment Gazette*, June, pp. 260-264.

Jordan, B., James, S., Kay, H. and Redley, M. (1992), *Trapped in Poverty: labour market decisions in low income households*, London: Routledge and Kegan Paul, London.

Joshi, H. (1987), 'The cost of caring', pp 122-133 in Glendinning, C. and Millar, J., (eds.), *Women and Poverty in Britain*, Wheatsheaf, Brighton.

Keithley, J. (1991), 'Social security in a single European market', pp 72-90 in Room, G. (ed), *Towards a European Welfare State?*, School for Advanced Urban Studies, Bristol.

Kemsley, W., Redpath, R. and Holmes, M. (1980), *Family Expenditure Survey: Handbook on the Sample, Fieldwork and Coding Procedures,* London: HMSO, London.

Konle-Seidl, R., Ullmann, H. and Walwei, U. (1990), 'The European social space: atypical forms of employment and working hours in the European Community', *International Social Security Review*, 2 (1990) pp. 143-178.

Labour Party (1990), *Looking to the Future*, Labour Party, London.

Lasok, K. (1982), 'The self-employed in EEC social security law', *Journal of Social Welfare Law*, September, pp. 323-331.

Law, I. (1994), 'Ethnicity and Eligibility: understanding the perceptions and experiences of eligible non-claimants within minority ethnic communities', *Benefits*, January.

Lee, R. (1985), 'The entry to self-employment of redundant steelworkers', *Industrial Relations Journal*, 16 (2) pp. 42-49.

Leece, D. (1990), 'Redundancy, unemployment and self-employment', *International Journal of Manpower*, 4 (4) pp. 35-40.

Legal and General (1985), *The Self-employed Report,* Legal and General Insurance, London.

Leighton, P. (1983), 'Employment and self-employment: some problems of law and practice', *Employment Gazette*, May, pp. 197-203.

Leighton, P. (1986), 'Marginal workers', pp. 503-527 in Lewis, R., (ed.), *Labour Law in Britain*, Blackwell, Oxford.

Lonsdale, S., Lessof, C. and Ferris, G. (1993), *Invalidity Benefit: A Survey of Recipients*, DSS Research Report No. 19, HMSO, London.

Lowe, S. (1992), 'Home ownership, wealth and welfare: new connections', in Corden, A., Tolley, K. and Robertson, E. (eds.), *Meeting Needs In An Affluent Society*, Avebury, Aldershot.

Luckhaus, L. (1991), 'New technology, social security and the self-employed'. Paper given to the European Institute of Social Security International Colloquium on Social Security and Technological Innovation, Florence, October 1991.

Lynes, T. (1988), 'The take-up of family credit among self-employed people is low - because the regulations are so absurd', *New Statesman and Society*, 16, p. 25.

Lynes, T. (1989), 'The self-employed deserve a better deal', *New Statesman and Society*, 6, 26 June.

Lynes, T. (1990), 'Confuse a cabbie', *New Statesman and Society*, 26, 25 May.

Lynes, T. (1991), 'Drumming up new business', *Community Care*, 9, 11 July.

MacAffee, K. (1980), 'A glimpse of the hidden economy in the national accounts', *Economic Trends,* 316, February, pp. 81-87.

MacDonald, R. and Coffield, F. (1991), *Risky Business: Youth and the Enterprise Culture*, Falmer Press, London.

Mack, J. and Lansley, S. (1985), *Poor Britain*, George Allen and Unwin, London.

Marsh, A., Heady, P., and Matheson, A. (1981), *Labour Mobility in the Construction Industry*, HMSO, London.

Marsh, A. and McKay, S. (1993), *Families, Work and Benefits*, Policy Studies Institute, London.

Malpass, P. (1990), *Reshaping Housing Policy*, Routledge, London.

McCarthy, J. (1993), 'Employee or Self-employed?', *Legal Action*, May, p.16.

McLaughlin, E., Millar, J. and Cooke, K. (1989), *Work and Welfare Benefits*, Avebury, Aldershot.

Meager, N. (1992a), 'Does Unemployment Lead to Self-employment?', *Small Business Economics*, 4, pp. 87-103.

Meager, N. (1992b), 'The Rise and Fall of Self-Employment (Again): a comment on Staber and Bogenhold', *Work, Employment and Society*, March.

Meager, N., Kaiser, M. and Dietrich, H. (1992c), *Self-Employment in the United Kingdom and Germany*, Anglo-German Foundation, London.

Meager, N. Court, G. and Moralee, J. (1994), *Self-Employment and the Distribution of Income*, Institute of Manpower Studies, Brighton.

Miles, M. and Huberman, A. (1994), *Qualitative Data Analysis: An Expanded Sourcebook*, Thousand Oaks, Sage, California.

Ministry of Labour (1966), 'Labour-only subcontracting', *Ministry of Labour Gazette*, 220, May.

MORI (1993), *Income Support for Self-Employed and Formerly Self-Employed People*, Research for the National Audit Office, London.

National Association of Citizens Advice Bureaux (1991a), *Barriers to Benefit: Black Claimants and Social Security*, National Association of Citizens Advice Bureaux, London.

National Association of Citizens Advice Bureaux (1991b), *Low Income Groups and Health Benefits*, National Association of Citizens Advice Bureaux, London.

National Audit Office (1988), *Department of Employment/Training Commission: Assistance to Small Firms*, HMSO, London.

National Audit Office (1991a), *Support for Low Income Families*, HMSO, London.

National Audit Office (1991b), *National Insurance Contributions*, HMSO, London.

National Audit Office (1993), *Quality of Service: Income Support for Self-Employed and Formerly Self-Employed People*, HMSO, London.

National Consumer Council (1990), *Credit and Debt: The Consumer Interest*, HMSO, London.

Newcastle City Council Housing Department (1991), 'Housing benefit: self-employed claimants'. Paper tabled at the Housing Benefit Standing Committee, HBSC 91 (23), October.

NOP (1990), *A Report of a Survey Conducted by NOP Market Research Limited on behalf of the National Audit Office: A Survey Among Family Credit Recipients*, NOP, London.

Organisation for Economic Co-operation and Development (1986), 'Self-employment in OECD countries', *Economic Outlook*, 43-65, OECD, Paris.

Organisation for Economic Co-operation and Development (1992), *Employment Outlook*, OECD, Paris.

Organisation for Economic Co-operation and Development (1993), *Employment Outlook*, July, OECD, Paris.

Oldfield, N. and Yu, A. (1993), *The Cost of a Child: Living Standards for the 1990s*, Child Poverty Action Group, London.

OPCS and Registrar General Scotland (1984), *Census 1981: Economic Activity, Great Britain*, HMSO, London.

Office of Population, Censuses and Surveys (1992), 'General Household Survey: Preliminary Results for 1991', *OPCS Monitor*, SS 92/1.

Office of Population, Censuses and Surveys (1994), *Social Trends*, HMSO, London.

Opportunities for Women (1990), *Care to Work*, Volume 1: Survey Report, OFW, London.
Pahl, J. (1980) 'Patterns of money management within marriage', *Journal of Social Policy*, 9 (3) pp.313-335.
Pahl, J. (1989), *Money and Marriage*, Macmillan, London.
Pahl, R. and Wallace, C. (1985), 'Household work strategies in economic recession', pp.189-227 in Redclift, N. and Mingione, E., (eds.), *Beyond Employment: Household, Gender and Subsistence*, Blackwell, Oxford.
Parker, G. (1989), 'A study of non-elderly spouse carers: final report', Working Paper DHSS 484, Social Policy Research Unit, University of York, York.
Parker, G. (1990), *Getting and Spending: Credit and Debt in Britain*, Avebury, Aldershot.
Payne, J. (1984), 'Young self-employed workers', *Employment Gazette,* November, pp. 497-503.
Piachaud, D. (1981), 'Peter Townsend and the Holy Grail', *New Society*, 57, p.82.
Pissarides, C. and Weber, G. (1989), 'An expenditure-based estimate of Britain's black economy', *Journal of Public Economics,* 39, pp. 17-32.
Pollert, A. (1988), 'The flexible firm: fixation or fact?', *Work, Employment, and Society*, 2, pp.281-316.
Pollert, A. (ed.) (1991), *Farewell to Flexibility?*, Blackwell, Oxford.
Prescott-Clarke, P. (1990), *Employment and Handicap,* Social and Community Planning Research, London.
Rainbird, H. (1991), 'The self-employed: small entrepreneurs or disguised wage labourers?', in Pollert, A. (ed.), *Farewell to Flexibility?*, Blackwell, Oxford.
Redpath, R. (1986), 'Family Expenditure Survey: a second study of differential response, comparing Census characteristics of FES respondents and non-respondents', *Statistical News*, 72, February, pp. 13-16.
Rees, H. and Shah, A. (1986), 'An empirical analysis of self-employment in the UK', *Journal of Applied Econometrics,* 1, pp. 95-108.
Ringen, S. (1988), 'Direct and indirect measures of poverty', *Journal of Social Policy*, 17, 3, pp. 351-365.
Ritchie, J. (1990), *Thirty Families: their living standards in unemployment*, DSS Research Report No.1, HMSO, London.
Rowlingson, K. and Berthoud, R. (1994), *Evaluating the Disability Working Allowance: first findings*, Policy Studies Institute, London.
Rowntree, B. (1901), *Poverty - A Study of Town Life*, Macmillan, London.

Rowntree, B. (1937), *The Human Needs of Labour*, Longmans Green, London.

Rubery, J. (1988), 'Employers and the labour market', pp. 251-280 in Gallie, D. (ed.), *Employment in Britain,* Basil Blackwell, Oxford.

Rubery, J., Earnshaw, J. and Burchell, B. (1993), *New Forms and Patterns of Employment: The Role of Self-Employment in Britain*, Nomos Verlagsgesellschaft, Baden-Baden.

Saunders, P., Hobbes, G. and Stott, H. (1989), *Income Inequality in Australia and New Zealand: International Comparisons and Recent Trends*, Discussion Paper No. 15, The University of New South Wales, Social Welfare Research Centre.

The Scotsman (1991), 'Fishermen's wives win family credit entitlement', 9 July.

Schumpeter, J.A. (1934), *The Theory of Economic Development*, Harvard University Press, Cambridge, Mass.

Sen, A. (1987), 'The standard of living: lecture 1, concepts and critiques', in Hawthorne, G. (ed.), *The Standard of Living*, Cambridge University Press, Cambridge.

Smeeding, T.M., O'Higgins, M. and Rainwater, L (1990), (eds.), *Poverty, Inequality and Income Distribution in Comparitive Perspective, The Luxembourg Income Study*, Wheatsheaf, London.

Smith, A. (1981), 'The informal economy', *Lloyds Bank Review*, 14, July, pp. 45-60.

Smith, S. (1986), *Britain's Shadow Economy*, OUP, Oxford.

Smith, S. and Wied-Nebberling, S. (1986), *The Shadow Economy in Britain and Germany,* Anglo-German Foundation for the Study of Industrial Society, London.

Stark, T. (1978), *Personal Incomes: Review of United Kingdom Statistical Sources,* Vol VI, Pergamon Press, Oxford.

Steinmetz, G, and Wright, E.O. (1989), 'The fall and rise of the petty bourgeoisie: changing patterns of self-employment in the post-war United States', *American Journal of Sociology,* 94, 5.

Tarpey, M. (1984), *English Speakers Only: a report on work on take-up of social security benefits with people whose first language was not English*, Islington People's Rights, London.

Taylor, M. (ed.), (1992), *British Household Panel Survey User Manual, Volume A: Introduction, Technical Report and Appendices*, University of Essex, Colchester.

Thomas, A. (1992), *Working with a Disability: barriers and facilitators*, Social and Community Planning Research, London.

Thomas, J. (1988), 'The politics of the black economy', *Work, Employment and Society*, 3 (2) pp. 169-190.
Townsend, P. (1979), *Poverty in the United Kingdom*, Allen Lane, London.
Townsend, P. (1987), 'Deprivation', *Journal of Social Policy*, 16 (2) pp. 125-146.
Townsend, P. and Gordon, D. (1989), ' What is enough? New evidence on poverty allowing the definition of a minimum benefit', paper presented at the International Sociological Association International Seminar on the Sociology of Social Security, University of Edinburgh, July.
Tremlett, N. (1993), *The Business Start-Up Scheme: 18 Month Follow Up Survey*, research for the Department of Employment, Social and Community Planning Research, London.
Twigg, J. and Atkin, K. (1991), 'Evaluating support to informal carers- part 2: final report', Working Paper DHSS 809, Social Policy Research Unit, University of York, York.
Unemployment Unit (1991a), Figures supplied in personal communication.
Unemployment Unit (1991b), 'Discouraging enterprise', *Working Brief*, July, p.6.
Veit Wilson, J.H. (1986), 'Paradigms of poverty: a rehabilitation of B.S. Rowntree', *Journal of Social Policy*, 15, 1, pp.69-99.
Waldinger, R. and Lapp, M. (1993), 'Back to the sweatshop or ahead to the informal sector?', *International Journal of Urban and Regional Research*, 17 (1) pp. 6-29.
Walker, R., Hedges, A. and Massey, S. (1987), *Housing Benefit: Discussion about Reform*, Housing Centre Trust, London.
Wheelock, J. and Baines, S. (1994), 'Dependency or Self-Reliance? The Contradictory Case of Work in the Small Business Family', paper presented to the Social Policy Association 28th Annual Conference *Families in Question*, University of Liverpool, July 1994.
Whiteford, P. and Kennedy, S. (1994) *Households Below Average Income: a comparative analysis*, Working Paper DSS 1065, Social Policy Research Unit, University of York, York.
Wilson, G. (1987), 'Money: patterns of responsibility and irresponsibility', in Brannen, J. and Wilson, G. (eds.), *Give and Take in Families: Studies in Resource Distribution*, Allen and Unwin, London.
Wilson, P. and Stanworth J. (1988), 'Growth strategies in small Asian and Caribbean business', *Employment Gazette*, January, pp. 8-14.
Windebank, J. and Williams, C. (1994), 'Defining Social and Spatial Inequalities in the Informal Sector in the European Union', in Mangen, S. and Hantrais, L. (eds.), *Unemployment, the Informal Economy and*

Entitlement to Benefits, Cross National Research Papers, Third Series - Concepts and Contexts in International Comparisons, Loughborough: European Research Centre.

Wood, D. and Smith, P. (1989), *Employers' Labour Use Strategies: first report on the 1987 survey*, Department of Employment Research Paper 63, Department of Employment, London.

Yu, A. (1992), *Low Cost Budget Standards for Three Household Types*, Family Budget Unit Working Paper No. 17, University of York, York.

Index